Bushman Shaman

"There is no question in the minds of the Bushman healers that Keeney's strength and purposes are coterminous with theirs. I know this from talking myself with some of the Kalahari shamans who danced with him. They affirmed his power as a healer and their enjoyment of dancing with him. . . . He knows whereof he writes, having traveled 'ropes to God' himself for much of his life, in many places in addition to the Kalahari."

MEGAN BIESELE, PH.D., cofounder and coordinator of the
Kalahari People's Fund, former member
of the Harvard Kalahari Research Project,
and author of *Healing Makes Our Hearts
Happy* and *Women Like Meat*

"Probably the most important book in the fields of healing and indigenous spirituality that's been published for many years. Keeney weaves together diverse threads of shamanic wisdom with deceptive ease—easy only because he became a shaman and lived the story on behalf of all of us. Anyone truly interested in the age-old questions of 'What is God' and 'Why are we here?' should read this book."

RUPERT ISAACSON, author of
The Healing Land: The Bushmen and the Kalahari Desert

Bushman Shaman

AWAKENING THE SPIRIT
THROUGH ECSTATIC DANCE

BRADFORD KEENEY

Destiny Books
Rochester, Vermont

Destiny Books
One Park Street
Rochester, Vermont 05767
www.InnerTraditions.com

Destiny Books is a division of Inner Traditions International

LIBRARY OF CONGRESS CATALOGING-IN-PUBLICATION DATA

Keeney, Bradford P.
Bushman shaman : awakening the spirit through ecstatic dance / Bradford Keeney.
p. cm.
Includes bibliographical references.
ISBN 0-89281-698-8 (pbk.)
1. San (African people)—Rites and ceremonies. 2. San (African people)—Religion.
3. Dance—Religious aspects. 4. Shamanism—Kalahari Desert.
5. Kalahari Desert—Social life and customs. I. Title.
DT1768.S36K44 2005
299.6'81—dc22
2004021164

Printed and bound in the United States at Lake Book Manufacturing, Inc.

10   9   8   7   6   5   4   3   2   1

Rock art images courtesy of Professor Emeritus David Lewis-Williams and the Rock Art
Research Institute, Department of Archaeology, University of the Witwatersrand,
Johannesburg, South Africa.

Text design by Priscilla Baker
Text layout by Virginia Scott Bowman
This book was typeset in Sabon, Avenir, and Eurostile
with Bubba Love and Elektrix as display typefaces

Dedicated to the
Ringing Rocks Foundation,
whose mission is to help
conserve global healing wisdom

ERIC *
My Russian
Found Friend ...
May THE BIG LOVE
find and teach/bless
us all .
BLESSINGS
:) Heidi
12, 2004

Contents

Acknowledgments

I AM MOST GRATEFUL TO MY WIFE, Mev Jenson, for her loving support and companionship in all of this work. And thanks to our son, Scott, for being a kind and joyful presence, as well as serving as my technical advisor to the ongoing fieldwork.

To all my Kalahari teachers, I express appreciation for your steadfast guidance and friendship. We will never stop dancing together!

I am deeply grateful to Nancy Connor, a dear friend and colleague whose organization, the Ringing Rocks Foundation, is helping conserve cultural wisdom traditions. Her foundation illumines how people can truly make a difference in the world.

Thank you, Nancy!

Special thanks to my friend and outfitter, Paddy Hill, who is an inseparable part of the Kalahari work.

And finally, I express gratitude to those who have made superb editorial contributions to the manuscript: Susan Davidson, Megan Biesele, and John Linthicum.

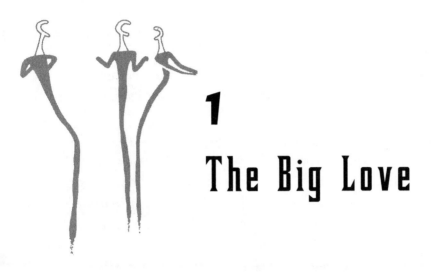

1

The Big Love

IT'S A HOT, MUGGY AUGUST NIGHT in Saint Joseph, Missouri, and my grandfather, Reverend W.L. Keeney, is preaching away in a revival service. "In the name of Jesus, we come here tonight to bring honor to his name." My grandfather welcomes all who have come to his red brick Savannah Avenue Baptist Church, the one with the lit cross hanging over the front entrance.

"Come on in and don't be ashamed to rejoice in our Precious Lord," my grandfather continues, as he looks out and sees that the church is packed, with extra folding chairs placed in the aisles to accommodate the overflow of worshippers. "It may be hot in here tonight, but someone once told me that there's a hotter place awaiting those who walk away." Handheld fans move in sync with the rhythms of his delivery while trying to bring relief from the sticky air. "Say Amen, somebody!" Time after time, the congregation erupts with bellows of the called-for responses. It feels as though a storm is about to take place, but this thunder and lightning will burst forth inside the church walls.

For most of my life I thought that my grandfather was a tall man. I would have guessed that he was at least six feet and two inches tall, if not a couple of inches taller. It was many years later, when my own son was an adolescent, that I learned that Grandfather Keeney, who I called PaPa, was not tall in physical measurement—he measured five feet, seven inches in height. As my dad explained, everyone thought PaPa was tall because of the way he lit up a room with his charisma, enthusiasm, compassion, and humor, his glowing smile, and most important, his booming voice.

Reverend W.L. Keeney was a giant of the spirit, and on that revival night in 1963 I sat in a chair right behind him, a twelve-year-old boy wearing a bright red bow tie. I was facing the congregation, seeing their riveted eyes transfixed upon my grandfather's delivery. Despite the serious mood he cast, they would find themselves laughing, sometimes gently and at other times more vigorously, as PaPa interspersed his sermons with carefully timed humor. Handkerchiefs ready for action, they would also cry as his stories touched the tender places in their hearts.

Grandfather's pattern was to begin softly, setting a stage with dramatic tension before weaving in a humorous anecdote for relief. Then, like a locomotive starting to gather power and steam, he would begin to perspire, and the volume of his voice would grow louder until he roared like a lion. His brothers, my great uncles, called him by his middle name—Leo; the name fit perfectly when PaPa got wound up in his revival preaching.

When my grandfather roared, you could see his white dress shirt become soaked with sweat. At that stage of his sermon he spoke with his whole body, stomping his feet, waving his arms, slamming his fist on the pulpit, walking back and forth. He turned into a fireball, a dynamo of evangelical fervor, and he shouted. That's what people sometimes called old-fashioned evangelical preaching—it was "shouting for the Lord." My grandfather was the best shouter on the circuit; that's what I heard others say and I believed it without a moment's doubt.

As grandfather worked himself up in those church services, his face turned redder, his breathing pumped more enthusiastically, and his movements became more spontaneous and vibrant. I recall hearing his parishioners boast that my grandfather worked himself into such a frenzy that he ended up reconverting himself every time he preached.

When he gasped, the congregation did so in kind, and when he became choked with tears, they wiped their eyes. At the height of his crescendo his voice would suddenly fall and become soft and tender, instantly pouring forth the message of surrender, compassion, forgiveness, and the transforming grace of God's love. As the church choir started to sing "Softly and Tenderly" or "Just As I Am," people would feel themselves being pulled to the front of the church by a mysterious force. They would come forward, weeping while reaching for PaPa's hand. He was a master at "bringing in the sheaves," as the old hymn put it. When they came to him, he was everyone's grandfather, standing there to cheerlead for them and to exclaim his celebration of their new lives born in spirit.

Although PaPa could preach fire and brimstone, he never ended a sermon without climbing up to the peaceful palace of heavenly love. Unlike the conservative Baptists and television evangelicals who broadcast judgmental condemnation and self-righteous morality, PaPa remained faithful to preaching love. He taught me over and over again that God was love, the Big Love that changed the lives of people. The Big Love he shouted, whispered, and wept about had the power to change the minds and hearts of those who asked for it to come into their everyday lives.

PaPa also carried a secret. He was a private mystic who had prophetic visions about the future of the world. Among other things, my grandmother and father told me that grandfather predicted how World War II would end before the atomic bomb had even been invented. PaPa practiced his mysticism with a fishing pole. Everyone knew his love for fishing, but they didn't know that much of his fishing time was spent just sitting still in the boat and staring at the water.

During my youth grandfather frequently brought up the importance of a great mystery in his life, but he never specified exactly what he was referring to. When I was in high school, he would fix my breakfast early in the morning before the rest of the family was up. Eating fried green tomatoes with biscuits and honey, he would allude to the mystery and then take a long pause before he'd wink at me, saying with a smile, "Someday you will understand."

I believed in the Big Love from my earliest childhood days and watched it transform the lives of those who walked down the church aisle and publicly surrendered themselves to it. I saw this take place in my grandfather's church and in my father's church; both men were missionaries of the Big Love. Both were the opposite of the arrogant, dualistic "judgmentalists" who gave Christianity a bad name among true God-loving people. Those who claim to be "fundamentalists" have little to do with the most important fundamentals of Christian agape, the love that forgives and helps (rather than condemns) others who suffer.

My father, who called himself a "Bill Moyers and Jimmy Carter Baptist," was devoted to fighting social injustice and emphasizing the social activism aspect of the Gospel. He regarded Jesus as a radical who began a revolution of the heart. I grew up reading the books in my father's office; I was inspired by the ideas of Dietrich Bonhoeffer, the German theologian who wrote *The Cost of Discipleship*. The Nazis hanged Bonhoeffer in the concentration camp at Flossenburg for his resistance to the racist nationalism of his time. Harvey Cox, the progressive cultural theologian at Harvard Divinity School, who himself grew up in a Baptist church, also caught my intellectual imagination.

With all the enthusiasm of youth, I too "signed up" for the Big Love. Walking down the aisle of my father's church, first as a twelve-year old professing his faith and later as a teenager who made a rededication commitment, I publicly declared my belief that God's love (or as I call it now, the Big Love) was the only thing worth sacrificing my life for and the only mission worth serving wholeheartedly.

During adolescence my place in the worship service was at the piano bench. I served my congregation as the church pianist. To me, music seemed to express the Big Love in a way that plain speaking could never match. I played those old-fashioned "runs," the arpeggios, up and down the keyboard as I accompanied a congregation filled with sunburned farmers, laborers with calloused hands, a suited doctor, and a scattering of business people, all standing side by side singing their hearts out to the words of the old revival hymns. They were joined to one another by the kind of music that folks said had "feeling." My job, as I understood it, was to amplify the music's feeling by embellishing it with improvised musical seasonings. Little did I know that I was learning the importance of music in bringing down the spirit, the oldest tool of shamans the world over.

The gift of being able to jazz up the music came from my maternal grandmother, Bess Gnann. She played the piano with a bit of stride and sang like Sophie Tucker. I loved to hear her "swing" the songs. It was rumored that somewhere in her bloodline was an African forebear, a conclusion based on how my mother (and grandmother) moved and sang, as well as on family gossip that went back further than anyone's memory. As a child, my unconscious mind heard that, in some way, I was from Africa.

In my childhood I didn't realize that my grandfather's high-wattage presence behind the pulpit was a teaching of how to work the spirit—bringing it into your soul and letting your body be moved by its energy. Without knowing it, I was being groomed to later become part of a Sanctified Black Church, a community of worshippers who first showed me what I call the "African body electric," their own bodies so filled with spirit that it inspired not only shouting but also dancing for the Lord. The term "African body electric" covers the whole range of home-cooked soulful expression, from the rhythms and chord colorings of blues, gospel, and jazz to the shaking, frenzied, dancing bodies in African ceremonies.

Given my country church upbringing and my delight in vibrant rhythms, it was understandable that I would connect with the Black Church. But never would I have imagined that I would go to the Kalahari Desert of Botswana and Namibia and dance with the Bushmen, the tribe regarded by many to be the oldest living culture on earth. Indeed, the Bushmen, who call themselves the First People, say that they practice the earliest form of spiritual expression. In Africa I was introduced to an even wider range of spontaneous expression than I had found in the Black Church, performed naturally and effortlessly by the African body electric.

Going past the familiar forms of improvised tongue-speaking, spirited dancing, and ecstatic shouting (and later to become familiar to me in the Sanctified Black Church), with the Bushmen I would enter a highly charged world of sound making, body movement, visionary experience, and interactive touch far beyond anything I had experienced in my formative years. At the same time, what I experienced with the Bushmen could be seen as the full blossoming of the seeds planted in my father's and grandfather's churches and watered by the tears released in joy and suffering, in the ups and downs that grace and carve every person's life.

I eventually recognized that it was my destiny to someday become a part of the Bushman spiritual healing tradition. They taught me to go all the way into the spirit, holding back nothing, having no limits to my reception of—and to the giving of—the Big Love.

When I grew up and left Missouri, I found myself traveling the world, meeting many shamans, healers, and spiritual teachers. Although they spoke different languages and wore different kinds of clothing, they all had one thing in common: they were devotees of the Big Love. In my odyssey I learned that there is an invisible and nameless ceremonial space that brings together all worshippers of the Big Love. The altar of this place of spiritual unity offers forgiveness and compassion, mercy intead of judgment. In this home of diverse spirits and presences, God is the Big Love.

I have spent my life being an explorer of the Big Love, including the way it can take us to what I believe is our spiritual origin, the African body electric, the body that improvisationally expresses ecstatic joy. I became a freedom soldier of the Lord of Love, a pilgrim of the spirit of eternal delight, an ambassador of the passionate Holy Ghost. And I did so by finding God in the Kalahari, among the people made famous by the movie "The Gods Must Be Crazy," the significant image of which was a Coca Cola bottle falling from the sky.

My story is about how the Gods truly are crazy, mad with a love that is capable of filling us with complete satisfaction and happiness. These Gods are transmitters of the Big Love and, like the Bushmen, they are ready and available to turn our bodies into instruments of divine celebration, making us lightning rods that bring down the spirit. These Gods of crazy wisdom love will transform anyone who simply says "yes" to their presence.

This story is my testimony of the living presence and availability of God, whose most honorable name is the Big Love.

2
Rapture in Missouri

IN MAY OF 1969, during my senior year of high school, I won a first-place award at the international science fair for a project entitled "An Experimental Study of the Effects of Hydrocortisone, Insulin, and Epinephrine on the Glycogen Content of Hepatic Tissues Perfused In Vitro." My award made the front page of the *Kansas City Star* newspaper with the headline "Small Town Boy Wins Big Prize."

The small town was the modest farming community of Smithville, Missouri, a place known for the way the Little Platte River overflowed every spring, flooding the streets. During one flood, characterized as the kind of flood that only takes place every five hundred years, the whole town was covered with raging waters. I remember the drama of watching that muddy water creep higher and higher until it flowed over the bridge and swept down the main street. It quickly became a torrential current. Boats and helicopters were on continuous patrol evacuating people off the roofs of their houses and barns. It rained for days. I remember thinking that this was what it must have been like in Noah's time.

When the waters receded, my father gathered our congregation to take notice of how the altar holding the church Bible had floated to the ceiling, leaving the Bible dry. Everything else was covered with thick mud. The dry Bible seemed like a small miracle that inspired all of us to pick ourselves up by our bootstraps, clean up the mess, and resume our daily lives. When everyone left the church service, I walked up to the Bible to see it for myself, turning the pages slowly. Sure enough, each page was bone dry. I believed what my father and my grandfather had said: this was the work of God's hand.

That event was one of the seeds from which my religious faith grew. I read my Bible and said my prayers every night as a young boy. Doing so left me with a good feeling. I was lucky—I didn't have a bad childhood experience of my family church. Naturally, I have heard that not a few people's early experiences of religion were not positive for them, and it saddens me that institutions whose purpose should be to bring the greatest joy can fall short of their mission. For me, living in the parsonage next to the Smithville First Baptist Church and being the church pianist at thirteen was an uncomplicated joy. I am grateful for the faith that was inspired in me in that time. In my childhood I also loved science projects and, of course, jazz piano. My life was church, science, and piano, and I was encouraged in all three realms.

In some ways, Smithville was a place where time had stopped. My family lived near a blacksmith shop that was so active I woke up most mornings to the sound of hammers hitting the anvils. My sister and I would gaze through the large open doors and see the bellows and fires in full operation. There was a lot of work to be done in that shop and the men, with their long black aprons and iron tools, seldom took a break.

The barbershop a couple of blocks up the street was said not to have changed since the 1920s. One wall was decorated with a painting of dogs playing cards at a poker table. My favorite wall hanging was directly across from the barber's chair. It was a rendition of the moment in history when Babe Ruth pointed toward the outfield stands before hitting his home run. Every time my boyhood friends or I went to get a haircut, we daydreamed about how long Ruth could hit a ball and what it would be like to hit a major league home run.

I recall a local farmer, old man Hans, who refused to use a tractor. He would work his field with a handheld plow. I don't recall anyone ever hearing him speak a word, but it was part of our daily landscape to see him out in the fields toiling away during the growing season. Once, while driving his wagon and horses down the highway, a truck came over a hill and was unable to avoid a collision. As soon as that truck hit the steel bar at the back of Hans's wagon, it catapulted old man Hans and his wife high into the sky, delivering them safely on a soft place in the pasture where some hay had been gathered. I can't tell you how much entertainment that story provided our town. We still talk about it.

Other characters also made for small town talk. The person in charge of testing and treating the water in the local reservoir, Robin Williams, was a self-made poet and inventor. I spent many an afternoon in his shop watching him build odd contraptions, like an everglade air boat that he converted to a sled to fly down the street in the middle of our midwestern snowstorms. His most amazing accomplishment was converting an old steam locomotive to an automobile of sorts and driving it down the country roads to the state fairs.

Then there was Ruben, the town hobo who slept in a chicken coop when he wasn't riding the rails. It was said that Ruben slept through most of the big flood of July 1965, snoozing away on the roof of the bank building as the waters roared just below him. Ruben wasn't an illiterate man. He read voraciously when riding the rails. He spoke as if he had been to every country in the world. As a child I never knew whether he traveled in his mind through the books he read or whether he had actually been to the places he spoke about—probably the truth lay somewhere in between. I remember the night my father baptized him in a revival service and how word spread throughout the rural area that Ruben had been saved. That was big news in our small town.

Although it may seem like an extraordinary feat for someone from Smithville to win the international science fair, it made all the sense in the world if you looked behind the scenes at how my mother, a school-teacher, filled my life with books, science equipment, and music. I grew up with three science labs in my basement, as well as a piano and a personal library. Most fantasies I would concoct, whether it was my plan to build a rocket, to collect old radios, or to start a jazz band, were encouraged by her. That was the home in which I worked, played, slept, and dreamed.

In high school I listened to Ramsey Lewis, Oscar Peterson, Bill Evans, Stan Getz, Louis Armstrong, and my main source of musical delight, Errol Garner, while religiously reading Albert Schweitzer and various theologians. I was in my own world, my own cave, and I thanked God every night in my prayers for being blessed with a wonderful family and home.

I don't want to sound as though I lived a utopian existence then. I was a sick little boy who ended up in a hospital oxygen tent several times a year. I almost died several times from pneumonia brought about by chronic asthma. I knew the doctors and nurses in town as though they were family members. My childhood bouts in the hospital provided early teachings on the importance of gentle touch and tactile communication for a human being's well-being.

I had my first religious experience as a twelve-year-old boy. In a revival service Dr. David Moore, chair of the department of religion at a nearby Baptist college, preached a sermon about how easy it was to run with the Lord but how much more difficult it was to walk with him through the steps of each day. That's all I remember Dr. Moore saying, but at the end of the service, as the congregation sang the old hymn "Softly and Tenderly, Jesus Is Calling," my body felt warm and tingly. Something inside me felt heated up. A force seemed to pull me out of the spot where I was standing next to my best friend, Ronnie Johnson. I was unable to resist the tug. Although my hands tried to cling to the back of the pew in front of me, my feet started walking forward to my father. He was waiting in front of the altar to accept anyone who was called to make a public profession of faith and commitment to the religious path.

He hugged me and I felt tears start to fall down my cheeks.

My father baptized me in the old way of going under the water in the church baptismal pool, like his father had baptized him in a river many years before. I walked down the steps into that pool while looking at the painted mural showing Jesus being baptized by John the Baptist. My father held me while he arranged my fingers so they would pinch my nose. As he spoke about me receiving a new life reborn in spirit, I went under the water. And then I was lifted up.

Even as a child, the power of that ritual was transforming and exhilarating. When you come up from that water you can almost hear a heavenly choir singing praise. It was the most important thing our family believed could happen to a person—getting baptized was a bigger deal than winning a financial fortune or (for a child) going to Disneyland. As my grandfather once said to me about his spiritual life, "Others may not see me as having much money but I'm the wealthiest man in the world. I'm speaking of spiritual wealth, grandson."

That baptism was my first step to becoming a shaman. That statement may come as a surprise, but I ask you to consider that the Siberian term *saman,* from which the word *shaman* is derived, refers to the excited state of one's body during a spiritual experience. It also refers to the inner heat of someone who is spiritually awakened. And finally, the etymology of *saman* reveals that the word has a Sanskrit root that means "song." When I say that I feel an inner heat and vibration move me while under the influence of a sacred song, please know that I am talking about shamanic experience.

I have met many shamans from around the world. From my perspective (and theirs), the root of their practice and the source of their gifts comes from loving God—or as I prefer to specify this, from loving the God of the Big Love, the God of many faces that provides compassionate grace to people and cultures all over the world. Accordingly, these shamans love and honor and speak highly of all efforts, practices, and traditions that love God.

I feel the same. I love all religions and any way that follows the Big Love. I have spent my life exploring many different religions and find that all of them reveal, for all their differences, the same central teaching: loving others through God's love. When you get a direct hit from God you receive a sacred gift. It may be in the form of inner spiritual heat, ecstatic dance, inspired vision, or songs of praise, among other possibilities. When you regularly receive the offerings of the Big Love, you are a shaman. Every mystic, religious pilgrim, and holy person who has wept at the touch of God's grace is a shaman. My hope is to help people return to God's love and to know that this is the originating experience for all religions and life in the spirit. When you hold the spirit, all kinds of unexpected and glorious things can happen to you, from receiving visions that direct your life to finding guidance in the world of mythic imagination to hugging the tree in your backyard or wanting to go back to church or temple.

There's a family story about my grandfather that we enjoy telling. As a young pastor, Reverend Keeney rode a horse to a country church to preach a revival. During one of the evening services the local troublemaker, a man named Mr. Black, stormed into the church and challenged my grandfather, saying that everything in the church was a lie. Then he stormed out. He and his gang of ruffians came back the next night and heckled the congregation from outside the church. My grandfather took off his coat, rolled up the sleeves of his white dress shirt, and walked right out of the church, waving his Bible over his head. He preached to those unruly men, looking them straight in the eyes as he delivered his message. Silenced by grandfather's lack of fear, Mr. Black had a religious conversion experience right there and then. With tears in his eyes, he asked for forgiveness and dedicated his life to the Lord; my grandfather baptized him in the river. But that isn't the end of the story. The town was so moved by what happened that every single person in the town, adults and children alike, asked my grandfather to baptize them. PaPa was a genuine frontier evangelical preacher man, a Christian shaman.

It was in this context of family support and religious expression that I made it to the international high school science fair in May 1969. At the close of the fair one of the judges, the director of admissions of the Massachusetts Institute of Technology (M.I.T.), offered me a full academic scholarship.

When I returned home from the fair another offer was awaiting me.

Dr. David Moore, the man who preached the revival service in which I had my first calling, had written a letter offering me full academic scholarship to a local religious college. My parents both graduated from that institution and my grandfather had given a prayer at one of its graduation ceremonies. I quickly dismissed M.I.T. and headed off for William Jewell College in Liberty, Missouri.

As a freshman in college, I began to come out of my (very cozy) cocoon and look out toward the world. Being from the "show me" state of Missouri, I didn't believe everything I was told, whether it was conveyed by the media, the government, or a textbook. I had to see it for myself. It was 1969, one of the most explosive years of the decade, and I saw how our society had become corrupt. I joined those in the counterculture who were angry at the way things were going, particularly in regard to civil rights issues, the capitalistic war machine, and the pillaging of the earth's environment.

I began playing more jazz piano and reading the literature of radical theology. This led to my creating an underground newspaper called *For Christ's Sake,* an outspoken collection of quotations and essays encouraging liberation on all fronts based upon the rhetoric of the spiritual leaders of diverse cultures.

I probably don't have to explain how this resulted in all hell breaking out on the conservative religious campus. A professor of physics singled me out in class, calling me a weasel and publicly blaming me for contributing to the violence in the streets by virtue of my social criticisms and protests. When General Maxwell Taylor visited the campus, someone painted the chapel walls with "Go home, Max! Make love, not war." I was blamed for the grafitti. When a group of conservative students approached the dean, encouraging him to ask me to leave the school, I finally decided to transfer to another place of higher education.

During my time at William Jewell College I had one ally on the faculty. An associate professor of physics one day suggested to me that he host a gathering of students in his home who were interested in discussing the issues being raised in my newsletter. This professor encouraged me to follow my own instincts and not to be unnecessarily distracted by voices of unreason and inappropriate castigation. He also took me to hear a public presentation by a renowned yogi from India, Swami Rama, who had been brought to the United States by Elmer Green, an innovative scientist at the Menninger Foundation. It was Swami Rama's first public appearance in our country. I sat in the audience and listened to him talk about a spiritual path that was very foreign to me at the time I heard it, but became much more familiar several months later in my next spiritual awakening.

During all the turmoil of social activism in my college years, I turned to the piano as a source of relaxation and inspiration. I learned to improvise jazz, put together a jazz trio, and played a yearlong gig at one of Kansas City's premier steak houses, the Hereford House. I found that music, particularly improvised melodies, opened my heart and gave birth to powerful experiences of connection with others. I was falling in love with the world through music and stirring up passion through discourse that urged us all to be serious custodians of our planet and one another.

This was the context of one of the most eventful nights of my life. I was a nineteen-year-old student filled with jazz, social concern, and a love for religion. Without knowing it, I had prepared myself to receive another spiritual gift of rebirth and awakening.

It was a late afternoon in January 1971. I was casually walking along a sidewalk at the University of Missouri, where I was now enrolled.

It was an extraordinarily warm day for winter; the temperature had risen to the midseventies. People were wearing short-sleeved shirts during a time of year when shovels and plows typically were out clearing away snow and ice. I was headed for a record shop, probably humming a jazz tune, when out of the blue I felt the most intense comfort and joy I had ever known. Sheer calm, relaxation, and happiness spread though my whole being. As I went along the way, I began to feel my body getting lighter and lighter until I felt I had no weight at all. I wasn't concerned; I assumed it was a consequence of feeling so good on a spectacular day.

This bliss continued to escalate and elaborate. I soon found myself in the midst of a kind of awareness I had never known before. An uncannily deep calm and wide-ranging peacefulness flooded my consciousness and I felt a certainty about life that no words can adequately convey. In that moment it seemed that all questions about life's meaning could be answered instantly and effortlessly. I felt complete peace and joy, but at the same time I did not feel in the least ego-centered. On the contrary, I was losing awareness of my individuality. I was floating in pure consciousness. This knowing did not reflect or analyze what was going on, nor did it show delight, amazement, curiosity, or celebration of the moment. It was more like a total centering of awareness and being that became compressed to a microscopic dot, pulling in the container that had once held it, setting it free of physical and conceptual weight and burden. Paradoxically, this getting smaller resulted in a feeling of also becoming larger, a state in which my sense of time and space was lost in a realization of eternal presence. As I write of this event now, it is obvious that I was having some kind of mystical experience. But at the time I experienced no outside evaluation of what was taking place. I was the experience, absent of all internal conversation.

My body moved without effort. It wouldn't be totally inaccurate to say that I felt as though I were flying—or at least as though I were gliding along the sidewalk, without a single muscle exerting any force to move me. It was automatic movement of a body focused entirely on a sense of pure knowing that was absent of self. My body walked me up the steps of a small university chapel made of stone.

There was no one inside. The place was dark, with only a little light coming from a dimmed iron chandelier. A dozen wooden pews faced a Gothic-style altar. I walked up to the front pew, sat down, and felt like

I had arrived at my natural place. I sat absolutely still, without thought or movement. In those moments I perceived what seemed to be the unity and wholeness of the cosmos.

I don't know how long I sat there, but I do know that what I am going to describe lasted throughout the evening.

It began as a baptism into a river of absolute love. My deep sense of knowing melted into an even deeper awareness, both of being loved and of loving all of life. To be more accurate, I did not feel separate from the beloved, and the beloved was the world. As I plunged deeper and deeper into this infinite ocean of love, the inside of my body began to get heated. The base of my spine felt like an oven that was getting progressively warmer until it burned with red-hot coals. As the inner heat turned into what felt like molten lava, my body began to tremble.

It may seem strange to you that I had no fear or anxiety about what was happening. I believe this had to do with the fact that I was not in a dualistic relationship with the experience. There was no "I" having "the experience"—there was only unexamined experience. The former boundaries of my self had simultaneously shrunk to an unseen dot and expanded to embrace the whole of the universe. As I went further into the depths of love's unlimited oceanic space, I also went higher into the sky, feeling both the heavens above and the underbelly of Earth below.

The fireball within began to crawl slowly up my spine. It had a purpose of its own and nothing was going to stop it. Like a baby, after the breaking of its mother's water, this birth was determinedly on its way. As the lavalike movement crept upward, heat spread throughout every cell in my body. I was on fire. My legs, abdomen, arms, and especially my hands felt as though they could melt through metal.

When the fire came to my heart, the spiritual lightning struck. It was like being pierced in some unintelligible way. My heart was opened and, rather than bursting, it grew and grew. The best way I can describe this is to say that both my heart and head felt as though they physically expanded, first getting larger by a matter of inches, then by feet. Soon my body had no boundaries—my heart and my head had encompassed all of space and time.

Now I was really shaking, trembling, vibrating, and sweating. The inner fire became even hotter, vaporizing the molten lava into pure energy as it entered my head. This steam went out of the top of my head and turned into a ball of light that then stretched itself to a kind of oval, egglike shape immediately in front of me.

My body didn't cool down or become still. It continued to shake and boil as I beheld a sacred light that filled itself with the image of Jesus. I was in such an intense state of focus that it does not do justice to the experience to say that I saw Jesus. I saw, heard, and felt him at the same time. Every sensory process in my body was fully alive, creating a multidimensional, holistic encounter of the sacred.

As I beheld Jesus, as I felt him, a realization came that my hands were still hot as fire. I felt that I could heal anyone at that moment. Jesus then showed me other holders of sacred wisdom and light. His image dissolved into the image of the disciples, the Virgin Mary, and many other saints, some of whom I did not know. On and on, this slow-moving picture show continued, a magical multisensory film revealing what seemed like all the holy people who had ever lived. My vision soon went beyond the Christian tradition, becoming a global revelation of what seemed to be the truths of all the world religions. I witnessed images of Ghandi, the Buddha, Mohammed, holy medicine people, shamans, yogis, mystics, and a host of other sacred beings, all residing in immediate luminosity.

In this way I was shown that all religions and spiritual practices come from and return to the same source—a divine light born out of unlimited and unqualified love. This love boils inside the inner spiritual vessel and makes the body quake at the slightest awareness of its presence. As I received what others later told me was "direct transmission," "satori," "cosmic consciousness," and "spiritual rapture," my body dripped with sweat and was baptized with tears that would not stop flowing. I knew, without any doubt, that I was having the most important experience a human being could ever have. And I have never doubted since that time that an experience of that kind is the greatest gift a person can receive.

I believe now that I was hooked up to a cosmic source of timeless wisdom that was principally about relationship and ecological connectedness (rather than particularity and linear cause-and-effect interaction). In this hookup to a spiritual "gas station," I was filled with some kind of spiritual energy and knowing. That night my spiritual insides were rewired. I was reborn and made into a completely different person. I felt as though I received my entire spiritual education that evening, although it is taking me the rest of my life to understand it. From that moment at nineteen years of age, I have carried an inner spiritual heat that precipitates body shaking and trembling as soon as I focus on spiritual matters.

But on that evening, thirty-three years ago from the time I am writing this account, I didn't know what to call what had happened. Nor did I know how to talk about it. I also wasn't sure what to do with the experience. I did find that it took several weeks to cool myself down.

I went to the university bookstore in hope of finding a book that would give me some clue about what had happened. As I walked along one section of the store, a book dropped off the shelf and landed at my feet. I saw that it was the autobiography of a man named Gopi Krishna. This was the first time I ever encountered the word *kundalini*. As I stood there reading Gopi Krishna's account of how kundalini, the yoga term for inner spiritual energy, could be heated and activated, I was astonished to find that other people had had similar experiences to mine. However, in Gopi Krishna's case the kundalini awakening was so strong that it hurt him. I was very lucky to have only felt pure love, bliss, and revelation. There was no pain or horror in my introduction to kundalini.

Later I learned that kundalini is the same as chi, ki, seiki, mana, wakan, jojo, voodoo, Manitou, yesod, baraka, Ruach, holy spirit, and holy ghost power. Whatever name you give it, it is the same. Somehow we all carry this wound-up spring of life force within us, at the base of our spines, and it can be awakened, causing it to heat up and ascend the spinal column. As I learned more about what had happened to me I couldn't help asking why kundalini had awakened in me. Was it an accident, or had I done something to prepare myself for this?

I entered early adulthood with a secret understanding of my place in the world. I was here to help others be touched by spirit, whether directly or indirectly, however circumstances led that to happen. At the same time, I felt I wasn't ready to reactivate the internal heat to the degree that it had already played itself out. I told nobody of my kundalini experience. Something inside me said it would take many years of preparation and training to be ready to return to that kind of experience again.

3
Turning Lines into Circles

ONE OF THE CONSEQUENCES of facing that rapturous illumination was that I became more skeptical about mainstream education. University classrooms seemed like dreary dungeons for the imagination, places where students were simply rewarded for being predictable and obedient. Memorize, regurgitate, and receive a grade: that was conventional education in a nutshell. I wanted to find the books and knowledge that would prepare me to hold and address the mystery that had recently touched my life. But before giving up completely on college education, I wondered what I would find at one of the country's most renowned academic institutions.

One early morning in the summer of 1971, I went to Cambridge and stood by the office of the director of admissions at M.I.T. Upon his arrival, he graciously welcomed me into his office where I reminded him of our meeting at the international science fair. As I had hardly dared to hope, my scholarship was still intact and I was admitted to the university the next week.

It was autumn when I started classes. To my disappointment, M.I.T. began immediately to feel like a soulless place. The buildings and the weather were cold. In spite of all the hype about its reputation, I found this place to be no different pedagogically from any other school that I had attended. It was only more competitive: students worked harder for their grades.

After being at M.I.T. for a month, I was invited to lunch at the faculty club by my academic advisor. There was an impressive grand piano in the lounge. After I played a few tunes on it, my advisor asked me to perform at a party he was hosting. One thing led to another and before long I had an agent setting up bookings to play in Boston society. Music stole my interest and I found myself escaping to the jazz clubs for inspiration.

One evening that autumn, in a smoke-filled basement club on Boylston Street, I experienced the live piano music of Errol Garner, the composer of the popular song *Misty*. Garner was the most joyous improvisationalist I ever heard. With his body keeping time, punctuated by ecstatic smiles and loud grunts, he hardly ever talked to the audience. He communicated solely with his body and through his music.

Garner's songs began with absolutely crazy introductions that gave his drummer and bassist no clue as to what he was going to play. Then he would fall into a groove and the song would be launched with a rhythmic pulse that made everyone in the room swing with him. Unable to read music, Garner was plugged into some mysterious music-making talent whose signature was surprise. Not even Garner knew what or how a song would come forth. His music came directly from the earth's roots. He was an original, unschooled artist, a natural genius.

On that chilly Boston night I felt as though I experienced a spokesperson for the gods. I felt connected to my previous rapture experience. Sitting at a small cocktail table, I wept during his performance. The beauty of that music permeated every cell in my body and I felt inseparable from the pulsing canvas of sound. The next day I found a piano at the university and sat down to play. To my delight, I had somehow absorbed the music from the previous night. I could play in the Garner mode; I felt as though I was plugged in to the same source that moved his fingers on the keyboard. At that moment I fully realized that there was a different kind of learning than what was being offered by high schools and universities. It was learning through absorption, a condition brought on by merging with one's source of inspiration—like my experience of learning Errol Garner's music and like my experience of rapture in the small chapel at the University of Missouri. This was education that happened by *becoming* something rather than by learning *about* it. It didn't matter whether you knew how to specify what *it* was. (Summed up in Garner's words: when an interviewer once asked him about his inability to read music, he quipped "Hell, man, nobody can hear you read.")

Hearing Errol Garner play the piano, you had no doubt that he was plugged into a primal source of creativity and joy. He was an instrument played by the gods. Extraordinary experiences would sometimes take place for him during the music making. Like a shaman who experiences his or her "double," Garner was no stranger to uncommon realities. He once felt he was in the audience watching himself play on the stage.

The night I first heard Errol Garner play live piano was a turning point for me. From that night on, book learning took second place to what I called "absorption learning." The latter only happened when my heart was wide open. Feeling joyous love—in this case, love of Garner's music—enabled the absorption to take place. When this occurred I was immediately transformed. The object of my affection was then with me forever, always alive and available in my heart.

I searched for books that addressed this kind of learning, where the learner and the subject of learning aren't separate. I didn't want the structure of my relationship with the "other"—whether music, wisdom, or people—to be considered in terms of straight lines. In a linear or straight-line relationship, "I" am on one end of a pole while "the other" is distantly located at the opposite end. That's the setup for mainstream dualistic learning: *you* must learn/observe/know/master *it*. I wanted to bend those lines of relational connection into a circle, bringing both sides together. To use Martin Buber's distinction, I wanted to turn an I-it relationship into an I-Thou relation. The only way I could conceptualize doing that was by turning lines into circles.

Thanks to a forthright guidance counselor at M.I.T. who spoke to me about the importance of following my heart, I quit school at the end of my third semester, packed my few possessions, and headed west in a dilapidated Ford Pinto that chugged along at 35 miles an hour. I had always wanted to live in Arizona; as a child I frequently heard the doctor tell my parents that if my health didn't improve, then perhaps the family should move to Arizona, where some people found relief from asthma. My grandfather suffered from allergies and he, too, liked to fantasize about moving west. It was a long trip, but the car finally made it to Phoenix.

I hit the streets with my love of music, playing piano in Phoenix wherever I could get a job. Sometimes I rented a tuxedo for playing at the Arizona Club; other times I wore a string tie to perform at the Moose Club. I eventually enrolled at Arizona State University and completed an undergraduate degree in psychology.

Phoenix provided an opportunity for me to build a sense of what I really wanted and to launch out in a new direction for my life. I learned that it was not all that difficult to follow my dreams and aim my compass toward where my heart and imagination called.

In 1974, several months after my college graduation, I came across the book *Steps to an Ecology of Mind,* written by anthropologist Gregory Bateson. It was the book I had been waiting for, without knowing it. I certainly had never found that book on my university reading lists. Bateson was also not satisfied with linear definitions of human interaction and causality; he turned to systems theory and cybernetics, finding that those scientific disciplines yielded some important directions for moving toward circular knowing, or what he called *cybernetic epistemology.*

Cybernetics can be defined as the science of circular causality, where constantly assessed outcomes help determine ongoing performance. We call such a guidance loop *feedback.* You can't land on the moon by using the geometry of a line—that is, by taking linear aim at the moon and trying to get there with one rocket blast. You must constantly monitor where the rocket ship is in relationship to the moon and make constant corrective adjustments. This circular process of using changes to maintain stability is the focus of simple cybernetics.

Gregory Bateson looked beyond the guidance and control mechanisms of engineering devices, applying the ideas of circular interaction to human conduct and social relationship. One of Bateson's favorite examples of circular relationship was the image of a man cutting down a tree in a forest. We are taught to see a man unilaterally acting upon the surface of the tree with his axe, chopping the tree down without any participation from the tree. However, if we construe the situation as involving a circular process, another description becomes possible. Every notch on the tree is actually directing and organizing how the man will take his next swing. Among other things, the notches determine where, and at what angle, the next cut needs to be located. The causality, if you will, is going both ways: the man acts on the tree and the tree acts on the man.

Seen circularly, you can construe a different understanding and appreciation of the interaction. Tree, axe, and man must all work together to get that tree to fall. Or, from another angle of viewing, they must all cooperate to get the man to walk away from that spot in the forest.

When I examined my music making in terms of this paradigm, I found that the best music arose when I felt as though the piano keys were moving my fingers. During those moments I had no sense of making music. Music was making my fingers move about the keyboard. The same kind of circular description can be applied to other venues of action—writing, painting, cooking, sports, dancing.

Even though I kept quiet and never told anyone about the kundalini awakening I had experienced in the chapel a few years previous, I couldn't keep mysterious occurrences at bay. In a replay of the event in the bookstore when I first learned about kundalini, walking through the university library one day a black book dropped to the floor in front of me. The book was a University of Chicago doctoral dissertation written by José Arguelles. Titled *Charles Henry and the*

Formation of a Psychophysical Aesthetic, the dissertation was about the genius savant and director of the Laboratory of the Physiology of Sensations at the Sorbonne. Charles Henry had been the muse for many post-impressionistic artists, most notably Seurat, Signac, Valery, and Mallarme. The book's appendix included a translation of Henry's ideas about creating a new kind of art, a therapy based on psycho-synesthetic experience, one that conjoined the senses for a kind of holistic revelation. It was a transformative therapy of the whole being that made little sense to me at the time.

I continued my academic studies as a graduate student, hoping to learn more about circular thinking while doing my best to keep the mysterious experiences at bay. I still wasn't ready for them to return. I eventually worked up the courage to call Gregory Bateson, who was living in California at the time, and met with him in October 1976. He became my intellectual mentor, though I didn't reveal my experiences of rapture to him.

Bateson and I organized a conference in 1979 that brought together poet Gary Snyder; essayist, poet, and farmer Wendell Berry; Jungian psychiatrist John Perry; and cultural anthropologist Mary Catherine Bateson, Gregory Bateson's daughter, and others at the Menninger Foundation in Topeka, Kansas. Titled "Size and Shape in Mental Health," the conference was meant to encourage psychotherapists to move away from simplistic cause-and-effect thinking, such as the idea that faulty biochemistry alone causes a mental illness, which can then be fixed by the right medication. Bateson also taught that we should not pay excessive attention to the materiality of things but should instead be more mindful of the patterns that organize a system, whether that system involves therapeutic change, family communication, musical improvisation, or Zen Buddhist learning.

Bateson did not believe in supernatural forces. He attended to the patterns of mind that brought one to what Blaise Pascal called the "reasons of the heart." This pattern-oriented way of knowing gave me a new way to think about my rapture experiences. To rearticulate our previous example, the circle of interaction that constitutes a unit of mind during music traverses the pathway of musician, composition, keyboard, and vibrating strings. From this vantage point it is only a partial description to say that the pianist plays the piano. The piano also plays the musician. More accurately, the mind of music plays both instrument and player.

Circular understanding is arguably a Western equivalent of Buddhist epistemology, with its deconstruction of the illusions that emphasize "thing-ness" rather than the "related-ness" of experience. I think it is accurate to say that my years of studying with Bateson provided me with an outlook similar to what would have been laid into my consciousness by studying spiritual texts. Bateson even mentioned the spiritual implication of cybernetics:

> The cybernetic epistemology which I have offered you would suggest a new approach. The individual mind is immanent but not only in the body. It is immanent also in pathways and messages outside the body; and there is a larger Mind of which the individual mind is only a subsystem. This larger Mind is comparable to God and is perhaps what some people mean by "God," but it is still immanent in the total interconnected social system and planetary ecology. (Bateson, *Steps to an Ecology of Mind*, 461)

Bateson's circular paradigm enabled me to examine my rapture experience without separating the sacred from its beholder. It also helped me realize that any overconcretization of the God that mystics try to experience may paradoxically lead to their separation from God. The more you try to prove the existence of either "yourself" or "God," the more that line separates and distances rather than intimately joins you with the object of devotion. When the mystic surrenders to being no different than the other beings within his range of awareness, the line starts turning into a circle.

Or, to say this differently, the successful mystic cares less about distinguishing himself from any imagined other, including the concept and/or reality of a transcendent God. Immanent God, on the other hand, emerges as the realization of the circularity that relates all things. Not surprisingly, we get closer to God by becoming less distinguishable from the lesser "things," including the sparrows and the smallest grains of sand.

I was fortunate to have another intellectual mentor steeped in cybernetics and circular thinking—the physicist and pioneer of biophysics, Heinz von Foerster, nephew of Ludwig Wittgenstein. Von Foerster believed that understanding meant "standing under another person" so that person could realize her fullest potential. Von Foerster taught me the following principles for what he called "human becoming":

1. to know, you must first act; and
2. always act so as to increase the choices for all involved.

Von Foerster enacted an idea proposed by Bateson: "The truth which is important is not a truth of preference, it's a truth of complexity . . . of a total eco-interactive ongoing web . . . in which we dance, which is the dance of Shiva" (Bateson cited in Stewart Brand, *Two Cybernetic Frontiers*).

In my quest toward absorption learning, I found that I had to first act to put any wheels in motion. It was not possible to first understand music and then bring forth its experience. If I waited for a complete understanding of how to make music, I'd never get to the piano bench. The first action necessary for absorption was nothing less than making a sound, any sound—or in my case, hitting any key on the piano. Music making was what you did next with the sound. To paraphrase jazz pianist Oscar Peterson, there are no wrong notes or mistakes in jazz because improvisation is all about what you do with the music at any given moment. Hitting a clunker note is simply a surprise that must be creatively woven into the ongoing flow of sounds.

This perspective asks the musician to be a servant of the music (and the instrument) as opposed to being its proud master. Here the musician's job is to pay close attention to what is happening to move things along in an aesthetically satisfying way. This is pure cybernetic process. From the circular way of knowing and being, one necessarily addresses and involves all the constituents of a given context. Acting for the good of all elements involved helps turn lines into circles. In the domain of mysticism, it requires a surrendering of the hierarchical importance of your life. You must get smaller to get the bigger picture.

In this time, during the late 1970s and early 1980s, when I was studying cybernetic theory, I was also learning to be a family therapist in my position as a "communications analyst" at the Menninger Foundation in Topeka, Kansas, and in being a doctoral student in family therapy at Purdue University. In its beginning days, family therapy was a paradigmatically different orientation to solving human problems than other therapeutic orientations. Rather than emphasizing psychiatric medication, the pioneers of family therapy, including Don Jackson, Milton H. Erickson, Carl Whitaker, and Virginia Satir, first looked for the circular patterns that organized people's interactions and experiences and then intervened in ways to help evolve more resourceful outcomes for all members of the family. Diagnosis, or understanding the client's situation, involved seeing what the client did with your efforts to help her to change.

This practice was called circular, or interactional, diagnosis. Looking more like shamans than medical doctors, the early family therapists promised to revolutionize the psychotherapy profession, showing how everything from so-called schizophrenia to clinical depression could often be efficiently alleviated by social interventions. Unfortunately, by the 1990s the economic power of the major pharmacological corporations pulled the carpet from underneath the feet of talk therapy, trumping it with a biomedical model that had facile explanations (and pharmacological treatments for) anyone within its reach.

In the earlier days of my academic and therapeutic careers, I proposed that being an effective agent of change had little to do with understanding the other person or group being treated. I thought it better to assume that you can never understand your client and that your client will never understand herself. Moments of temporary illusion of

understanding may punctuate one's life, but all in all any grand understanding or narrative structure of a human being's existence is absurd.

Setting aside understanding—and doing so in a culture addicted
to the myth of understanding, particularly psychological explanation—leaves us free to act. We take more responsibility for our
actions when we accept that what happens around us is intimately
related to how we act. In this radical constructivist view, I followed
R.D. Laing's dictum to see the world in terms of *capta* (capturing,
construing, constructing, assuming invention and fiction) rather than
data (representing, objectifying, concretizing, assuming discovery and
realness). Giving a client a psychological exam constructs pathology
more than it identifies one. Such action needs to be judged as to
whether it is the most ethical way to commune with another human
being. As an alternative, acting so as to help spring forth surprise, joy,
absurdity, or just plain difference is arguably a more responsible way
of being with others.

With all this as foreground, I abandoned any pseudoscientific con-
textualization of psychotherapy over two decades ago and invented a
therapy based on improvisation; that is, inventing a unique therapeutic approach for every session and client. During the 1980s I used the
performing arts (rather than psychology or medical science) as a con-
textual framework and encouraged therapists to create a theatrical
encounter for their clients, with the goal of moving both client and
therapist into being more imaginative in approaching the issues at
hand. I eventually called this improvisational approach "resource-
focused therapy," to accentuate the positive thrust of this nonpatholo-
gizing orientation.

During my days of pursuing circular thought and therapeutic action
I was consciously aware of holding a lid on my inner spiritual awakening. I even stopped playing the piano for several years out of concern
that it might reactivate the inner heat. I did this while writing books and
teaching throughout the world. Working in a variety of psychotherapy
training centers, including the Menninger Foundation, the Ackerman
Institute for Family Therapy in New York City, the Philadelphia Child

Guidance Clinic, and as director of two doctoral programs in family therapy, I learned more about teaching others how to use circular thinking and interaction in the helping professions.

In 1982, at the height of my involvement in the field of family therapy, I wrote an essay for one of the field's leading journals, *Family Process,* that created a stir similar to the one brought on by my radical newsletter back at the Baptist college. Following in Bateson's footsteps, in the essay I challenged the importance of the "power" metaphor in understanding human experience. I argued for an aesthetics of therapy that would temper any false sense of arrogant knowing brought about by overly pragmatic, technique-oriented approaches to helping others.

That suggestion caused quite a commotion in the psychotherapy hierarchy! One article after another criticized me for even asking the question, Does the metaphor of power provide a resourceful way of conceptualizing therapy? In tones of anger and disgust, I was accused of being irresponsible: how dare anyone think of human relationship outside the explanatory theme that depicted people as being all about exercising power and hierarchy over one another? Lynn Hoffman, one of the key historians in the field of family therapy, called this the "dark period" in the field, when the revered assumptions about human social behavior were challenged. During that time I found out how deeply allergic many of the leaders of psychotherapy were to concepts of love and beauty; they had instead made a pact with the epistemology of power and control. And I had bumped smack into the same cultural beliefs that fuel materialistic greed, ego importance, and social hierarchies. Bring in the word *love* and the rhetorical rifles come out. What a strange cultural climate we had created. I longed to find a culture more committed to the tenets of compassion and forgiveness, sharing and stewardship.

I responded to all of these attacks and criticisms in 1982 with an essay in *Family Process* entitled, "Not Aesthetics, Not Pragmatics." I argued that each voice was a partial truth and that it was the whole ecology of the discussion that was vital to respect and maintain. I took the one-down position of declaring myself no wiser than any idea I had critiqued.

It had been over a decade since my experience of rapture in a university chapel. Since that time, I often worked day and night to cultivate a circular way of knowing the world. My monastery had been the university and the academic worlds of family therapy and cybernetic theory. Those were the days when I battled the "line people," trying to encourage them (along with myself) to turn lines into circles.

Now, battle worn and somewhat wiser than in my youth, I felt a big change in the air. I wondered whether I was ready to return to the mysteries that originally shook my whole being and gave birth to visionary experience. Before going to sleep each night, I prayed for the next chapter of my life to begin.

4
Starting Over

IN 1988 THE INNER HEAT and mystical excitation announced itself again. One day in October, while sitting at my desk at Nova University in Fort Lauderdale where I was creating a new doctoral program in family therapy, I suddenly felt the same sense of calm and knowing come over me as that one time many years before. This time, however, I did not walk to a chapel and I did not approach the experience alone. I went to Mary, a good friend and natural synesthete, who encountered the world on a multisensory level; Mary would often speak in terms of "hearing color" and "seeing sound." I asked Mary to walk with me, and she came without hesitation.

We silently strolled to a park in the middle of a sunny day in south Florida, then sat on the ground and faced one another holding hands. Soon the inner heat started and my body began to tremble and vibrate. Mary's hands also started tremoring and we shook together. We sat as close as we could and embraced, holding on to one another lest some hurricanelike force whisk us away. The inner heat began to feel like fire, while the shaking escalated. We both shook in synchrony, closely linked through pulse and rhythm.

As the shaking energy amplified it seemed to me that my body was evaporating. I was only aware of vibrations. This time when the energetic

33

heat came out of my head, it was different from my early rapture experience. The inner heat did not turn into a cloud of light. Instead, it felt as though my whole head propelled itself into space. I saw specks of light, like stars in a galaxy, scattered amid a great black void. I was floating in the dark, perhaps the outer space of my imagination. And I only felt bliss. Mary, too, was powerfully moved by the experience. We both began weeping, feeling overcome by the ecstatic, shaking embrace.

We laughed when we tried to talk about the experience, thinking how anyone overhearing our conversation might imagine that we were talking about sex. I didn't know what we had just experienced, but I wanted to explore it further. I proceeded to study the experiences that take place when two people interact with body vibrations and shaking. I wanted to explore this phenomenon with any person who was willing to share that adventure with me.

In these relational encounters the world of interactional shaking was opened to me. Years later I was to learn that this practice and teaching also takes place in various parts of the world, from Tibet to Africa, but is usually done in secret. In these explorations I learned that it was possible to initiate vibrating in another person—the "shake" could be passed on to others. Sometimes that person would experience an opening of his heart and enter a blissful experience; some people reported seeing a divine light. I spent years experimenting with different ways of instilling this spirited feeling into other people, both privately and in small and large groups gathered for ceremonial purposes. I called this stage of my spiritual development "tinkering in the carnival of the spirit" because of the number of imaginative experiences that surrounded this kind of play.

Some six years before I had my interactional mystical experience in Florida, I made a visit to Minneapolis, Minnesota. It was an evening in the winter of 1982, one of the coldest nights I can remember. I was there to give a lecture on how circular and systems thinking can help us change our ways of helping others. In the audience was an Ojibway medicine man named Sam Gurnoe. At the end of my talk Sam came up and said "My people know about the circles of life. It's our natural way to be systemic and circular. Why don't you come visit us and see a culture that lives what you are talking about?" I had a feeling that some day I would return to Minnesota and learn from Sam.

While in Florida, almost immediately after the interactional shaking began, an opportunity came to teach at a college near where Sam lived. I took the job and moved to Minnesota. That's when my life started all over again.

I went to Sam in the fall of 1989, offered him some tobacco—the custom in his culture for asking someone for help or teachings—and told him I was ready to learn. Within a month Sam arranged a sweat lodge in a Minnesota woods on the edge of a serene lake. With a group of men, I crawled into a dome structure made of willow branches and covered with blankets. As the hot rocks were brought in and filled the room with a forceful heat, Sam prayed and sang his sacred songs.

Sam had a vision of placing me on a cliff. There in the sweat lodge, through the eyes of his inner seeing, he saw me ask the Creator for guidance. He told me what he saw, saying, "I hope that my cultural tradition may help you find strength in your own." He graciously suggested that we pray as brothers and find nourishment from the spiritual homes we had grown up in.

Over the next couple of months Sam prepared me for the vision fast, teaching about the cultural history that embraced it. In the middle of the night before we were to drive out to the wilderness area, I woke up inside of a visionary experience. Standing in the corner of the room was an elder medicine man who waved me over to a group of elders standing in a circle, all in traditional dress. They began to speak about their sacred pipe and holy ways. Although they were speaking in their native language, I intuitively understood what was being said. I was fully conscious and awake as I listened to the words of these spiritual teachers.

That morning we drove to western Minnesota, to a forested area with many cliffs. We built a sweat lodge and made prayers. Sam was a strict teacher, always making sure that I understood the culture's traditional way of doing things and giving me constant lessons on language, history, and customs. The next morning he woke me up and offered me a plate of hot cinnamon rolls, something he knew I craved. I turned them away and Sam replied, "Okay, now you are ready to begin."

We hiked out to a cliff and Sam helped me set up my prayer flags and tobacco offerings. He gave me a pipe to pray with and then left me alone to seek guidance and vision. I prayed all day; nervously, I waited for night to approach. I was a complete virgin to the forest, having never been camping in my life. It was early spring in Minnesota and it gets very cold during that time of year. I was there with only a blanket, a pipe, and tobacco. My responsibility was to pray with as much sincerity as I could. I still remember when the stars came out and the beauty of the night cast its spell. I fell into a deep sleep.

It wasn't long before I was awakened by a sound that made my whole body shiver. Peering out from under my blanket, I saw a coyote standing quite near to me. I recognized its sound as a musical intonation heard in many American Indian songs. Rather than being frightened into stillness, I began singing with the animal. In that moment I learned to open my voice in a spirited way.

The same energy that had been known to shake my body now came out of my mouth as sound. I sang and sang, feeling related to the coyote. It was gracing me with this visit, and I wanted to honor its presence.

The coyote eventually walked away and I collapsed into sleep again, exhausted by the vigor of the song vibration that had just moved through me in the wild night.

The next time I woke up I was momentarily confused as to where I was. Fog was everywhere around me and there was a slightly glowing light in its midst. It seemed as though I was lying in the middle of a cloud. Then, seemingly out of nowhere, an eagle flew in front of my face. For what may have been only a second I stared into its small eyes, but that moment seemed to go on and on; I felt a bolt of energy enter my eyes and travel down to the bottom of my spine. My body jolted upright and I let out a loud shout. With my coyote's voice I began singing and started dancing there on the cliff. I danced and sang myself into rapture.

My intimate contact with that eagle erased the differences between us. The emotional relationship was so vitally present that it overtook any intellectual distinction between a winged being and a human one. In our contact and subsequent expression, I became inseparably interwoven with what I beheld. The eagle sang through me and with me, touching currents that had been experienced once in a small university chapel and again with another human being in a park. Now I knew the vibrations of that inner heat, that shaking and song making, in the context of being absorbed into relationship with nature.

I spent the day giving thanks for the experience and the way in which it opened my mind to a greater mind of the wild. I came home recharged to continue my journey. What I did not know was that I had somehow opened the door to an inner dreamscape that would take over the direction of my life. I found that the visitation of those medicine men in my bedroom and the encounter with the coyote and eagle were the beginning points of a new life, one in which I often received visions and dreams. The visions would not be symbolic enigmas to decipher for deep meaning; most times they were direct prescriptions for action, giving me information on a place to go or a person to meet and what to do and say once there. On that cliff in Minnesota I became a pilgrim guided by my visions.

In my journey from becoming a circular thinker to an improvisational therapist to a vision-seeking, shaking shaman, I did not abandon my previous ways of thinking and being with others. I found that being an improvisational therapist made me a more complete circular thinker; similarly, becoming a shaman expanded my circular participation in therapy. Most important, I found over and over again that, no matter what system of metaphor or practice I was working with, all paths led to the same affirmation of love and its fostering of circular relationship, where we feel one with the beloved. Love is the holiest circle, holding the only tonic that can quench our deepest intellectual, creative, and spiritual thirsts.

As a matter of curiosity I once tried a clinical experiment. I went to a hypnotist and asked him to put me into trance and regress me to the time when I had my original rapture experience. Would I re-experience what took place then or would there be something new? The hypnotist placed me into a relaxed state and reminded me of where I was at the time of the experience, with all of its sights, sounds, smells, and body sensations. In my imagination I was taken back to that campus chapel. Sure enough, I again saw that light. But this time there were no images: there was only a white light. I then heard an inner voice calmly say, "Your heart is the instrument of divine perception. Find a copy of *Creative Imagination in the Sufism of Ibn 'Arabi* by Henry Corbin."

I had no idea who Ibn 'Arabi or Corbin were, but when I came out of that trance state I located a bookstore that carried that book. When I opened it I found these same words: "Your heart is the instrument of divine perception." The passage within the book went on to describe the heart as the organ that produces the gnosis of God. Furthermore, the heart's power is a secret energy that enables direct perception of divine realities, "like a mirror in which the microcosmic form of the Divine Being is reflected."

Time and again this sort of experience presented itself, pushing me toward learning more about mystical illumination and love through the practices of circular thinking, psychotherapy, and shamanism. In my pursuits I found that the wisest shamans and traditional healers of indigenous cultures seek to address and make a relationship with circular patterns of mind rather than getting caught in the back-and-forth oscillations (and battles) of linear causality. As more encompassing circles of connectivity are brought into play, the sacred becomes more easily revealed and experienced. Here dreams direct healing encounters and provide vision for one's life. This is the realm of the active divine, where interventions, like spiritual lightning bolts, arrive unexpectedly to shake up one's life.

As I studied the traditional healing practices of shamans and medicine people throughout the world, armed with the premises of circular thinking, I felt fairly immune to the temptation to "draw lines" upon my experience. I was not interested in making theories that underscored the differences between anthropologist and subject, therapist and client, observer and observed. I interacted as a means of participating in a circle of connection. To know the Bushman experiential universe, for instance, I danced all night with their traditional doctors, allowing the ecstatic interactions to vibrate and shake my body into synesthetic experience. In that heightened state of awareness, I could see what was felt and hear what was touched. The shaman's world revealed not an inner world of private hallucinations but an opening into other circles of being.

Shamans first move the locus of mind to the heart and whole body rather than to the inside of the computational cerebral brain. This whole-body knowing is, in turn, a vehicle for stepping into relational mind, allowing for "the other" to be felt in more intimate and expressive ways. As we are absorbed into the greater relationships around us, whether with another person or a redwood forest, we enter the domain of sacred mind. This broader mind touches, awakens, and deepens our connection with one another and brings us inside the mind of nature, an ecology that holds diverse ways of knowing and being.

The most powerful experience shared by all shamanic healers is the deep bond and love in their relationships with others. Ecstatic bliss arises when they throw themselves into spirited shaking and dancing, which serves to open their hearts. Shamans help bring forth the spirited interactions that open the doors to circular, absorptive relations with others. I hold that this is an entry to the Big Love.

An ecosystem, when left alone from human intervention, takes care of itself. The processes that generate life also sustain it. When shamans bring a community into the mind of ecology, every member becomes linked within an unbroken circle. This becomes a pattern of healing that naturally connects and corrects, without anyone having to do a thing. Seen this way, the actions of a shaman are not directed toward curing a specific symptom but are meant to carry a community into a different circle of mind. When this relational, communal, ecological mind prays in harmonic resonance, the whole system reverberates with the pulse of life. Then it is life that heals.

Stated differently, the solution to a problem in life is stepping more fully into life. Doing so doesn't necessarily mean that everyone's symptoms will disappear. Sometimes a symptom appears, and at times even death is required, to keep the ecosystem vibrant and appropriately alive: the ecosystem exercises its capacity to initiate healing responses. We, too, must sometimes be ill, and we must sometimes "sin," to activate and tune the processes that keep us alive and redeemed. Individual death and various forms of social crucifixions provide the ecology with an opportunity to exert its capacity for supporting life and human transformation.

Circular thinking provided me with a means for recognizing the shaman's way of being. As a double agent of change, the shaman attempts to break open the closed circles of psychological mind and reconnect us within other patterns of circular process. Whether involving the inclusion of an exterior other (imagined or material) or the relational dance of a family or the choreography of a vibrant ecology, shamans open and reconnect us with larger circles of mind. Doing so facilitates the self-corrective natural healing of whole systems.

As a circular thinker climbs the sacred ladder toward what some dare to call spiritual realizations, we find more and more paradoxes, absurdities, and nonspecifiable expressions of the heart. The experiences that come to us when we stand inside the circle of sacred mind evoke the ancient riddles of relationship. From this vantage point, paradoxical complementarities spew forth never-ending teases and tensions: love is found to be a companion to hate. The manure of relationship is necessary to fertilize its garden of delights.

In the loftiest spiritual realms reside the secrets seldom discussed by anyone other than the high priests and priestesses. Here we find the sacred in bed with the profane. God's bearded face is found on the same body as the hooves of Satan, as William Blake once envisioned in one of his illustrations for the biblical Book of Job. In God's court, fools hold the holiest powers and wisdom. To enter and stand still in this locale requires that one not overindulge in either good or evil. Judgment must be absolutely stilled to maintain balance in the middle of this whirlwind. The middle place of intersecting contraries gives birth to the circular movement of spirit, the very breath of life. This is the view from on high that, in turn, is mirrored in the view from way below.

The flat-planed, straight-line world of naïve legal judgment and psychological explanation is removed from this greater mind of knowing. Attorneys and therapists are not asked to seek sacred visions to help their communities. They extract a slice of the ecology of human interaction and draw simplistic lines that mark victims and villains and then set themselves up to punish and reward.

Overfocusing on any variable in an ecosystem as a way of trying to fulfill the greater good is antithetical to circular (and shamanic/spiritual/religious) wisdom. In the greater ecology of being, we should not take any event out of its context. In a sacred ecology, the agents of evil foster and maintain a dance with the saints. It is the dance that is divine, not either partner in the interaction. However, when "do-gooders," liberal and conservative alike, ban the dance or limit the sacred alternatives, the whole ecology suffers and we are assaulted by the devastating consequences of those who naively and unwisely march for the general good. Cutting a circle and straightening it into a line constitutes ecological violence.

Healing, therapy, and correction do not necessarily require judgment (or diagnosis) and singular attention to any particular part, whether that be an action or interaction, a person, group or nation. Circular wisdom traditions teach forgiveness and love for one's enemies. In the most important matters of our lives, circular thinking joins hands with the spiritual truths of the world's religions.

5

Meeting the Bushmen

FASTING ON A CLIFF HELPED open the inner sight of my imagination. In the wake of my experience under Sam's tutelage, I began to dream of shamans, healers, and medicine people from all over the world. These dreams were not the stuff of psychological fantasy, suitable for metaphoric examination and analysis. Rather, I would see a person, a book, a map, a ceremony, a place—I would literally hear a voice telling me where to go and what to do. I would do my research to see whether the visionary information held up. Most times it did.

I could not explain how or why this was happening. I did nothing consciously to open this line of communication. I didn't even know such a relationship with dreams was possible. In some way, my time with Sam Gurnoe and his cultural tradition had turned on a switch that connected me to a wider sphere of knowing.

When it dawned on me that I was being taught by dreams, my life changed dramatically. I organized my schedule according to the directions I received in visionary states. These dreams took me to various American Indian elders as well as to an inner city African American church; that was how they enhanced my local relations. But the dreams also called for me to travel to faraway cultures and meet elders who practiced shamanic ways.

From the time that I began shaking with the spirits, back when I had that first rapturous awakening, I always wondered whether there were others having the same experience. Although it was reassuring to discover yoga traditions that accessed and handled what they called kundalini energy, they weren't quite the same as the practice that I had stumbled upon. I never meditated or had a spiritual teacher who gave instructions about how to move the inner life force—after being hit with spiritual lightning, that just happened automatically. Furthermore, I stumbled upon the fact that this shaking and vibrating experience could be passed on to others, like an enthusiastic and natural (though somewhat strange) game of spiritual tag.

In the summer of 1990 I came across the short documentary film *N/um Tchai* about the Bushman healing dance. I immediately recognized familiar territory: I watched people shaking and passing the ecstatic body trembling on to one another. The oldest living culture's ecstatic expressions were readily identifiable to me; the movements, sounds, and interactions recorded on the film were all part of my experience. Without knowing it, I had been practicing a form of vibrant touch and ecstatic encounter similar to the Bushmen's.

I wanted to visit the Bushmen. In an experience that was coming to be oddly familiar, within weeks I had a vivid dream in which a mark on a map of the central Kalahari Desert indicated where I should go. The marker pointed to the southern border of the Khutse Game Reserve in Botswana. I went to the library and looked up a map of Africa. What I had seen in my dreams was an actual physical place.

Not long after that dream I received a phone call from the University of South Africa asking me to come teach as a visiting professor. I replied that I would accept the invitation on one condition: that someone take me to the Kalahari to meet the Bushmen. I was told that a professor named Peter Johnson would organize a field expedition.

The following year, in March of 1992, after being in South Africa for a while, I told Peter how I had arrived at my decision to accept the visiting professorship. I could see that Peter wasn't quite sure that I knew what I was talking about; on the other hand, he had already heard about my visits to traditional *sangomas* (healers) around South Africa and how I had experienced dreams that enabled me to talk openly with them. He knew that I had had an extraordinary experience with his colleague Stan, another professor at the university. I was in Stan's home, looking at a certain mask, when I went into some kind of a shaking trance. In that dreamlike awareness, I remember:

Giant crocodile, taking dead aim at me. There is nowhere to go. My soul has already entered this fate. Jaws up, teeth sinking into my flesh, a bloodcurdling voice shouts "Now we will never let you go!" Drumming starts, pulsing through the scales of the prehistoric beast. Dark odors linked to oldest fears. Primitive power unknown by any man. Built to destroy, life married to clashing teeth and bloodthirsty slaughter feeding a frenzy of insatiable desire. Instantly, without warning, mangling and devouring the delicate and soft.

Mythodile, neither good nor evil, takes me under water, and another opening is born. Whatever I had known is now destroyed, then taught again, in this hot belly. After the death I breathe water, seeing currents underground. "Hey-shee-moh-ka-may-hem!" Chants emerge, like bubbles rising from final underwater breaths. "Moh-key, nah-soma!" Lions roar, monkeys scream—thundering bellows, screeching pitches—and then deep, gutteral staccato breaths, sounds, and snorts. I am delivered to earth wet, limbs folded into fetal position, convulsing on the floor, ready for the final gasp. It is impossible to breathe the air. Desperately wiping sweat into my mouth, I long for the water but must remember how to breathe as man.

I enter a tunnel of black. Accelerating through the dark, I am suddenly thrown backward. Again my body hits the floor. Eyes still above, I look down and see a man naked, covered in mud, wearing a necklace of crocodile teeth. My university friend greets me, "Good morning, ancestor, welcome back."

Seeking an explanation of this visionary journey, Stan and I climbed into his jeep and went to consult the local sangoma, an elder woman traditional healer well versed in crossing the crocodile boundary. Covered with beads and holding a stick with animal hair, she brushed me and gave me the dried blood of a crocodile to swallow. The bubbling waters of the African dreamscape took me down again, this time into the skin of a snake. Slithering across the floor, I felt at home. In that impoverished shack with the dirt floor and leaky tin roof, gateway to a universe beyond a midwestern boy's imagination, my body proclaimed "Africa, I embrace thee."

As I regained consciousness of the others in the room, the sangoma spoke for the first time. "You must immediately go find those crocodile teeth that ate you and make a necklace of them." I looked at her with eyes of fire, trembling hands of animal being hunted and hunting at the same time. I recognized her truth. I allowed my body to continue shaking, opening further the lens of wider viewing that is the compass of the hunter. "Take me to the center of the village," I asked of my colleague. "There's a shop there that I will recognize."

We drove around a settlement outside of Pretoria where poverty was displayed in every shanty's nook and corner. Cookfires burned, the smoke-smell everywhere. Then I saw the place: in front of us was a tin shack that sells traditional medicines, a *muti* shop. I walked into that small, barely-threaded-together structure and looked at the monkey skins and skulls, jars of strange bones, herbs, and other unknown things. Then, without equivocation, I walked to the back counter, stood on a wooden box, and reached behind a glass jar. My hands felt a bag. I pulled it out. Inside was a complete set of crocodile teeth. Shocked, the woman attending the shop nervously cried out "How did you know that was there? Are you a sangoma?"

She rushed out of the shop, mumbling as she went, and I worried that she was fetching the police. Had I broken some taboo?

The shop attendant came back shortly with an old man, the local sangoma, beside her. He asked why I was interested in the crocodile teeth. When I told him my story, he said, "You must come to my home.

We need to make a ceremony and call forth the ancestors."

His hut had symbols painted at the threshold: snakes in vertical ascent. Stepping inside the mud-molded entrance, I saw a lion's skin hanging on the wall. The sangoma called for the people who were nearby to join us. They picked up drums—some small, others large, all covered with elephant skins—and began to beat them. The rhythms of spiritual seduction and intoxication sent me where I needed to go. "Eeh-shee-moh-ka! No-sho-ma-kah!" I was back in the void where animal and man pass through one another, exchanging archetypal sounds and postures: shapeshifting, morphing into one form and then another, moving through earth, fire, water, and sky.

The old man, now covered in his shamanic paraphernalia, came over and spoke words I did not understand, but the wild beast inside me knew fully well the poetry and music of this other shamanic voyager into the night. I died another ritualistic death and went to another place, found another voice, not beast from lost time but old African man from an unseen crack in historical memory. I spoke with him, lips moving at the same time, followed by a silence that screamed until it wept. I reentered the light of day, smelling sour beer trickling down the top of my head. I was told to dance. I had to dance the spirit, respect its presence in my body, honor its wisdom, and then let it go back to sleep. It would then reside deep inside my body, ready for the next call of African drum and pulsing command.

The old man was very pleased. He patted me on the back, making congratulatory gestures. "You are welcome here. This is your home. I see that we are the same. The spirits already own you, my child. You belong to them. Your grandfather is very strong. He is taking care of you. Oh, if I was young again and able to walk like I used to, I would take you to African places no one has ever seen or heard about. But I know that somehow you will find your way there. Makhosi, Makhosi." (Makhosi is an honorific title used by Zulu sangomas when addressing the ancestral spirits.) When I was about to leave that day he offered me his lion skin, which he had received from his grandfather, himself a respected sangoma. I declined the skin, remembering Sam Gurnoe's teaching that I should be careful about what I accept as a spiritual gift, never taking something of spiritual power that I did not dream. I thanked the old man for the gift of the crocodile teeth.

The next day, in another bizarre and yet increasingly common experience of crossing between worlds, I went back to the university to teach a class on psychotherapy.

That was the kind of story Peter had grown accustomed to hearing about me, so when it came time to follow a map I had seen in a dream, it did not come as a shock to him. An ethnographer who interviewed street prostitutes to understand their social reality, Peter was ready to observe and query the visiting professor who hung out in the streets, embracing old men and women who wore beaded headdresses and beat drums made of metal cans covered in elephant skins. He was curious to see how this adventure would turn out.

When it came time to go we had a small truck packed with water, food, and the necessary supplies. We headed north for the Kalahari to meet the Bushmen shakers.

Across the desert sand we rolled, kilometer after kilometer. The thick sand rested upon a layer of basalt rock 200 to 400 meters deep, where the water table is most often located. We were heading to a small reserve that adjoins the Central Kalahari Game Reserve, the latter covering 52,800 square kilometers (20,000 square miles). It is the second largest protected area in the world. Gemsbok darted by our side, a reminder of the remarkable capacity they have to survive without water.

We repeatedly got stuck in the sand and had to dig out a path for the truck, a routine chore for a Kalahari voyage, as Peter assured me. While it is commonly known as a desert, parts of the Kalahari actually receive an annual rainfall of 150 millimeters, making it hospitable to wild grasses and hardy trees. It would be more accurate to call the Kalahari a "thirstland." Here the tree roots go down to the rocks to reach the water table. Though a deadly place for the unprepared, life abounds in the Kalahari.

Peter wiped the sweat off his brow. His voice carried a worried tone. "We may not have enough fuel to make it. I did mention, I think, during the second day out, that there's no way to get any out here. If we're not careful we could get stuck. I think we should turn around."

With my faithful optimism I replied, "We've come too far not to go on. A little trust, please." Peter shrugged his shoulders, heaved a big sigh, and headed further north.

I thought about how the Kalahari was considered the largest continuous sand body in the world, an expanse of two million square kilometers. The sand below us was as deep as 100 meters, although sometimes it could get as shallow as 20 meters. I thought of how my mother used to sing me to sleep when I was a child with the song verse, "Mr. Sandman, bring me a dream." I began to sing; Peter's frown dissolved into a smile. We were entering the Kalahari Dreamtime.

At just about the time that we were out of fuel, I looked along the horizon and saw a distant gathering of Bushmen. We stopped the truck and I ran toward them. I went up to the oldest of the men, recognizing who I had seen in my dream. Our arms reached out for one another and we embraced as if it were a homecoming. Immediately the old man, whose name I was later to find out was Mantag, the chief of his village, began to shake. I shook with him. Without words we were already communicating; we were meeting through our bodies, expressing through vibrations what I had traveled across the globe to "discuss." As we shook, some of the women in the community gathered around us with their children and began singing a song and clapping their hands to make a vibrant rhythm. That was my first experience of shaking with a Bushman.

Other men came up to us. We all exchanged these shaking hugs and began to make the songs and noises characteristic of Bushman shamans. When we settled down, I introduced myself with the help of our translator. I told them I had received a dream that instructed me to come visit them. Old Mantag replied, "Yes, we know. You are the Bushman we have been waiting for." Pointing to a tree in the distance, he continued, "That camelthorn tree over there is your home. It is where you belong and it is where your spirit will return when it is time for you to die. Tonight we will dance and I will tell you all that I know. I can see that it will be a very good dance."

The day before we had arrived at their village, I had a dream in which I saw a thin man with brilliant brown eyes and a smile that shone. In the dream he said "I am Twele and I will serve as your guide." When I told Peter, he was teasingly apprehensive. "Well then, we shall see about this dream business. I'll keep my eyes and ears open for a Twele." Peter, the quiet ethnographer and systemic therapist, couldn't help but show his enthusiasm for our adventure.

As we set up our tents, Peter reminded me to be on the lookout for wildlife. "We might see some giraffe, cheetah, kudu, honey badger, leopard, or a lion." I looked up and instead saw a thin man walking toward me. He was wearing an olive-colored work shirt; as he approached I saw that he had three deep wrinkles etched into his forehead and a circle that outlined his nose and chin when he smiled. He walked straight to us and introduced himself. "I am Twele. I am here to be your guide. You can ask me anything about our culture because the shamans said you were one of them."

With great excitement I clapped my hands and hugged Twele. We both began shaking, as had happened earlier with the elders. Then I said, "Let's get started. Please tell me what you experience when you are in the dance." Happy to meet a white man who could communicate in their most intimate mode of expression, Twele began talking.

"For me, it is a very special time. I love to dance. It is the favorite thing for all Bushmen to do. We dance when we are happy and we dance when we are sad. When we get ready to hunt we dance because it helps us find the animal, and then after the kill we bring home the meat and dance again. We also dance when we feel sick. It helps us take away the sickness and it keeps us well. The dance is the most important aspect of our lives. It is our prayer, our medicine, our teaching, and our way of having fun. Everything we do is related to that dance."

"For shamans, the dance helps them feel the power that causes the shaking. We see that you already understand this. For me, I feel my hands getting very hot when I touch others in the dance. When the people sing loudly and I dance, the power comes into my feet. It is the power from the music and the seriousness of the occasion that makes me very hot. It comes into my head and I feel it as a kind of steam that makes my head feel larger. A light then comes over the dance. My body also seems to become lighter in weight and I feel like I am floating over the ground. It will be good to dance with you tonight!"

As night appeared on the horizon, the community gathered to prepare for the dance. Twele told me that there were still herds of elands in the area, a very special animal for the Bushmen. While he was talking, I spotted an ostrich in the distance; a black-breasted snake eagle flew overhead. Branches gathered from nearby trees were brought to make a fire. The women arranged themselves in a circle to clap and start the songs. All of the community came to the dance, ready to put electricity in the air under a sky filled with onlooking stars.

At first I stood outside the dance circle watching with Peter, who was unusually serious, not teasing as he had done so far throughout the trip. Peter was fully into the moment, and his silent presence encouraged me to jump right in. It only took a few minutes for me to feel the now-familiar tingling in my legs. My calves and thighs felt like sharp needles were being stuck into them. They twitched and jerked as the pricking gave way to the flow of an inner current. I told Peter, "I feel the electricity. Look at my legs." He smiled and said, "Yes sir, you are definitely plugged in." Then, without expectation, I felt my hip muscles start to move. It was as if there were strings attached to my hips held by some puppeteer in the sky who was lifting them up and down. The dance had caught me. The Bushmen noticed and clapped their hands, shouting with joy. They, too, knew that I had been snared.

I didn't dance that night. It's more correct to say that I was danced—I exerted absolutely no effort or willful intention. Twele and Mantag gracefully moved over to me and brought me into the line of men who were dancing around the fire. I had entered the dance and was doing it with no choreography, dance lessons, or understanding of what was taking place.

I looked up to the sky and saw the Southern Cross, which to the Bushmen represents two male lions in their pride. As I received that thought of the lions the women ululated, shaping sound by the movement of their hands in front of their open mouths. Feeling the tug of unseen hands, I turned and watched as more wood was thrown in the fire. As sparks streaked toward the heavens, parts of me switched on, an internal power station setting up for some heavy work in the night. Waves of sounds, sand, and stars began to merge as I surrendered to the moment, allowing myself to be moved by the rising and falling tides of human energy.

Improvisation is my modus operandi, even in the Kalahari. Years before I had written a book entitled *Improvisational Therapy;* in it I argued that therapy should be invented for the situation at hand. All clients require a unique therapy, tailor-made to enable their uniqueness to be fully met in the most resourceful fashion. I argued that therapy should be considered a kind of improvisational theater. I extended this way of thinking to teaching, seeing each class session as an opportunity to improvise an experience that might make a difference in the lives of each there. As I met shamans around the world I saw that they, too, often improvised their conduct to evoke and touch a soulful gathering.

As I traveled between cultures, I did so with a devotion to spirited improvisation. When I attended a ceremony I waited to be inspired, "grabbed," moved by the spirit of the moment to bring forth expression that was spontaneous and natural. I didn't go into the experience wanting any specific outcome—in fact, I was content even if nothing happened, okay with simply standing outside the circle and observing. I chased away any sense of purpose and intention other than the purpose of being fully present and freely available to what was going on. I kept quiet the mind that judges and evaluates, following whatever happened to move me at the moment, as long as it served the God of the Big Love. What I found was that whenever the deepest part of my being—my unconscious mind, if you want to call it that—felt the spirit or life force that was in the air, my body would move automatically: quivering, vibrating, jerking, shaking, dancing. I just moved out of the way and let it happen, whether the gathering was of Buddhists, Christians, Jews, Ojibway, Guarani, Zulu, or Bushmen. I simply allowed myself to be moved by spirit at the moment.

I discovered that spirit would grab me whenever it wanted, whether I was filled with pure thoughts, nasty thoughts, or no thoughts. In fact, it seemed the less I tried to be "spiritual" or "religious" or "serious," the more likely spirit would arrive. I learned how to be available for shamanic experience by not caring, not trying to make anything happen, just letting things be. I aimed to have no mind for no experience.

On that night of my first dance with the Bushmen I danced around the fire and felt ripples of energy traveling up and down my body. Shadows flickered on the faces of men and women, seeming to close out this world and open another one that belonged to the night. That was the homecoming I had waited for all of my life. I had been shaking by myself for nearly twenty years until I started experimenting with passing the vibrations into others, but I had never communed with a culture whose whole way of life valued and practiced this experience of and interaction with spirit.

Round and round that fire we went. I felt more and more heat build up inside my body as sweat dropped off every inch of my skin. When I began to feel dizzy I stepped outside the dance and staggered a bit, under the influence of the Kalahari spirits. Twele came to me. His hands touched my belly. I almost fell over. They were the hottest hands I had ever experienced. By this point in my life I had already felt the warm (and sometimes hot) hands of healers from various cultures but that had not prepared me for the red-hot hands of Twele. He was in a league all by himself. For a moment I wondered whether he was holding a hot coal, but when I looked there were only his hands gently touching and stroking my belly.

I started to touch Twele in return, feeling the heat in my own hands.

The other men doctors came over to us and joined in. Our hands were all over one another, pulsing and vibrating as deep tonal moaning and high-pitched shrieks filled our auditory space. It was pure ecstatic interplay, multiple bodies holding and collapsing onto one another. Down to the ground we fell, a heap of vibrations. I forgot where my skin began and another person's ended. Our boundaries dissolved. There were only vibrations, energy, heat, sweat, and sound. We had merged through unencumbered spiritual expression. Held by old Mantag's arms, Twele hugged both of us. Around us other doctors were touching and shouting while women sang, clapping their hands and sometimes dancing nearby. I fell to the ground and stared at the sky. I closed my eyes but I still saw the stars in the sky. Staring at a star, unsure whether my eyes were open or closed, I watched its twinkle get brighter and brighter. As its illumination grew in intensity, it began to form a tunnel, a line of light from the far distance in the sky to the middle of my head. "My God," I thought to myself, "that star is making a connection to me." Through the tunnel of light that shown down upon me I felt the star as inseparable from my body.

The star spoke. "We are the old shamans. When we die, we become stars in the sky. It is we who want to come dance with you. One of these days old Mantag will be one of us. He will still be with you, but in the sky rather than on the ground."

I was awakened by someone shaking my head and another shaman blowing into my ear, but the call of the stars was stronger. The tunnel of light reappeared, this time taking me to a woman wearing a necklace of stars. "And we will wed," I heard her say, "when I am brought down again to earth."

Several men, including Montag, were tugging on me, pulling my arms and trying to get me up. I could see in their faces that there was serious concern about something. I assumed there was a crisis and I was being asked to help. They all spoke rapidly with a chorus of click sounds, the most distinctive part of their language. I was flooded by the music of their voices and stopped trying to hear the lyrics of their spoken words. I began to understand what they were saying. I am not insinuating that I understood the words themselves, although in that state of altered consciousness nothing would have surprised me. I felt that I knew what they wanted to express from a deeper communion than linguistic exchange.

They took me to another Bushman doctor who was lying on the ground, looking as though he were in a deep trance or a coma. He had the signs of being unconscious. Later I learned that the community felt that his spirit had left his body and that he was in danger of dying. I was called to his side to help bring him back. Without thinking, I fell on top of him along with the other doctors; we pulsed vibrations into his body. I made sounds, fast and furious, congruent with the Bushman music and noises surrounding me, and fell again into feeling part of a larger body comprised of Bushman shamans held together by pulses and waves. We were one large heart trying to pump life into another.

All of us wiped our sweat onto the man, making shrieking sounds and shaking, hands touching him everywhere. Suddenly the man jerked as if hit by lightning. He began to shake, at first spastically and then smoothly, in sync with the rest of us. It was as if he had been brought back to life. This was healing in its most ecstatic form—skin on skin, heart to heart, mind within mind. This was the Bushman way to heal and it brought truth to every experience in my life as a secret shaker. Now I was in the open, available to every member of this faraway Bushman village, free and spiritually naked underneath the Kalahari canopy of living stars.

The dance went on through the night and I never tired, although I fell to the ground from time to time and was reenergized by other shamans coming over with their shaking hands. A shaman is like the mechanic you call when your car battery is weak. They hook up some cables to the battery and then crank up their engine to give you a fresh start. Here the cables were the shaman's arms; the shaking of their bodies brought in the juice.

That was my first dance with the Bushmen. It was as transformative an experience as my spiritual baptism in my childhood church and my later experience of being hit by rapturous lightning in that university chapel. Now I understood that my experiences were more "normal" than I had ever otherwise imagined. This was a way of being with others that was known by the oldest living culture on earth. Even without scholarly reference, I had no doubt that this was the oldest and purest form of healing, prayer, and spiritual worship. I had found a home in Africa with roots to my heart and soul.

The next morning I was eager to see Twele and discuss what had happened. He came with a small carving he had made for me. It was a stick man that danced when you shook it. "Yes, the healing dance was very strong. We are very happy to find another shaman. You are very strong and everyone wants to feel your touch. By the way, did you know that some of the shamans saw the light last night?"

"The light?" I asked. "Please tell me more about that."

Twele continued. "I saw the light for the first time when I was a young boy. I was sitting in the dance and the light just came in and I started to feel things. It didn't startle me; it felt natural. I can tell that you have also seen the light."

"Yes, Twele. The first time I ever saw it was the most important experience of my life."

Mantag stepped in to join us and I handed him a cup of coffee. "Yes, that's the way it has always been." The old man added his voice to our conversation. "All the strong shamans have seen this light and it is what makes us who we are. Without the light there would be no dance, no healing, no hunting, nothing. We wouldn't be alive."

Twele interrupted. "I see a light that makes me float. The experience is very wonderful and it feels good. It is the best feeling. The people know when I am seeing the light. They know it is a special gift."

As the other shamans joined us they told their stories about the light. For some it appeared as a thread or rope to the sky. Like Twele, others saw a diffuse light that hangs over the dancing community. One old shaman said he saw a light inside each person's body, enabling him to discern sickness because it appeared as a dark spot. All the shamans, men and women, were familiar with the light. It was perhaps the most important experience in their spiritual universe.

Mantag reached out for my hands. "The Big God gave you special hands. Please touch me with them. We all want to be touched by you."

For the rest of the time we were there, Bushmen came by our tent to be touched and shaken. Sometimes they would break into a dance with everyone joining in. This around-the-clock shaking made me drunk on spirit. My consciousness became deeply altered and I experienced one waking vision after another, along with voices that gave instruction. I continued seeing the threads of light that connected to the stars. I was out of my culture-of-origin mind and inside a more caring and relational mind, the mind of the Bushman shamans.

Again I see a line that connects me with a star. I see a woman. She says, "I, Sister Elize, do wed with thee." We are married in the celestial sky, we make love while she gives birth to me—all occur simultaneously. She is both Mother and Bride. We are brought together within holy matrimony.

A few months later one of the great healers of Soweto, South Africa, Mamma Mona, passes her spirits into my body. At her home she says, "I see you already have become acquainted with Sister Elize. She is my main guide."

Spirits enter, impregnate, and give birth over and over again. There is no end to the creative cycle of life in spirit. The Dreamtime regenerates, all differences giving way to union and propagation . . . .

The community told me that Mantag was their eldest healer. He could pull the sickness out of another person and pass his shaking energy into another, causing the other person to shake as well. They said that I had that same spiritual gift. Mantag and I talked about how the vibrations and shaking would come upon us. He explained that it was the spirit inside us, a spirit that came from the Big God and had many different manifestations, including our grandfather's ancestral spirit and various spiritual essences from other times and places.

I learned that no one had taught Mantag to be a healer. As a young man he had simply gone into the bush one day; there he met God and was given the power. Afterward he had a dream in which he saw how he would heal others. Before I left Mantag he said, "I have prayed that someone like you would come here to help me. You have done a lot to help save our ways."

At times I didn't know when I was awake or asleep. I was deep inside the Kalahari Dreamtime. Sometimes my grandfather would smile upon me, singing the old church hymns as I danced with the Bushmen. Then I would hear a chorus of my former teachers' voices: "The lines are circles and the circles feed upon themselves." And the stars would call, "We are the circle. Come home."

My life was never the same after that first visit to the African bush. As of my return to the States in June 1992, I no longer cared about keeping my shaking a secret and was open to sharing it with anyone who sincerely wanted to be touched by this kind of ecstatic contact. When I left the Kalahari I started introducing myself as a shaking shaman. Or, after sharing my enthusiasm over what I learned, I might ask a person, "Would you like to try some shaking?"

In my travels in Africa I was taken all over the southern part of the continent—through Botswana, Namibia, Zambia, Zimbabwe, and South Africa—meeting one kind of healer, shaman, and witch doctor after another. I would go into ceremony with them and then tell what my inner visions, voices, and intuitions revealed. From one village to another, I was greeted as a shaman who had contact with the ancestral spirits and the forces of nature. I was offered many spiritual gifts, from crocodile skins to beaded necklaces to sacred objects I had never seen before. I only took what I had dreamt. The professional paraphernalia of my life changed from university diplomas to skins and bones. I was a White African shaman who numerous sangomas and African spiritual elders proudly introduced as "a White man who had the same color skin as us."

With the Bushmen I learned that the light, inner heat, and shaking I first experienced was the same experience that gave birth to their shamans. I also discovered that there is little one could be taught about the shamanic arts from the words in a book or from another person's talking. This profession can only be learned through experience. One becomes a shaman through being lit, shaken, and spiritually turned on. Once that starts, the rest of your life continues as a journey into spirited expression, with further heating, shaking, and lighting.

The Bushmen believe that I am a Bushman shaman no different than any other of their shamans. I can't say that—I wasn't born and raised in the Kalahari. But I can use this descriptive as a metaphor that helps evoke an awareness of a natural way by which human beings can find themselves shaken and heated up, bringing forth an endless array of spiritual experiences.

Kundalini yoga, chi gong medicine, tai chi, Quakerism, Shakerism, Judaic davening (torso-rocking prayer), the swaying zikhr and whirling dervish of Islam, Goddess circle dancing, Dionysian ecstatic mysteries, flamenco, belly dancing, Reichian bioenergetics, holy ghost dancing, or Bushman medicine: there is an aspect of all of this that involves being a capacitor of spiritual energy that is transmitted into others. At least that's how it feels, and that is how many cultural traditions talk about these energized experiences.

I don't believe anyone will ever understand ecstatic shamanism. And I say that about all teachers, from the past or present, who have spoken about any aspect of shamanism. We are talking about mystery here, and the more you are with it, the less you will believe that it can be understood or turned into a mathematical equation. When I read abstract treatises on matters of the spirit, I start laughing as I imagine a group of Bushman shamans reading it. They would fall to the ground laughing, wondering why anyone who knew how to be in spirit would ever spend so much time trying to understand it. If you are filled with spirit, then pass it on. All that can be said about this ecstatic way of being is that it happens.

Shamans sometimes discuss how they strive to become empty vessels—"a hollow bone," as the Teton Sioux medicine man Fools Crow referred to it—so that the spiritual current may flow through them. On one level, this means that the shaman should be humble and not boast about her relationship to the divine. Some traditions urge their practitioners to keep silent about their practices for fear that they may swell the ego and shut down the efficacy of spiritual transmission. But there is as much danger in being quiet as there is in being loud about these matters. If silence and secrecy lead to smugness and piety, the silence backfires and closes the spiritual valve.

I learned from my Bushman teachers that the best way to keep the vessel empty and ready for use is to wallow in absurdity, always teasing yourself and others about your most serious concerns and practices. I found that the more comical and outrageous you are about this kind of work, the more spirit will flow. So rather than saying that you are a shaman or choosing to stay quiet about it, consider carrying a business card that introduces you as a "Real Deal Shaman" or "Lunatic Trickster Being" or, as I once suggested to a close colleague, "Genuine Weather Reverser." Show this card to yourself or a close friend who shares your sense of absurd spirituality and it will keep you giggling. You'll find that the vibration of chuckling will cleanse and empty any clogged spiritual arteries, allowing swifter movement of divine play.

The Bushman shamans are remarkable teasers and tricksters. As in many other indigenous traditions, they have a trickster-god motif that keeps their mythological view slippery and always changing. It's fair to say that from their point of view, any spiritual rhetoric or text that becomes too clear, logical, and persuasive should be avoided like the plague. Taking yourself or someone else too seriously is a sure way to keep the spirits at bay.

During my development as a Bushman shaman (metaphorically taken, if you please), I learned to move with the spirit when it was natural and effortless to shake, either solo or with others. I also acquired and cultivated a deep respect for the practice of absurd thinking and performance. These two sides of the coin display the reverent and irreverent aspects of shaking—trembling with awe as well as jiggling with humor.

Over a ten-year period I returned many times to the Kalahari to learn from Bushman shamans from all over Botswana and Namibia. My earliest teachers were Mantag, Twele, Mabolelo, Motaope, Matope, Ngwaga, and Xiaxe, all from Botswana. Later I learned from Cgunta /kace, Kgao Temi, Cgunta !elae, and /oma Dham, along with the powerful women healers Texae, Tlixgo, !ae, Lesua, and Tcqoe from Namibia. I found that each shaman had his or her own style of moving, vibrating, shaking, and touching others with a trembling hand and ecstatically charged body. Every one of them loved to laugh and tease as well as shake themselves into sacred delight, journeying into the furthest reaches of mythical mind.

One of my guides, Izak Barnard, who took me out on many of those expeditions, established some of the first trails to reach the Bushmen. We used to talk about what the Bushman culture was like before the government resettled them in villages with schools and health care. Prior to that, the Bushmen were completely self-reliant and trusted their spiritual ways to lead them to food, water, and wellness.

Izak told me a story about a band of Bushmen he met many years ago in the southern Kalahari. They had a word for the Big God that meant something like "the God Who Looks over Things." However, a couple of years later when he returned to see them, he learned that they had changed the name of their Big God. Now he was called a word that meant "frog." There had been a long drought and when it finally rained, the frogs were heard once again. Why not change God's name (and meaning) to fit the circumstances at hand?

Although their stories, metaphors, and understanding may constantly morph into new forms, what remains constant in the Bushman experiential universe is their belief in and practice of working with the vital life force, what the Ju/'hoansi Bushmen call *n/om*. This is one of the most important ideas in the Bushman worldview. To the Bushmen, the living world is filled with this vital force, this spirited life energy; without it nothing can live. Shamans devote their lives to arousing it within their own bodies and heating it up so that it transforms them into an altered and heightened awareness, doing so to help cure, resolve problems and tensions, and provide hope to others.

What is most important about this spiritual energy is that it is least potent when it inflates any sense of personal power. What makes the spirit get as thermal as it can—that is, boiling hot—is moving away from a power/warrior outlook and surrendering to a love/maternal presence. This shift from what some might call the masculine to the feminine allows n/om to fulfill its destiny, becoming the trigger for healing and transformation. The Big Shamans are the Big Lovers. They hold nothing back and allow their hearts to open fully so that the n/om can circulate through their own beings as well as flow into others. Perhaps the best translation of n/om, as well as kundalini and holy spirit, is that all refer to the "love current," an invisible but life changing vital charge that is capable of sweeping us into the ocean of divine mystery.

A Bushman shaman is a love doctor, someone who puts the arrows of love into another. Like Cupid, these shamans touch others with vibrant love, an intimacy that surpasses eroticism and agape. It is the love that seeks union with the divine. The deeper you allow yourself to be punctured by these arrows, the closer to God you come. That is the Bushman shaman's secret.

6

Shooting the Arrows of Love

I ARRIVED HOME FROM THAT FIRST TRIP to Africa during summer 1992. Within days of my return I received a letter from Japan, inviting me to give the keynote address to the tenth-anniversary gathering of the Japanese Association of Family Psychology. It was a real honor and I immediately replied to Dr. Kenji Kameguchi, professor of clinical psychology at the University of Tokyo, thanking him and accepting. I wrote that I had recently heard about a traditional healer in Japan whom I would like to meet. Could he help me locate her?

Ikuko Osumi, Sensei, a Japanese woman in her mid-seventies, was one of the last living masters of *seiki jutsu,* the art of handling the life force. She was legendary for the ways she could instill the life force, or what she called *seiki,* into others. One of her patients, Dr. Takehi Hashimoto, a professor of anatomy at Toho University Medical School, had written the foreword to a book about her life.

After doing some sleuthing for me, Professor Kameguchi wrote that Dr. Hashimoto had recently passed away and that he had no other way to learn where Osumi, Sensei lived.

Several months passed. Then the night before I was to depart for

Japan, I received a fax from my host saying they had located Osumi, Sensei. She lived very close to the hall of Showa Women's University, in Setagaya, Tokyo, where I would be giving my speech. My hosts contacted her and she agreed to meet with me.

I traveled to Japan that October. Following my talk I was taken to meet Osumi, Sensei. She greeted me dressed in a traditional kimono made of eggshell-white satin with a single-lined angular design of tan trees whose branches wrapped around each other. Osumi, Sensei lived with her household staff in the lifestyle of an old samurai family. To the surprise of my host and interpreter, I was addressed and treated like a returning son, as indicated by how Osumi, Sensei spoke, bowed, and gestured to me.

Osumi, Sensei brought me into her home. Through gold-rimmed spectacles she looked into my eyes as if reading some kind of hidden record. She then began talking. The interpreter could barely keep up with her. She somehow was tapping into the history of my life, telling me where I had traveled, what I had learned, the challenges I had faced, and other details not only about my life but that of my family members as well. Then she concluded, "You must phone home and tell them that you are canceling your return. You must live with me. I am going to teach you ancient knowledge that will change your life. It will bring together everything you have learned."

I was momentarily frozen by the unexpected demand and didn't know what to say, but the old woman's authority was not to be challenged. I slowly nodded in agreement, not really sure what I was getting myself into. My olfactory sense registered burning incense. I visually scanned her home, seeing a family shrine, a collection of rare orchids, and numerous gifts from her many patients. I remembered reading stories about how people trying to learn from her quickly felt as though they were going mad. You had to sacrifice yourself to be her apprentice, her *deishi*. That was the old Japanese way. From a Western perspective, the sensei-deishi (master-apprentice) relationship was brutal and to some, excessive and cruel. But the Western obsession with appropriate teacher-student relations may obstruct teaching the wisdom that begins with a deconstruction of the self. In days of old, a Japanese student or apprentice had to give up any self-importance and become completely obedient to his or her master. Osumi, Sensei was that kind of teacher. She was obedient to her cultural tradition.

I hoped that she wasn't going to put me into some kind of seiki-jutsu-Zen-monastery or Marine boot camplike training program. I imagined cleaning temple floors all night and being whacked on the side of the head by a wooden board. I was respectfully going along for the ride, a trip I hadn't planned but a journey I was nevertheless unable to refuse.

Without further adieu I moved in with Osumi, Sensei. To my welcome surprise, she was a firm but tender and caring grandmother. She taught me many things about the nature of loving touch and healing energies.

I observed how she worked with her patients, many of whom were very sick and had been released from the care of such medical establishments as the Mayo Clinic and Massachusetts General Hospital. Some clients were influential scientists and prominent businessmen in Japan, including the CEOs of several of Japan's top industries. Osumi, Sensei would take me to clients' houses so I could watch how she worked with them. I visited several of the homes of Japan's national living treasures, including the director of the national Noh theatre. I was astonished to observe how much influence this traditional Japanese woman had over the leaders of Japan's artistic, business, and scientific communities. They listened carefully to the advice she gave.

Osumi, Sensei didn't teach them to memorize any esoteric textbooks, undergo complicated exercises, or do anything that a five-year-old child couldn't master. She simply asked them to take time each day to sit down and move their bodies in an automatic, effortless way. Through her touch, she showed them how to circulate their life force and how to draw upon it—how to "milk seiki," as she called it—to help them gain and maintain physical and mental well-being. Her clients described how this practice connected them to their inner resources of creativity and clear thinking. Her clients became healthy;

without exception, they attributed their achievement to her teaching.

One day Osumi, Sensei opened her vault and took out a historical document written by Jozo Ishii in 1928 entitled *The Essentials of Seiki Self-Healing Therapy*. It discussed how the practice of seiki jutsu had been part of the daily regime of ancient samurai warriors; they used the practice as a means of keeping themselves in optimal condition. This was clearly a very old discipline. During the first years of the Showa era, in the second half of the 1920s, there existed a popular health movement in Japan called "self-improvement life force therapy" and this book on seiki was one of its main texts. In it, the author proposes that "seiki stimulates the exhausted nerves of the body and causes a reflex movement in the muscular system," referring to an automatic rocking motion and the spontaneous movements seiki practice brings about. Explaining how it contributes to healing, Ishii offered this account:

> Seiki stimulates any afflicted part of the body and sparks the cells in that region into activity. This influence spreads to surrounding areas until finally the cells of the body are aroused to action. This fires activation of the metabolism, quickens the flow of blood, brings forth active secretion, piques strong respiration, and induces proper and steady circulation. The result is that stagnation within the body is washed away. Seiki excites the nervous system. The nerves of any afflicted organs react. This produces the physiological movement of the nerves that are required for rehabilitation.

I am wearing a white and blue kimono, sitting on the seiki bench given to Osumi, Sensei by her aunt many years ago. "Yes, very good"— Masako translates her mother's words. This morning in her Setagaya, Tokyo home, Osumi, Sensei is teaching me about circulating seiki. "Forget what you have been told about chi gong, tai chi exercises, or any of the other Asian disciplines. I don't want you to be purposeful about anything. Do not attempt a preconceived form or choreographed sequence of motions with names like 'grasping the bird's tail' or 'wave hands like clouds.' In this approach, which I feel is more natural, I want you to become empty and available. Wait for the seiki to move you."

"This is how those other practices were born. People were naturally and effortlessly moved by the life force and then only afterward did they try to teach others in a backward way. They want you to start with the forms, memorize them, become them, and then forget them, hoping they will come back on their own, without any effort. I want you to start in the opposite direction. Wait for the seiki to move you and find your own forms—or more accurately, let seiki form you."

As I am moved by seiki, my arms wave like a flying bird and my feet shift across the floor as if they are buttering toast. I think to myself how amazing it is that I have been led to an improvisational practice. It fits my nature and the way I believe spirited things work. "Thank you, Osumi, Sensei, for teaching me this free-of-form practice, this way of falling into the forms that nurture the flow of the life force."

"Yes, Keeney, Sensei, you are becoming a good teacher. I want you to work with many people and give them seiki as my aunt and I have done for several generations. Your life has a purpose. I knew it from the first time you made contact with me. It is now time for you to rest. Please wait while I go bring us some tea."

At the corporate headquarters of Sony, I learned about a secret laboratory they established for the scientific study of the life force. It was headed by Dr. Sako, a client of Osumi, Sensei. Dr. Sako had earned his doctorate from the Massachusetts Institute of Technology, where he made early advances in the field of artificial intelligence. He went on to contribute to the invention of the DVD. He told me that the cofounder of Sony, Dr. Masura Ibuka, was a student of kundalini yoga, another practice concerned with circulating life force through the body. Dr. Ibuka's spiritual teacher was a former jazz saxophonist turned yoga master named Masaharu Naruse, whom I also had the opportunity to meet several times.

I demonstrated how the Bushmen gave the life force to one another, and the Sony scientists, in turn, were enthusiastic about sharing their research findings. Dr. Sako and his colleagues had developed measuring instruments, based on the principle of supersensitive microphones, for detecting the life force and were in the process of formulating mathematical descriptions of its function in the physical world.

In July 1995, several years after teaching me her ways, Osumi, Sensei witnessed my giving seiki to her daughter, Masako, a contemporary artist and interpreter of postmodern philosophy. Masako collapsed to the ground when she received seiki and reported that she felt infused with a warm energy of love. Osumi, Sensei was very excited about what had happened.

I told her how the Bushmen did this and showed her a videotape of the Bushman healing dance. Sitting in her living room, underneath a silk rendering of cranes that was hanging on the wall, she smiled and pointed to the television monitor, saying "seiki, seiki, seiki." I told her how the Bushmen shamans believe that there are concentrated forms of the life force, what they call n/om, residing in their bellies in the shape of little arrows, thorns, and nails. These arrows, when heated by ecstatic dancing, are shot by the shaman into another person. What they call "shooting arrows" (or "nails"), the "arrows of n/om," are comparable to what Osumi calls "giving seiki." Whether n/om or seiki, its truest transmission takes place under the auspices of unconditional love.

I told Osumi, Sensei how there are different sizes of Bushman arrows. Some of the arrows are short and some are long, but they hold the same power. The size of an arrow has to do with the animal it is associated with. The long arrows come from the giraffe. There are also eland, gemsbock, and kudu arrows, among many others. Bushman shamans regard the invisible arrow as a condensation of the Big God's love. When the Big God sends affection to an animal, the love is first condensed into an arrow and shot into the animal. Once inside, the arrow melts and is expressed as a song. It is the song that is subsequently transmitted to the shamans. When the song touches the shaman's heart, there is a soulful piercing that feels like the entry of an arrow. When the emotion settles down, the song, now residing inside the shaman, turns into an arrow that is stored in the abdomen for future use.

When the Big God sends love directly to human beings, Bushmen shamans refer to it as "sending nails" rather than arrows (in the old days they referred to this as "sending thorns"). These are the Big God's songs that come directly to the shamans without first being sent to an animal. Practically speaking, arrows, nails, and thorns are the same. They are metaphors for the way it feels when the Big God sends the Big Love.

One night, sleeping on the floor on a traditional mat, I fall into the dreamtime.

Cupid, spirit in white, reaches for an arrow, but not the ornate kind on Valentine cards. This is a Bushman's arrow, a stick with a sharpened tip. He dips the arrow into his heart, a pulsing fire, and the arrow turns red hot. Showing it to me, Cupid says, "This feeds the hunger of Eros and the thirst for skin." Placing the arrow back into his heart, he now heats it up again and I watch it become blue hot. Cupid laughs and says, "Same arrow but hotter. This is the heat of familial love and agape. It is so strong that you are only aware of the other. With this arrow, you would sacrifice yourself for your beloved." Finally, he heats the arrow until it is absolutely white hot, saying, "This temperature is used to open the Divine Love, the love that melts away all differences and reveals a unity of all living forms. Here you feel and give the love of God, neither experience separate from the other. Same arrow, hotter arrow."

Awake, I reflect on all the many ways I have learned to heat up the arrows of love—Cupid's arrows, if you wish. I think about how every person has seen an arrow of passion shoot across a room, even if he or she didn't know it was happening. In the energetic dancing and moves of the great soul singers like James Brown, Ray Charles, and Little Richard, their bodies periodically express a climactic release of energy that looks like a sudden jerk of arm or head, a shaking of the body, or a wild shout. These moments of heightened expression are what Bushman shamans regard as releasing arrows of emotional intensity.

The opening scene of the Robert Duvall film *The Apostle* shows a Black Church in the rural south. As the preacher enthusiastically conveys his message, his body jerks from time to time, looking as though he has released something from inside himself. What he releases, from the Bushman perspective, is an arrow of ecstatic expression—in this case, an arrow of God's love.

No doubt, one of the best places to witness arrows of love is in Black Church services. Some of the oldest practices of shooting arrows, still found in the oldest tribes in Africa, remain preserved in the ecstatic worship services of African Americans. These celebratory services demonstrate a wide variety of arrow-shooting styles: jumping, shouting, jerking arms and body, trembling, and shaking are some of the ways the body naturally releases its built-up feelings of excitement, passion, and love.

Bushmen shamans probably refer to the passing on of n/om to another person as "shooting an arrow" because the bodily sensation of feeling an inner tension being quickly released is comparable to their experiences of hunting with a bow and arrow. This spirited transmission is the heart of their healing practice, serves as the way someone is initiated into shamanism, and constitutes how shamans recharge one another's vitality.

Shamans from diverse cultures taught me a variety of methods for shooting arrows. Among the Bushmen, a shaman flutters his hand and touches another person, usually on the belly, back, heart, or head, as a means of giving them some arrows through vibratory motions. In lower basin Amazonia, the Guarani Indians dance themselves into altered consciousness and the shaman uses a sacred wand of feathers to disseminate the sacred arrows. Among the Ojibway and Cree Indians, in an old ceremony called the "shaking tent" or "shaking wigwam," a medicine man goes inside a tent and gets moved to do some spiritual shaking. Not only his body but the entire tent shakes wildly back and forth, releasing arrows with each movement. I've also seen shamans point their fingers at another person as a means of releasing an arrow. Others may point a seashell or bone at someone and shoot the arrows. Or a shaman may stare into someone's eyes so intensely that arrows are felt.

Osumi, Sensei beats the walls and shouts to accumulate and energize the life force and then aggressively fans the atmosphere above a person's head to guide the seiki into the top part of the client's body. I have experienced her giving seiki to me in this manner and have witnessed her giving it to others.

One day in the middle of summer in 1994, I received a call from an interpreter in Japan saying he was calling on behalf of Osumi, Sensei. She believed it was important to visit my home in the United States to give seiki to my wife and son.

She and her entourage arrived at my hometown airport the next week. Accompanied by a translator and several assistants, Osumi, Sensei cleared the furniture in our living room and made arrangements to gather the life force in an accumulated manner and then transmit it. I stood by her side as she asked me to feel the space over my son's head while she swirled the seiki. Although I wasn't expecting to feel anything, I actually did feel a thick taffylike substance directly above his head. Although it was invisible, I felt it to have mass and texture. It was warm and sticky. Perhaps I was in a trance that enabled me to have an altered perception of the air over his head. Whatever the reality, Osumi, Sensei believes that when she heats up the seiki enough, she can instill it into a person through the top of the client's head.

As she did this to my ten-year-old son, Scott, I watched his body start to rock forward and backward. A trancelike movement overtook him. This is what usually happens when Osumi, Sensei instills seiki into the recipient. It happened to me and I noticed it taking place with every single person I observed receiving seiki from her.

There is a Hollywood ending to my son's encounter with seiki. He played his last Little League baseball game the next day. Our Japanese delegation came to his game, which was held at a field in St. Paul, Minnesota. As always, Osumi, Sensei arrived in her traditional kimono, accompanied by her respectful Japanese colleagues. They patiently watched the entire game, clapping for Scott every time he did anything. When he stood up, they clapped; they clapped when he sat down. Whether on or off the field, their eyes were glued to him and they seemed to cheer for every breath and movement he made.

The score was tied going into the final inning. Scott went to bat with the bases loaded and worked himself into the classic baseball situation: three balls and two strikes with two outs already chalked up. I can still hardly believe what happened. With the cracking sound of the hardball making perfect contact with his bat, Scott hit his first and only home run. The ball flew over the left-field fence—Scott had hit a grand slam to win the game. Ikuko Osumi, Sensei not only gave him some arrows of love; she instilled in him the confidence of believing he was capable of doing anything with his life.

Osumi, Sensei came to my house several more times over the years and we have been with her in Japan on numerous visits. She became part of our family and her teaching will always be an important foundation of our lives. The key to her success as a healer and personal advisor has to do with her total devotion and caring for her patient. Her eyes never miss a thing. She tunes out everything that distracts her and becomes completely focused on the person she is helping. I have watched her treat many patients and am amazed by the intensity of her connection. She taught me that it is important to establish "skinship" with every person you want to help; that is, you must create a relationship through touch. Through tactile contact she is able to transmit arrows like the Bushmen, a practice she prefers to call "instilling seiki."

In the autumn of 1996, Osumi, Sensei flew to the States, having told me that there was something important she wanted to convey to me and that she had to say it in person. We waited, nervously wondering what she was up to. Why wouldn't she send a letter or have an interpreter talk by phone? What was so important that she had to organize a special trip to the United States?

She arrived carefully tending to a box she carried. She wouldn't allow anyone else to carry the box for her. We took her to a hotel, allowed for time to rest, and later met her for dinner, still wondering why she had come. Osumi, Sensei was waiting for us in the lounge, carefully holding the box on her lap. We went to the St. Paul Grill because she is fond of American steak. After a multicourse dinner, she told us this story.

"Many years ago when I was a little girl, I had a special gift that amazed everyone. I was able to predict the weather and when it would change. Because of this ability, the community asked me to get up early each morning and stand on a mountain. There I would hold up a colored flag telling the fishermen what weather and wind conditions they could expect. I had a different colored flag for each weather situation. I also could see the sickness inside people and tell them what was going to happen to them. I was very loved by the village people and I grew up expecting that those kind of things would always take place naturally.

"Sadly, I lost my mother when I was a young girl and then my husband was killed within a few years after we married. I experienced great suffering during the war. There were times when I wasn't sure I would survive. In spite of these difficulties, my aunt believed that I should carry forth the ancient tradition of seiki jutsu. The Shinto priests told us that my spiritual talents came from the spirit of my ancestor Eizon Hoin. There is a shrine, Makiyama Shrine, built for him on top of Maki, the sacred mountain outside of the city of Gamo on the northern coast of Japan. When I was a little girl I would visit his shrine, where a white snake would come and talk to me about taking care of others. One day it said it was tired and could no longer help the family. 'You must do it now,' the snake said to me. The white snake, a messenger or manifestation of Eizon Hoin, called me to be a helper to others. When I returned home I felt his presence in the left side of my body and realized he would always guide and protect me.

"My aunt watched over me and passed on her traditional knowledge about how to charge the atmosphere and instill seiki into others. Like in the film of the Bushmen that you showed me, I, too, learned how to activate the life force, seiki, and shoot it into others.

"There is a tradition in my culture that when a master passes this knowledge and spirit to another person, we write that one's name on a piece of sacred wood that comes from our ancestor's shrine and temple. The wood carries the name of the person who has inherited the ability to give seiki to others."

Osumi, Sensei reached into her box and pulled out a bundle wrapped in an old piece of silk cloth. She went on, "This silk is the only thing that I have left from my aunt. We lost everything else in the war. It is wrapped around a piece of wood. I have written your name on it."

I bowed my head as she placed these gifts in my hands, knowing that she was handing over a great responsibility. I took a pledge to tell the world about the importance of her loving touch and healing presence.

Osumi, Sensei's love is not a dramatic performance. It arises from a still, internal place, a place where emptiness prepares her to interact with others with no attachment to a particular outcome. She never asks for the spirits; they come. She is never separate from her patient, but becomes one with them. Her love is a disciplined devotion, an unbending commitment to honoring the heartbeat of life, seiki, practiced by sharing it with others. Her teaching is simple: follow the wisdom of your body; there you find the source of healing.

I learned from Osumi, Sensei that every human being makes many natural movements as a child. With no conscious knowing, this spontaneous expression helps circulate the life force. Children are always rocking, swaying, bouncing, tapping their fingers, shuffling their legs, jerking, and wiggling. They seldom sit still. For some reason, this constant movement often annoys adults in our culture. Consequently, parents and teachers admonish children to sit down and remain still. These natural and spontaneous movements are thus repressed. When we become adults, we find that our natural ability to circulate the life force in our bodies has been put to sleep. What Osumi, Sensei does is reawaken her client's childhood ability to move without effort and bring it back into adulthood's daily life as a practice of revitalization.

In September and October of 1999, I had the opportunity to conduct field research on traditional healing in Bali, where my academic mentor, the anthropologist Gregory Bateson and his former wife and colleague, Margaret Mead, conducted some of their early research. There I was able to validate Bateson's finding that Balinese parents encourage their children to make automatic movements. For example, Balinese children are taught to stand with the body leaning on the ball of one foot in such a way that it brings about an oscillation or tonus of the large muscles in the legs. When you feel this vibration, it seems as if your body is moving on its own without any conscious effort. This experience of automatic body motion is a natural hypnotic induction that easily leads a person into trance.

I learned more about trance states brought about by automatic body movements from a pioneering Brazilian psychiatrist and medical hypnotist, Dr. David Akstein. His landmark work was conducted in Rio de Janeiro, where he studied the trance dances of spiritual groups such as Umbanda and Candomble, syncretic blends of Catholicism, African religion, and indigenous Indian beliefs and worship. He wasn't interested in their religious origins; instead he paid attention to how natural body movements alone could bring about trance. He named this form of trance "kinesthetic trance" and developed therapeutic ways of enabling his patients to benefit from it. He once taught a national ballet troupe in Brazil how to trance dance, and they began reporting spontaneous recoveries from medical and psychological difficulties. That gave his work early publicity. Dr. Akstein went on to live in Paris and write classic texts about the use of movement, trance, and therapy.

In Africa, Japan, Brazil, and elsewhere, people have benefited from automatic body movements that arouse their emotions and often bring forth ecstatic experiences. I have spent decades traveling the world, tracking down these practices and learning how they facilitate the shooting of love arrows. I found that the majority of both Westerners and Easterners have little understanding of—and less practice with—heightened states of arousal brought about by movement. In the West and the East, people tend to emphasize quiet forms of meditation and relaxation as the royal road to biological, psychological, and spiritual recovery. Healing is defined as the "relaxation response."

The cultures I have spent most of my time studying emphasize arousal rather than relaxation. If you have a problem in an African village, there is no psychotherapist who says, "Sit down and relax. Let's get to the bottom of this. Are you having trouble relaxing? If so, I'll prescribe some medication to settle you down." In Africa, things work in an opposite way. There the shaman shows up and says, "It's time to dance you. Let's build a fire and gather the community."

My field observations suggest that relaxation is only half of the equation that governs healing. Healing must also include arousal. In an African ceremony you are danced until your body collapses from fatigue. At that moment you fall into a deep state of relaxation and inner stillness, receiving the same benefits of classic meditation. When your body recovers, the drums call you to be danced one more time. The arousal-relaxation cycle is repeated three or four times in the course of an all-night ceremony. I believe that the next frontier work in natural healing will involve bringing these arousal-relaxation cycles into the lives of those who seek both personal healing and optimal well-being.

In June 1997, I am conducting a demonstration before an audience of medical doctors and psychotherapists in Belo Horizonte, Brazil. The volunteer, a distinguished psychoanalyst in her early fifties, is sitting on the seiki bench, waiting for me to instill seiki. I remember what Osumi, Sensei taught me and I feel her at my side. A heavy vibration begins at the base of my spine. "Ahh-hi! Ahh-hi-hi!" my voice shouts, while my arms begin whirling about in a manner similar to martial arts moves. Soon the movements begin slowing down, becoming gentle while being carefully danced.

All my teachers, those in flesh and those of spirit, are moving inside my being, bringing in the sacred winds. I whirl the air around the woman's head and feel waves of life force, n/om, holy spirit, seiki above me becoming in sync with the waves of rippling muscles within my torso. One crescendo after another voices itself in sound. A storm is gathering.

I close my eyes and see white clouds roll into the room. At any moment lightning will strike. I know it with the certainty of long experience. In this work, thunder comes first and then the lightning. The sounds are pulsing, thunder is building, and then out it comes. There is a crackling of energy inside both our spines. She feels and hears it with me. We are whipped from one side to another by an unseen cyclone that enters the top of her head and extends to the furthest edge of the Great Void. Seiki is shooting down through the atmosphere. The cloudy sky outside now bursts with sunshine and the room inside becomes fully illuminated. The Great Mother of light is delivering her newborn ray. Into the sway we fall, rocked gently by unseen maternal arms.

I fall into the Dreamtime, arms wrapped around a newborn spirit. I am stretched across two oceans, pulled so far that I become elongated until I am nothing but a thin line, a line of light extending between Grandmother Africa and Grandmother Asia. To the north and south, and in all points in between, I see other lines stretching across shaking tents, dowsing rods, gyrating bodies in a holy ghost dance, masters teaching tai chi from chi rather than form, musicians being played by the music—all manifestations of the same current, all cross-cultural and spontaneous yogic movements—*kriyas*—playing themselves out with eternal might and delight.

With quivering flesh, we all reach to hold hands with both longed-for Mother below and Father above. Not choreographed, unrehearsed, this childlike quest seeks marriage of wildest movement and deepest stillness. We plunge headfirst into the Mystery, juggling life and death in absolute free fall.

I see the starry lines again and hear their voices united: "The lines are circles and the circles, when moved, become the Wheel. We are waiting."

7
Surviving the Ordeals of Spirit

SPIRITUAL AWAKENING IS THE EASY PART; learning to hold spirit is another challenge altogether. Shamans around the world talk about the difference between receiving spirit and surviving the ordeals as it settles down within you. After you first open yourself to an infusion of spirit (or kundalini, holy ghost power, n/om, or seiki), your body is like a cowboy trying to ride a bull in a rodeo. You literally can be flopped around as though some wild current of energy is inside you. It is no surprise that outsiders looking at this phenomenon would think they were seeing someone possessed. In a way, you are—you are possessed by the life force: pure vibrant, flowing currents of spiritual energy. It can take a long time to negotiate how you and spirit will come to terms with one another.

It took me nearly two decades for spirit to comfortably "settle into my body," as the Guarani Indians from the lower basin Amazon refer to this adaptation. Before that, I never knew when the shaking would come upon me or what form it would take. At first I did everything to stop it—I even stooped over, since looking upward could trigger the internal lava flow. I stopped playing the piano at times and limited listening to music because it would arouse ecstatic states. All opportunities for spiritual experience were avoided like the plague because they too easily sent me into spiritual rapture. I often refused to attend church or read any spiritual literature and I would not dare put myself in any opportunity to be religiously inspired in any significant way—no lighted candles, altars, praying, or dancing. I had to stop practicing spiritual rituals so as not to be overwhelmed by spirit.

Spirit would still flow, finding a crack here or there in my armor. I might seek a massage for a sports injury and within minutes on the table, my whole body would start vibrating. (Several sessions ended with me giving vibratory treatment to the bodyworker.) I can now appreciate how my dedicated plunge into mastering the theoretical world of cybernetics and circular thinking was motivated by disciplining my mind to avoid being overtaken by spiritual experiences and to find a different way to hold and relate to these phenomena.

As my years of academic study reshaped the interior space of my thinking, I grew more comfortable reflecting on spiritual themes. I was inspired by Alan Watts' book *Psychotherapy East and West,* written while Watts was hanging out with Gregory Bateson in San Francisco in the fifties. The world of Buddhism, particularly the Zen variety, was valuable in seeing how it created a means for the mind to remain still and empty while the hurricanes of experience, spiritual and otherwise, stormed through everyday life.

The journey to becoming a shaman is filled with many treacherous ordeals. I had to learn how to be calm with the transformative processes that were taking place in my body, mind, and soul. In the beginning of the entry of spirit, novice Bushman shamans feel as though they are losing control; sometimes they think they are dying. It takes a long time to get past the fear and anxiety associated with out-of-control experiences.

There were, for example, times in my early adulthood when I would awaken and find myself in a bed that was moving. The vibrations in my own body were so strong that they were shaking the bed, though it seemed the bed was being moved by outside forces. More than once I jumped out of bed in the middle of the night thinking there was an earthquake. The whole room felt as though it was shaking. That's how strongly I would experience the vibrations.

When I began expressing the shaking with another person or group of people, I found that the interaction could become a self-corrective circuit. Being in relationship with another person helped calibrate the flow of spirited expression and seemed to offer a natural way of cooling it down when it became too strong. The Bushmen long ago knew this secret and they still practice it today.

The yogic traditions offer many stories about kundalini accidents or overfirings resulting in physical or mental injury. But the Bushmen don't have such problems. They attend to one another, helping cool down the other when it is necessary. When this happens, a Bushman shaman may rush over and stand on the person's bare feet. I have found that anything that gets you more firmly grounded to the earth helps when the inner heat gets too overwhelming. I once told a client suffering from an uncontrollable kundalini outburst that she should dig a hole in the earth and stand in it barefoot, covering her feet and ankles with the dirt that had been dug out. In her case, that was enough to help her manage the situation.

Bushmen shamans also use their hands to wipe the belly of an overheated person. They blow in their ears, brush their sides, and give them a sweet fragrance to smell, all of which facilitate the cooling-down process. I believe that the technique you use is less important than finding any way to make a pathway of connection to the earth or to another person (which is also the earth). The problem is when the vital force can only circulate within your own physical (and imagined) boundaries. Since many of the prescribed lessons and protocols of meditation themselves indirectly underscore a context of solitary isolation, they may sometimes, without meaning to do so, paradoxically contribute to bringing about a crisis, which I define as circulating inner energy with no place to exit. We have much to learn from our Bushmen elders who do this work in social interaction and community; their approaches make the situation more accident free.

During the eighties and nineties, I found friends who were interested in and respectful of what was taking place within me. We would interact in a deeply spontaneous way and allow a transformation of our experience and relationship. This work had the appearance of improvised bodywork; the aim was to allow touching and movement to happen on their own, with no prescribed sequences of action. I was learning how to use my hands as dowsing instruments—my body learned to "listen" to the "call" of another person's body. When I played with (rather than "worked on") another person, my hands and feet became dancers on that person's skin. I considered this all to be an aesthetic performance moved by spirit. I later met healers from many different places in the world who believed that healing came forth when their work was improvisational in this way.

Most traditional healers I have met believe—like Osumi, Sensei—that a shaman must learn the art of establishing "skinship" with those with whom they work. Through improvisational touch, a shaman holds a whole-body conversation with another. During my years of learning to be naturally comfortable with shamanic ways of expression, I experimented with many ways of being in touch with others. Some of these experiments were counterproductive or just plain silly; other encounters proved beautiful, transforming. I discovered firsthand how any effort to make tactile interaction happen with a specific purpose or outcome was doomed to skid off the road, while "letting it be" resulted in movements being right on track.

I was fortunate to find a partner who was open to exploring in this way with me. My wife, Mev, and I have enjoyed the private theater of improvisational tactile contact. Both of us have learned how to shake, how to move about the various energized zones, and how to use touch as a way of entering altered consciousness. In our touching interactions, we have felt the presence of powerful healing and direction.

I found early on that when two people open themselves to tactile improvisation they enter a sacred school of higher learning. This includes learning how to recognize the various forms of eroticism as well as how to navigate from one form of tactile expression to another. It is not only our sexual energies that can be aroused through touch; so can our spiritual energies be aroused this way. Sometimes one form of touch leads to another; at other times one can short-circuit the other.

For years, my hobby was vibrating with others. Throughout the late eighties and nineties, if I visited someone open to this work, everyone from the children to the family pets got shaken. I became a dedicated vessel for improvisational touch. At times, it would cause spontaneous yoga postures and trigger natural vocalizations, sounds that were highly charged vibrations. I would sing tones into spines and internal organs and charge the atmosphere of a room with improvised sound poetry. This was an exploratory stage of development, where free-spirited, improvised contact could be played out at a moment's notice.

In a ceremony in northern California, I once worked with several hundred people, shaking every single one of them throughout the night. I found that I would not tire or be physically or psychically drained if I was obedient to the call of improvisation. If I worked without any predetermined outcome or form of expression in mind, the interaction would be natural and effortless.

I was aware that some people came to me thinking that there was some particular expression I should do for it to be the "real experience," such as screaming like a wild animal or shaking them into human butter. If I fell into the temptation to give them what I thought they wanted, then forcing the conduct would immediately exhaust me and I would not be able to do much of the work. On the other hand, if I simply didn't care about what happened and instead made myself available to the callings of the moment, I could do anything all through the night, including lifting people over my head, wrestling them to the ground, or dancing energetically. Or I might be silent and relatively still in movement with a person, blowing gently on the top of the head or lightly lifting the arms with slow movements. I found that if I consciously thought I knew what I should do with another person, then that was a good sign that I didn't know what I was doing. But if I didn't "know" what to do, then I would be guided into what seemed, in retrospect, an appropriate expression for that moment.

Since my body, rather than my speaking, became my principal mode of communication with others in the shamanic encounter, I found that I received a different kind of voice. I would spontaneously make sounds I did not know I was capable of making. Some of these were animallike cries; others were long, heavy vibratory expressions that started soft and grew to a feverish volume. I learned to make and use sounds of the wind through energetic huffing and puffing interspersed with gentle blowing. My sound making was becoming as important as my body movement. I later found that this form of sounding was a disciplined practice in various experimental theaters, such as the Roy Hart Theatre of France and Duke University's Archipelago Theatre, under the direction of Ellen Hemphill. These traditions encouraged me to respect the sound making as much as the body shaking. Each fed the other. In fact, they were the same, because a shaking larynx *is* a shaking body.

Professor Hemphill wrote me a letter in 1996 describing her experience of these sounds:

> I'd also like to exchange with you about the sound that you have tapped into in your work. It is not foreign to me and I have spent eighteen years using and teaching and understanding these "sounds" of the human voice, which are, I believe, a passageway into the holy voice, and the healing voice. Holy because used/discovered in the right way, they make us more whole. Healing because when heard on stage the centered voice heals, soothes the listener, and [is] clearly a tool for healing the body, in connection with "the laying on of hands." A sound misused or imitated for the sake of imitation leads to disembodiment, [makes the encounter] dis-spirited. We used to call the moment of inauthentic vocal work "vocal gymnastics," and today there is a lot of that in the art/discovery world. Your connection is genuine and rooted; it is a pleasure to have been in your sound waves. Your own experience with the different masters you have worked with

has obviously held you to the fire to be true to yourself. Because I am a theatre artist and director and voice teacher, and because I work with "truth in art" . . . there is never a question (for me) about the healing moment.

An ecstatic shaman learns that the body is more like an orchestra than an individual instrument. Unfortunately, most of us only play and listen to one section of our orchestra, whether a "body" piccolo, trumpet, violin, or drum. As I learned to be aware of the orchestral dimension of my body and other bodies, I found that my shamanic interactions with others became polyphonic.

In my work with others I found myself beginning to use both hands and all of my fingers, as I would to play a piano; at the same time I would use my voice as an instrument for healing expression or blow out air as if I were playing a horn or reed instrument. Meanwhile, my knees might grab another person's knees or my feet might touch them to keep a bass percussion line going. More and more, shamanic interaction became the improvised performance of many instruments. It became jazz.

In 1989 I began consciously moving from one spiritual context to another, learning more about how to become a facilitator of shamanic expression. On Wednesday nights and Sunday mornings and evenings I would attend the Minneapolis African American church, New Salem Missionary Baptist Church, shaking and dancing down the aisles. On Saturdays I might be in a sweat lodge or at a spirit-calling ceremony in South Dakota or a shaking-tent ceremony in Canada. Throughout the week, I'd be freely improvising with others who wanted to play in that way. I continued to take trips to faraway places where I would shake in all-night ceremonies and healing rituals. For years, I lived this way, building my personal curriculum for this school of shamanism.

Life wasn't always easy and comfortable after I received these initiatory spiritual awakenings. One thing that all of us can be assured

of is that each and every one of us will get a considerable dose of difficulties, problems, symptoms, illnesses, and suffering in life. That is part
of the deal of being alive. It also may be that those who enter the
"school" of shamanic studies find that the number of issues needing
resolution and the amount of pain to attend to gets turned up a notch.
Maybe this is necessary to move outside of a habituated way of being.
We somehow live the suffering we need to receive the lessons necessary
for our growth and evolution.

I have experienced my share of suffering and pain, surviving scary
physical challenges, relationship impasses, political injustices, economic
calamities, and social fallout from disappointing or upsetting people
who didn't share similar expectations. But I have walked (and often
crawled) away from them. I did so not by being immune to suffering
but by throwing the pain into a spiritual fire that aimed to burn away
my ego and strip me down to being more human.

Most of the shamans I've met have advised that one must learn
about both the dark and light sides of nature, your own as well as others. An old Cheyenne medicine man, William Tall Bull, told me, "Son,
you must not only learn about the bad ways—you must know them
firsthand. How can you help others unless you know what it feels like
to be sick, drunk, financially broke, and filled with guilt? You know too
much about being good. Go out and make a fool of yourself. Then you
can come back and I might teach you something else."

At first I thought he was kidding, but I kept hearing the same thing
from other shamans and spiritual elders. I remembered that after I had
my original spiritual awakening, a voice woke me up in the middle of
the night, saying "You are too good now. Go sin boldly. Start by flunking a course or two." I have to admit that hearing that made me laugh.
It sounded absolutely ridiculous. I had a straight-A average in college,
had graduated as valedictorian of my high school class, and now I'm
being told to flunk a class on purpose? Yet the more I thought about it
the more interested I became in flunking a course. I became obsessed
with this idea and it led me to be aware, for the first time, that I was
not studying for the love of learning as much as I was doing it for fear

of failure and for maintaining the image and social expectations of someone who is intelligent and capable.

Before I knew it, I was committed to staging a minirebellion against my well-practiced form of trivial learning. I deliberately flunked my class in American government. It seemed to me that I learned more about self-politics in that act of defiance than I would have if I had attended every class and aced every exam. As harmless as this act may sound, it was my first step toward learning about the dark side of my being. And, over the following years, I continued to learn what could be learned by being a "bad boy"—drinking, cussing, annoying professional organizations with pranks, stirring up trouble with overly serious authority figures, going "over the top" in a variety of situations. Yes, William Tall Bull was right. There is a lot to learn from carousing with the troublemakers.

The view from the bottom was a big lesson for me. I had a reversal of understanding as I learned to recognize and appreciate the integrity of scoundrels, gangsters, tricksters, and outsiders. Different truths are revealed when you change where you stand in life. From the muddy swamps, the successful city slickers look rather moronic in their manicured suits and sterilized fingernails. As all good and low-down radicals know, from the outlook of Deep Truth the whole culture appears as a greed machine devoted to making profit off of ignorance and addiction. I went way down and got some views that changed me forever. That was part of my becoming a shaman.

Old Tall Bull taught me something else. He told me a story about how you become a shaman. Long before the Catholic orphanages and mob-affiliated casinos, a band of Cheyenne Indians was preparing to move their campsite before the cold of winter set in. One of the young men had a dog that was his best friend. The trouble was that his dog was old and blind, too lame to make the journey. The dog probably only had a few months left and his buddy felt sad about the creature. The dog had been his loyal companion for many years and he wanted to honor its life. With that in mind, he told the others that he would stay behind with his dog and catch up with them later.

During the next several months the man did everything he could to make his dog's life comfortable. He rubbed its worn fur, gathered food and water, and talked with it, remembering all their good times together. He even sang to the dog. Then one cold early winter morning the man had a dream. In his vision the dog spoke to him, thanking him for all that he had done. The dog said, "I'm moving on now, but I am going to leave you with a gift. When you wake up, you will see that I have died. Take your knife and cut out my eyelids. Then place them in a leather pouch and use it as a medicine bundle. You will find that when people come to you with eye trouble and snow blindness, you can hold that bundle over their eyes and they will be cured."

Startled by the dream, the man woke up and saw the dog lying on his leg. The dog had died, just as the dream predicted. Obedient to his dream, the man made his medicine bundle and became a great shaman.

"That's how you get the medicine," Old Tall Bull explained. "The visions teach and direct you. Sometimes you have to step away from the direction everyone else is following and reorient toward the calling of your own heart. Doing so makes you more accessible to receiving a guiding vision."

The teacher of Zulu spirituality, Vusamazulu Credo Mutwa, once asked me, "What do you do with good and evil?" This, he added, was the final question given to a shaman after years of training and supervision. If I had said, "You must devote yourself to good and destroy all evil," I would have flunked the test. The correct answer is that one must not overindulge in good or evil. Spiritual presence is in the middle, where the contraries yield their maximal tension.

This systemic insight should not be understood as giving license for debauchery and undisciplined living. What it warns against is falling into either the pole of being piously self-righteous about one's purity and importance or the pole of mindless and reckless living. Seeing that each extreme masks the same underlying error gives us compassion, rather than anger, toward those who have become enslaved by the grip of either pole. The goal is to stay small and alert, floating in the middle of the two extremes, neither surrendering to being a Boy Scout or a bad boy, a Girl Scout as opposed to a bad girl. Whatever the dichotomy, whether good/bad, healthy/sick, smart/dumb, or sacred/profane, I was taught to stay clear of the end zones, the places of existential quicksand.

Rather than pushing away what is unpleasant or trying to hold onto what is satisfying, the unattached middle neither pushes nor holds. It neither complains about pain nor boasts about pleasure. In the exact middle of our dualities, where differences are both joined and separated, the shaman and spiritual pilgrim learn to be thankful for suffering and losses while cautious of comfort and gains. This paradoxical reversal of common sense helps keep us spinning in the middle, not on one side, not on both sides, but spinning in the middle ground.

I learned to be thankful for having one of the largest bone tumors on an ankle ever seen at Harvard Medical School. I became grateful for a disastrous first marriage that was filled with a spouse's unexpected alcohol-inspired (and sometimes violent) tirades and my contribution to the cycles of desperation fed by my being an overly self-righteous critic. I hadn't yet learned that a white knight must necessarily coexist with a dark adversary, and that neither role is superior to the other.

Many a Tibetan monk has, in a weak moment, wished for angry revenge on China. That's why the Dalai Lama is able to thank the Chinese for being an important teacher in his life. They, on one level, are the same as His Holiness. Through his example the Dalai Lama teaches us that each can have compassion for the other only when the other is seen in oneself. There is no room for one-upmanship in the politics of the spirit. No one is above any form of low life; no one is better than another.

Becoming a shaman is like climbing up and down a spiritual ladder. You must go up the ladder and see God but then get over it and come back down. Then you must go down to the underbelly and be leveled by dark, musty, infectious evil and then get over it. Up and down you go, each turn bringing you more into the center, where with a little luck you finally take notice that up and down are not separate. They are partial arcs of a circle, a circle that is not broken until people think good must combat evil. When the circle of light and dark, right and wrong, right and left, is made whole again, you come home to the center, feeling the strength brought about by the coexistence of all opposites and polarities. That is where you find the eye of all the spiritual winds, the deepest cave of the mystics, the hottest fire of the shamans.

I am daydreaming about the 1870s, when //Kabbo, Dia!kwain, and other /Xam Bushmen spoke to linguist Dr. Wilhelm Bleek and his coworker, Lucy Lloyd, about their beliefs and worldview. That was the first time people outside Bushman culture heard the story of the Day-Heart Star. I remembered what I had read from their studies of Bushman folklore:

The Dawn's-Heart has a daughter called Dawn's-Heart-child and she has a mysterious relationship with her father. He calls her My Heart; he swallows her and then he walks alone as the only Dawn's-Heart Star. When his child grows up, he spits her out. She then becomes another Dawn's-Heart and, in turn, spits out another Dawn's-Heart-child. And on and on it goes.

Since we are stars, we must walk the sky. We do so for we are heaven's things. Because we are stars, we do not sleep. We who climb the sky become the sky's things. I am the day's star for my name is the Day-Heart.

I came out of the daydream to see the old Bushman shamans, men and women, gathered around me, teasing me about the way they think of life in terms of changing forms, one thing coming out of another. Cgunta Boo, wearing a hat I brought for him on a previous visit, lights up his pipe, a metal tube filled with tobacco, and leans back to enter in the discussion. "Yes the ancestors want to help us," he explains, before being interrupted by another voice.

"But if they miss us too much, they might make us sick and try to bring us over to them," says Texae, the old woman who is the most powerful shaker in the region.

Cgunta Boo retorts, "They only love us and would never want to harm us."

"They only help." "They can hurt." "They hurt in order to help." "They would never hurt"—and the more they talk the more inconsistent it all sounds. I begin to surmise that there is some circular thinking going on with my Bushman teachers. Help/hurt, good/bad, stable Big God/shape-shifting trickster god—the two sides of the pairs are related and yet remain distinct. I am being pulled into the mind of circularity, the mind in which the mythical snake, Ouroborous, swallows its own tail (and the storyteller swallows her own tale).

As the Bushman elders continue talking, my attention is distracted by a memory, a time when I taught at the university. I see myself explaining how cybernetic thinker Francisco Varela calls this complementary framing of distinctions *star cybernetics*. For example, as I told my students, the dualistic, antagonistic pairing of predator/prey is itself the side of a more encompassing distinction, ecosystem/species interaction. In this world of circles within circles, whatever appears as an opposition is, on another level, cooperating to maintain a more encompassing circularity. In the past I have explained therapeutic change with this circular way of understanding.

I am brought back to the moment by the sound of laughing Bushman shamans. Noticing that I have drifted away, they are standing up, waving their hands toward the sky, mimicking a dancing shaman who reaches for the stars. I realize at that moment that when the Bushmen speak of stars, they imply circular connection. I mix their words with those of my earlier (academic) teachers: "Circle or star swallows itself to give birth to offspring, with subsequent unbroken continuance of destruction and creation, death and life." I remember the first time I danced with the Bushmen, a time when I made relationship with a star, joining it, listening to it. . . .

No one of right mind would choose to be a shaman. The price of getting to heaven is always going to hell. The cost of gaining a spirited life is losing it. The fullness of meaning only comes after silencing all understandings. Give it up to get it, be here now to get there, and go further down before you can find your way starting up. These paradoxical reversals, in all their infinite variations, comprise the wisdom of the world's ancient religions.

As I learned to be in a shamanic state of mind, I discovered over and over that the most important compass setting was the arrow of love. My wife and I have spent over a decade tracking down spiritual elders from all over the world and writing about their life stories. When people ask us how we find these people and inquire about our criteria for selecting someone to write about, we always respond that it depends on the person's "A.Q." That's our shorthand for "Amos quotient," the love that a person exudes in his everyday being. We don't look to write about people who are clever in the "I.Q." sense. We are looking for love beings, the saints amidst us who have become beacons of love, "sunbeams for God," as my grandmother used to call them.

We believe we have met a few actual saints in our travels. One of them is Amos Griffin, the head deacon of an inner city Black church. Amos grew up in a small town in Louisiana where his family, particularly his grandmother, taught him about what he calls the "sweet love of Jesus." This love, according to Amos, is a love that does not judge but accepts, unconditionally forgives (no matter the offense), and kindly serves all people no matter their color of skin, economic position, educational background, or social status.

We observed how Amos lived his life. The love that he exudes on a day-to-day basis is truly inspiring. Amos rarely sang a song in tune, but when the spirit and love of his church got hold of him, his song was the purest of them all and it always touched everyone in the congregation. If a person in his community was sick, hungry, or without a roof over his head, Amos was there to help, and he served all of his sisters and brothers with joy and delight. It was easy for us to feel the love arrows shooting from his heart. He touched and moved every person within his reach.

Amos told me an amazing story about his life. When he moved from the country to the city, as a young man, he was desperate to find a job so that he could feed his family. He had grown up picking cotton but didn't have any skills required in the big city. As he walked down a sidewalk in the industrial part of town, he saw a sign on a window that advertised a job. He went inside the building and the company manager asked him if he knew anything about fixing engines. Before he could say that he didn't know a single thing about them, he heard a voice whisper in his ear, "Just have faith and place your hands on the engine."

Amos took a moment to gather his composure and replied, "Show me what needs to be fixed and I'll see what I can do." The employer took him to the workroom and showed him an engine in need of repair. Amos took a deep breath, brought forth his inner faith, and placed his hands on that assemblage of metal. Like dowsing rods, his hands reached for the correct tools, aimed them where attention was necessary, and fixed the engine. He was hired and he spent his entire career in that company, fixing many different kinds of engines and doing so with no training or conscious expertise. His pure heart opened a door to a faith that mysteriously helped him deliver what was required. Whether helping man or machine, Amos and his heart of faith connect him to a wellspring of wisdom, the source of which will always be a mystery.

The shaman's starting point is a burning sun of passionate connection with all of life, the original source of love, taken to its purest and most intense form. Agreeing with most of the shamans and mystics I've known throughout the world, I call this originating source of love the Big God. As my grandmother and grandfather taught me, "God is love." This is all I need to know about God. The alpha and omega of all that existentially matters is found in love. In its purest form, love does not judge, harm, or punish. It embraces all people in its arms, whether saints or hard-time criminals. Love is the great democracy—all of us are equally deserving of its welcome. Supreme love brings grace with no disgrace. It is the Bushman's brightest star.

Among the Zulu

ONE OF MY TEACHERS IS THE ZULU ELDER and cultural storyteller Vusamazulu Credo Mutwa. One of the more illustrious and controversial characters in South Africa's recent history, he is regarded by some as one of the great African shamans, indeed, he is even referred to as "the Pope" among Africa's witch doctors. Others see him as a scoundrel. I believe he is a little of both.

Credo is a dreamer of mythic proportion, an original artist, and a world-class storyteller in addition to being a clever therapist.

I had the privilege of writing Credo's biography; it was no easy task to approach the complexity of his life. When we started work on that book in the early 1990s, for example, Credo hadn't seen his aunt Mynah, who originally initiated him, for many years. He didn't even know whether she was still alive but he could remember how she used to look: "a slender statue in living ebony." Credo recounted childhood memories of Mynah's hair smeared with red ochre and how she walked about barebreasted with strings of pulped and dried herbs crisscrossing her body. She wore necklaces of seashells and an animal-skin skirt smeared with red ochre and adorned with more seashells. As she walked, the rattles around her ankles made a haunting sound.

In September of 1998, I had a dream that Credo and I must undertake an adventure to find out whether Mynah was still alive. I have told the story elsewhere about how he and I found her in the remote hills of Zululand, in the Babanango area (see *American Shaman: An Odyssey of Global Healing Traditions*). Aunt Mynah was in her nineties at the time; she has since passed on.

Aunt Mynah was one of the old sangomas who lived in a traditional *kraal* away from modern conveniences and technology. She still danced wildly when the spirits moved her. Among the Zulu, the spirits are believed to live inside a sangoma's shoulders. You must be careful not to touch a sangoma's shoulders or you will awaken the sleeping ancestors. I found this out the hard way. By accident I touched Mynah's shoulder; immediately her voice and facial expression changed dramatically.

Mynah had the ability to make very strong muti—"medicine"— particularly the kind that can protect you from harm. She would fill a brass bullet shell with all kinds of secret things and pray over it, using a strongly focused visualization method that directed her spirit to imbue the muti with a protective power. I have seen this medicine exercise dramatic influence, whether brought about by activating faith and unconscious suggestion that causes a turn in events or involving something more mysterious that can never be quite discerned. Whatever the case, I would tremble in my boots if I were ever to be seen as interfering with any of Mynah's muti. Believing in the work I was doing with Credo, she made me one of those bullets and took me under her ancestral spirit's protective eye.

We tried to visit Mynah a second time, but we lost our way. While waiting for someone to bring us directions, I took a nap and had a dream of seeing another *sanusi,* an elder holder of sacred knowledge and healing. (Both Credo and Aunt Mynah are sanusis, or highly respected sangomas.) In my dream the woman I saw was the grandmother of one of our bodyguards, a young man named Blessing Makhoba. At dinner, I asked him straight out, "Blessing, is your grandmother a sanusi?"

"Yes, she is," he answered with a look of surprise. "How did you know that? She has never met a white person."

I told him I had dreamed of her and that I would like to visit her as soon as possible. We took off the next morning and drove past all the highways and narrow dirt roads, going where outsiders seldom visit because it was an area known for frequent ambush attacks. Bodyguards were necessary to take us in safely. Crossing a river and hiking up a mountain, we finally arrived at her home, an old kraal with a thatched roof and a floor of hardened earth smeared with cow dung. The horns of a cow that had been sacrificed for the ancestors hung over the main entrance.

When she came out to meet us her head and face were covered with beads. Blessing told his grandmother who we were and why we had come. She replied, "My name is Bhidliza Sicisini Nzuza, but everyone calls me Ntshiki. The records show that I am at least 110 years old. I have seen many things in my life. You are the first white person who has come to my home."

"Now, choose anything that you own and go hide it in the mountains. When you come back, I will tell you what you hid and where you put it. Then you will know that I have real power. I don't want you to have any doubts."

I didn't have to hide anything. I could see already that she was a link to the past, an old-time sanusi. She had chosen to have little to no contact with the modern world and stayed in her village nestled far away in the hills. She looked into my eyes and spoke without hesitation. "I see that you know the Bushman way of healing. I was also taught by a Bushman when I was young. I see who you are. You are welcome here."

Out came the drums, and Ntshiki and I danced inside the kraal to the sounds of singing, vibrant rhythms, and undulating. When the celebration died down, she and I embraced and shook one another, speaking in improvised sounds, as our sweat mixed and brought us in closer contact. She presented me with her sanusi beads and said, "I will tell you anything you want to know." We spoke of how difficult it was to be a shaman, and how, if you weren't careful, all kinds of suffering and challenges could easily come into your life.

I told Ntshiki, "All imaginable opposites seem to be kept in balance by the universe."

"Yes," she replied. "Go out too far on a limb in one direction, good or bad, and a mighty wind will blow you back to the center. The further out you get, the more tempted you may think that you can go even further, when the truth is that you are within a few steps of being blown back."

I added, "When people or groups or cultures gloat about their extreme position, they don't realize that it's simply stretching a slingshot that'll send it hurling back in the other direction."

With a smile, Ntshiki responded, "Yes, and whenever you get the bright light, be careful that you don't go so far out that the dark shadows catch up with you. There's a way out of this dilemma: never get too excited about either the light or the dark. When big things happen, favorable or not, don't make too much of them. Stay calm and accept everything as if you were in the middle. Be still in the middle of the wind and let everything get blown around your perimeter. The source of your power comes from knowing how to find the middle resting ground. It's like being in between two opposing forces. You feel each side pulling you back and forth. That's why we shake. It's the four winds that keep us vibrating back and forth, up and down."

The next time I went to visit Ntshiki, she wanted to bring forth her ancestral spirits so they could meet me. With the help of another sanusi named Sanelisiwe Gertrude Khanyile, who claimed to be one of the spiritual advisors to the king of the Zulu, we set up a ceremonial space for Ntshiki to get in touch with the spirit world. I sat facing the small elderly centenarian, whose head was covered in beads, her body wrapped with a sangoma's cloth bearing the image of a guinea fowl. As the drums beat, she bowed over and then suddenly jerked about. Her face started to alter; soon her voice dropped to that of a man. She had become an ancient Zulu warrior and she wanted to go to war. She picked up her shield and spear. The rest of us had to settle her down.

As Ntshiki sat there, serving one ancestral voice after another, I felt currents of energy begin to ripple in my belly. Ntshiki looked at me and asked that the ancestral spirits come forth. Without warning, I felt my face and body and voice change. I spontaneously entered the drama of performing various roles, first one and then another. It wasn't hard to get into being an imaginary other, but it was extremely difficult to come back to my everyday habituated consciousness. It actually hurt to do so, with my face grimacing and all my muscles tightly stretched, as if trying to pull the old me back to the present. I have no idea what I said because I went far away from any consciousness of my discourse.

I recall a time several years before when I was teaching in Sao Paolo, Brazil. One of my hosts was a gracious older woman named Maggie, one of the leaders of the therapeutic hypnosis movement in Brazil. A brilliant and charming therapist, she had earlier hosted Stan Krippner, an American dream researcher and parapsychologist, in some of his expeditions to Brazil when he studied traditional healers there. When I arrived to teach, a sad episode had taken place. Maggie's granddaughter had been killed several days before in an accident. She had stepped off a curb and been run over by a car. Even stranger, Maggie's son had died at the same spot in the same way several years before. She was in such grief that her friends arranged a gathering to support and pray for her.

I was asked to try "contacting" her granddaughter. Only because I loved Maggie and had known her for several years did I say yes. I immediately initiated some shaking in my body and went into a trance state. I saw a thin white tunnel appear and I shot through it until I came to a dark void. There I saw a man who said he was Maggie's grandfather. He said, "Don't worry, Maggie. She is here with me. I will see to it that she has a big wedding ceremony when she grows up. And one more thing: don't forget the white carnations." I then felt a need to come back to my normal awareness but found that it was not easy coming back. It took tremendous effort to retract my alert state of consciousness. When I came to, I shared what I had seen and heard. Maggie began crying and spoke. "My grandfather raised me when I was a girl. Every morning he asked me to go out and bring back some white carnations."

Many of the Zulu shamans are powerful mediums. They learn how to send their consciousness to another circle of mind and then have to find their way back. If someone does this with no apparent struggle or transition, I would suspect her of being a fraud. All the true mediums I have witnessed find it challenging to come back. You would think it would be difficult to leave, but that is the easy part. The deathlike experience is in becoming reborn.

Ntshiki, Baba Credo Mutwa, and Aunt Mynah, among other sanusis and sangomas in Africa, taught me many things about being a shaman allowing spirits to pass through them. I also found that the Zulu have a clear way of describing the process of becoming a shaman that applies to most of the global traditions I have personally known. The beginning stage of being a shaman is an experience that dramatically, and often traumatically, shakes one's being. Hit by something inexplicable, the shaman begins to shake, have uncontrollable visions, and wrestle with keeping his bearing. This "shamanic crisis," as it has been called, is the birth of a shaman. The first stage, what Zulu sangomas call the *indawu* stage, typically involves anywhere from several months to years of learning to activate the shaking and allowing it to express itself. In this stage, you feel a spiritual power inside you that you can't control. Your body may convulse and whip around, and you may shout out spontaneous sounds. During this time, the novice often lives with a senior sangoma in a community of trainees and other sangomas who can keep a watchful eye over them.

Speaking of her own development as a traditional sangoma, Ntshiki said, "My teacher's name was Mhlewsi Ntuli. I lived with him for six months. Some people stay with their teacher for three years or even longer. During the apprenticeship, we are called *amatwasa*; we wear the inflated bladders of sacrificed animals in our headdress. Beads are strung around us in loops so the spirits have a place to sit when they want to visit. My teacher gave us herbs and teas to help us learn. He would also take five liters of cooking oil and put some stones inside it to make a noise. When we'd work with it, strange noises would come. This was part of the training."

Every day the beginners dance to the drums and receive treatments that foster their relationship with spirit. As Mutwa once told me, "All African dances are invented for one reason only—the expression of tribal religion and the release of that beneficial life force dormant in every human being." This is the wild stage of being a shaman. Sometimes you look completely mad to the outside world. You don't know what is going on when the spirits come. You are lost. This is the most difficult time, because you sometimes feel as though you are losing your mind (and you may be); you may fear you are dying. You often dream of being tortured or slain, even chopped into little pieces. Over and over, you experience death and rebirth.

The next stage, called *indik,* involves learning to focus one's spiritual energies. Rather than making one wild sound after another, the chaotic multicurrents of spirit are focused to a single voice, giving you the ability to interact with others through meaningful speech and touch. Here you meet a spirit that, as Ntshiki put it, "is like your personal bodyguard." This one guides and protects you wherever you go. You finally learn to understand what that spirit is saying to you.

The third stage, *inlozi,* connects you with your relatives who have passed away, particularly grandparents, parents, uncles, and aunts. This is when you have direct communication with your ancestral spirits and begin to show signs of maturing as a shaman. While the first stage presents an opportunity for learning to bring forth spiritual power, you are still spiritually ignorant, deaf, and blind. In the second stage you learn to focus and understand. Then the third stage teaches you to work directly with your ancestors. This is when you get your songs and dances. The ancestors give them to you. They will tell you where to go and what to do at certain times. They teach you through your dreams. When you are awake, they may also whisper in your ears. It can sound like someone is really there talking to you.

Ntshiki recalled, "I felt something shocking my body when the spirits first came to me. I could feel it all over, through my shoulders, head, stomach, even my heart. In the beginning, when you're learning, you just start crying when this happens. After that crying stage, the spirit is able to talk to you. There is no specific amount of time for learning each stage. Furthermore, a few people, like you, are taught directly by the spirit. Each person is different. Some sangomas don't hear a voice. The knowledge just goes to them directly. It simply comes on their mind."

The fourth stage is called *mlozi*. Here you learn to hear the whistling sounds. You know when the spirits are coming because you hear them whistling. When they arrive, you feel them inside all of your body. It feels like something extraordinary is happening to you. When your heart starts to whistle, you see the sky opening. The whistling voice comes from the sky. It will tell you exactly what to do or it will tell you when someone is coming and say why she is visiting. If the person is sick, the voice will tell you about the sickness. You will know what is wrong before the person arrives. Few sangomas get to this fourth stage.

Some Zulu sangomas believe it is possible to have three more stages of learning. Those stages belong to the Christian faith and may be combined with traditional Zulu ways. The fifth stage is "becoming a member of a church." Here you become an active participant of a spiritual community. This is where you learn to pray in a strong way. You receive a special prayer. The sixth stage, called "the spirit of God," is when you begin helping people. You learn to light the candles when you pray and listen for the spirit of God to tell you what must be done. The last stage, stage seven, referred to as "getting your gift," is when you receive a special gift from God. You may receive more than one gift and it is your ancestral spirit(s) who help you find it.

Ntshiki has four ancestral spirits who help her. They are the older ones, Coco and Nkulu, as well as Ntshiki's father and her grandfather on her father's side. Ntshiki is very strong and never has to throw the bones to make a divination. Her ancestral spirits come to her immediately, requiring no elaborate ritual or paraphernalia.

Ntshiki told me about a special ceremony that was similar to what had happened to me early in my own development as a shaman. "We have a ceremony that helps us get strong. It involves a man and a woman being together and holding each other. They shake together and feel like a big power. If you have more power than the other person, you will feel like you are being pulled up. Your spirits may teach something to the other person's spirits. Teachers use this kind of close contact to teach their students. It's part of how we give power to the student. We may hold each other and fall to the ground. There are times when you feel like you are becoming an animal. You may sniff, bite, lick, or give special attention to the other. It is all up to the ancestral spirits."

On another occasion, Ntshiki summoned her ancestral spirits and went into trance. A loud, masculine voice came forth, speaking directly to me. "Where am I and why am I here? We are not friendly with white people. I was a strong Zulu warrior. I fought the white people and killed many of them. But the other spirits and I are happy with you. We will talk with you. We want to help you because your spirits are very strong. We want to give you something. You are a sanusi who has gone through all the seven stages. Your grandfather wanted to be a sangoma but he didn't go all the way. He has waited in the spirit world to help you make it as a sanusi. Your grandfather's spirit has been teaching you. He makes it possible for you to know the spirits of different cultures around the world. You don't even have to know the language of another culture. The spirits are talking to you directly. Your grandfather has another big gift for you. It will come to you soon. We are happy to meet your ancestral spirits."

As Ntshiki came out of her trance, Sanelisiwe began entering one. Sanelisiwe is regarded as one of the strongest sanusis in Africa. When Ntshiki was an old woman, she believed she needed a spiritual boost. She had been a sanusi since her youth. She had a dream that she should go to Sanelisiwe and live with her for a year, receiving even more knowledge and power from the woman, a highly respected teacher who had advised important Zulu leaders ever since she was a young girl.

As Sanelisiwe closed her eyes and began to change her voice, I waited for her words.

"I see you are like me. You have ancestral spirit groups from both the Christian side and the traditional African side. You can also work with the plants and trees. You have the powers from all sides. Your spirits work together and you can't separate them. That is good. Your dreams are clear. It is very good for us to be together. When the king comes to me for advice, I always tell the truth to him like I do with everyone else. I am telling you that you must come back to us. Live and work with us. There are more mysteries to explore."

Like the strong Bushman shamans, Ntshiki and Sanelisiwe are completely open and available to the expression of spirit. Among the most powerful sangomas I ever met, they share my belief that the Bushmen are the strongest holders of spiritual power. These women taught me to not worry about what anyone thought about these ways. After all, their cultures have been living successfully in this open-spirited way for thousands of years.

Credo Mutwa has lived an extraordinary life, having once taken a pilgrimage in his young adulthood across much of Africa, learning from one spiritual elder after another. In his old age his memory is exceptionally strong, making him a living library of remarkable stories, often apocryphal, that echo the voices of Africa's past. As much as anyone, he taught me to accept the way in which I was made to commune with spirit. He described his own experience of ceremonial ecstasy in his younger days.

"When you dance, you dance in a circle stomping your feet firmly against the ground and kicking your feet. You must kick your feet high and shake every inch of your body. When the dancing reaches its height, a strange spell comes over you. It feels like you are no longer dancing but like you are floating in air. You are one with the earth and the sky, at once. You continue to dance. And then a strange thing bursts from the small of your back. A pot full of hot water suddenly jets up from the small of your back between your buttocks right up to your spine to the top of your head, where it explodes into space and seems to float towards the stars. Your vision changes. Your mind suddenly flies. You are covered in sweat but don't feel any pain as you continue to dance ... I can't describe it any other way than to say that you feel as though you are one with every animal, tree, river, stream, and mountain on earth. You feel united with creation."

During the 1990s, there was a very troubling time in my life when some people assumed that my association with African spiritual traditions meant that I was a practitioner of evil ways. There were death threats and organized plots against my life and I had to return to Africa for safety. I grew afraid that I wouldn't see my son for a very long time. I lived with and was spiritually and physically protected by these sangomas and African witch doctors. It was a very dark time when I learned firsthand how misunderstood the spiritual expression and practices of the African diaspora can be. In that difficult moment, Baba Mutwa made a tape for my son, in the event that something happened to me. He wanted Scott to know how African traditional elders viewed his father.

"Scott, I see you. Years ago I met your father, Dr. Brad Keeney, a man we all respect and love in this circle of traditional healers whose ritual leader I happen to be. Master Scott, I want to tell you this, and in saying this I am not indulging in any cheap flattery. I am telling you the truth. Your father is one of our healers. Even though he is a white man, the oldest spirits of Africa come out of him. We call him the 'one who works with the human soul.' He comes from a very ancient branch of healers who made animal sounds when they healed or when the spirit was on them. The men and women who are called 'the priests of the shining one,' 'the repairers of human souls,' were very close to animals throughout their lives and were often possessed by the spirits of animals. When your father is healing people, I have often heard him make sounds of animals, some of which are no longer on the face of this planet. Your father releases from within him the mother spirit, a type of spirit that heals people with great rapidity, but unfortunately can invite attack from those people who fear the releasing and the manifestation of this ancient mother spirit."

"Scott, the law of our people says that the little hawk must always cherish the crag on top of which it has its nest. I am asking you to cherish your father and your mother. I want to open your eyes to the unique parents that you have. They are parents who have earned our admiration, deserve our prayers, and merit our respect. We, in this far and foreign land, believe this and say this to you."

Do I believe what these sanusis say—that I carry an ancient healing knowledge? In their context, and in their way of telling the truth, I respect their words. But the moment I step outside of their kraal, I am a preacher's kid from Smithville, Missouri, who got hit by ecstatic lightning and went on a global pilgrimage, led by visions, spirited experiences, and a grandfather who lives inside my dreams. However, my African teachers helped me identify what is essential about visionary and ecstatic experience. What the Zulu and Bushmen shamans, as well as the other African shamans I have known, have to say about the development of a shaman reflects my own experience. You first get hit by spiritual lightning, then you learn to settle the spirit in your body, focusing it to be utilized in various resourceful ways; then you get out of the way, allowing it to evolve and take you to many surprising experiences. Usually a spiritual gift or two gets thrown in along the way. If you are lucky, you attain the final stage, where the music, whether vocal or instrumental (or whistling), starts pouring in. This is what shamanism is all about.

But there is more to shamanism than visionary and ecstatic experience. Inner heat leads you to vision, but after vision you must bring the world of spirit into the everyday world with your working hands. Thus, it is good for the shaman to have a craft or art to express and transform the ways she is inspired. And following creative works, there must be never-ending transfusions of absurdity and humor to keep the vessel clean and empty.

There are four "corners" to shamanic practice:

1. Ecstatic experience that revitalizes one's being and helps open the gates to imaginative (mythopoetic) realities;
2. Entry into the visionary dreamtime;
3. Creative expression that crosses and recrosses the boundaries of rigor and imagination; and
4. Absurdity that deconstructs any overripened beliefs and concepts—that is, that deflates any ideas that are portrayed as too real, fixed, or concrete.

The matrix of shamanism encourages constant movement between these four corners. This tetrad of movement keeps the shaman alive. Being stuck anywhere sends the shaman to hell. There, what was once ecstatic experience yields to habitual routines and rituals, dreams give way to textual norms, creativity hands itself over to examinations and measured outcomes, and absurdity surrenders to overserious professionalism and pseudoethics.

The systemic web of shamanism is held together by circular trickster wisdom, the frame of mind in which everything is seen as constantly shifting and transforming. A spirit of experimentalism (act to know), improvisation (one step leads to another), ethics (act so as to increase the choices for all), and aesthetics (behold and honor the patterns that connect) prevails. On this slippery ground the shamanic conjurer makes noise while stirring action, makes prescriptions for bringing forth mystery, instigates transformational interaction, and provides a Zen-like no-therapy for no-mind as a way of awakening deeper presence in the greater Mind of systemic wisdom.

The Bushmen shamans are masters of these ways of transforming and being with one another. They live in a world organized by spirited play and playing with spirit. Nothing and no one can escape their spears of humor and relentless teasing. And when there's time to rest in the shade, that provides an excellent opportunity to make something with their hands, whether it's an arrow, a bow, an ostrich egg bead, or a musical instrument. Visitations from spirit, rather than dreams, revitalize the shaman's presence in the community, which in turn calls for a dance that pumps the life force, circulating it around all four existential corners of daily life: absurdity, creative work, vision, and ecstatic experience.

Guiding
Kalahari Star

IN DECEMBER OF 1992 I received a letter from Botswana. It was from Mantag, the first Bushman shaman I had ever met.

Bradford,

I have been requested by Mr. Mantag Kefeletswe to tell you that he is kicking and alive, even though at a very low standard. He still remembers you as his saver [*sic*] and he is still expecting help from you. If you still remember him, could you please write me and I will convey the whole information to him.

I am working for the Wildlife Department stationed at Khutse Game Reserve as Assistant Game Warden. I have been here two years.

You are welcome to visit Khutse any time to see the old man, Mantag, who says his days are numbered.

Yours Faithfully,
Odumeleng Radar Kaketso, Department of Wildlife
Molepole, Botswana

I remembered how I had given Mantag my business card and watched him stare at the small rectangular piece of white paper. I told him that if he ever wanted to send me a message, he must send a young man with the card to the game warden. My last memory of Mantag was watching him meticulously examine the ink markings on that strange piece of stiff paper.

I sat down and wrote him a response:

Dear Mantag,

Thank you for sending word to me. My friend, Peter, who came with me to see you, has made arrangements to send you and your people some food and clothes.

The fire still burns in my belly. I will be forever thankful for your accepting me and giving me a home under your tree. It remains my true home and I carry it with me in my heart.

. . . I believe you and I will always be connected no matter which worlds we live in. This is our destiny. I believe I will be in touch with you whenever either one of us crosses over. The spirits make that possible.

I love your people and I believe you have the most to teach the rest of the world about how to live. If we don't listen to you, we will all die. I am giving much of my life to encouraging people to support and learn from your people. You were the first people of the world, the first to learn how to heal, how to love, and how to live together. We must be led by your old ways of knowing and being. The wings of our hearts make us one.

All my deepest respect and love,
Brad

It took over a year to get back to Mantag's village. When I arrived, I saw Twele and Mantag's wife, Gabanthate, running toward me. Before I could ask the question, Gabanthate said, "Yes, Mantag received your letter. It made him very happy and he never let go of it. He was holding the letter when he died. We buried him with the letter."

We wept and hugged one another as our bodies began to shake. She went on, "His spirit is happy to see you. He waits for you by the camelthorn tree that is your home."

Twele walked with me and we talked about how the Bushmen believe that when a Bushman shaman passes on, his heart comes out in the sky and becomes a star.

"Yes, Mantag's star will guide you. You will learn many things from many of our elders. Know that he is guiding you. You will face many challenges. That is part of your becoming a Bushman shaman. But Mantag's spirit will help you. My heart tells me that this is true."

Twele then started clapping his hands and shouting with great joy, "Tonight we will dance for the stars!"

We danced through the night and from that night onward, I regularly came to the Kalahari, following my dream to meet and learn from every living Bushman shaman. In Botswana, I traveled to Ngwatle where I met the blind healer, Motaope Saboabue. Then on to Diphuduhudu, Zutshwa, Moithomelo, Metsiamonong, Molapo, XaiXai, and back to Khutswe. I also went from village to village in northeastern Namibia, dancing with their elders, learning from both men and women shamans. I danced myself throughout the Kalahari, pausing from time to time to follow whatever dream took me to another place. I was living as a Bushman shaman.

10

Working the Spirit

ONE AFTERNOON IN THE FALL OF 1993, I was contacted by a couple who asked me to visit their home in Saint Paul, Minnesota, and meet with their father, an elder physician named Dr. Jim Crowley. I found him hooked up to a respirator in the final days of his life. He had been raised by the Lakota Indians in South Dakota and wanted to talk about his spirituality. Eighty years before his father had moved to this country from Ireland and wanted to buy some farmland from the Indians, but every time he asked, the chief would respond, "We can't sell our Mother." The Irish immigrant was determined and finally the chief made him an offer. "We'll trade you some farmland for your first-born son." The Irishman reluctantly accepted because he felt it was the only way he could make a living for his family.

That's how Jim Crowley came to grow up with the Indians. The elders named him Iktomi, the Lakota word for spider, a trickster spirit in their mythology. As a young boy, Jim was an Indian. When he became an adult, he left the reservation and went to work. He supported himself as he later went to college and medical school. As a student, he met his biological family of origin and was introduced to their Irish Catholic culture.

He practiced Christianity while secretly holding onto beliefs that were born in Lakota spirituality. He always doubted whether the two traditions were compatible. In the last days of his life he hoped to resolve this issue once and for all.

I sat with Dr. Crowley and told him about my journeys. His eyes lit up with delight. You could see that he was pleased with receiving the opinion that it was all right to live simultaneously in different spiritual universes, since they were all derived from the same God.

Dr. Crowley died soon after our talk; his family asked me to provide a ritual during the funeral ceremony. They told me that at the moment of his death, hundreds of crows surrounded the house and called out for several hours. Wondering how I might honor this man's early childhood roots in a respectful way, I decided to set up an altar inside the Irish Catholic funeral home, beside Dr. Crowley's casket. The altar consisted of a buffalo skull, a medicine bundle, and other holy instruments, including Dr. Jim Crowley's pipe.

During his funeral ceremony, the crows came back. It was eerie.

At the funeral I made a prayer and sang a holy song with the doctor's pipe in my hand. People were touched to hear the story of this quiet man's life. They knew he had been a highly respected anesthesiologist and inventor of medical devices, an architect and acquaintance of Frank Lloyd Wright, a painter, carver, and poet. They didn't know that he was raised as an Indian with the name of Iktomi.

His children remembered a father who would speak an unknown language that brought animals and birds right up to him. He could heal wounded creatures that came in from the woods—they would come to the clearing around the house and wait to be touched by him. When Dr. Crowley was an old man, he returned one more time to the reservation in South Dakota where he had grown up. There the elders remembered him and pointed in his direction, uttering the word *wakan,* acknowledging that the spirit resided within him. They recognized him as a holy man.

Dr. Crowley remained a publicly devout Catholic and a privately devout Lakota, never quite settled about how these two traditions could live harmoniously side by side until the last two days of his life.

Our conversations about the inherent unity of all spiritual paths helped him hold onto both spiritual trails up until his last breath. As he was laid in the ground, the family and I saw a bald eagle and a golden eagle circling overhead.

What he didn't know was that our discussions helped assuage my own unspoken discomfort about being a traveler on so many different spiritual roads. Dr. Crowley gave me peace about those differences and helped me continue walking on diverse paths. We discussed how, if we squinted our inner eye, all the spiritual roads would converge as one. And that road headed straight toward the Big Love.

As a child, Dr. Crowley's Indian relations gifted him with a spider crafted from silver and turquoise to help him remember where he came from. When he passed on his family gave that spider to me, so I would never forget Iktomi.

It comes naturally to be spiritual in the sweat lodge, church, temple, ashram, or around a Kalahari fire, but it's a very different challenge when you try to bring spirit to the workplace and home. The holy shrines are a spiritual kindergarten compared to the graduate-level training of bringing spirituality into daily relations.

One of the first lessons of home-schooled spirituality is finding out how easy it is to be seduced by spiritual materialism—that is, by collecting experiences of the high and miraculous kind. Some experiences are simply outside the limits of commonsense understanding; they are rationally unbelievable. These often involve materializations and having influence over external events. I learned that these astounding experiences, whether my own or others, are not that important. The Zen folks get it right when they acknowledge that many distractions are waiting for us along the spiritual road. We must learn to not get caught up in them, lest we miss getting to the deeper learning and love that can renew and transform.

I have run into many of the magical performances that spiritual teachers (and charlatans) use to impress others: mind reading, lying on a bed of nails, breaking bricks with your bare hands, causing others to fall over with chi, bending spoons, levitating, standing on your head for twelve hours, practicing impossible yoga postures, living a long time without food, swallowing a string and pulling it out of your anus, drinking acid and surviving with no injury, walking on fire, and changing body temperature on different sides of your torso. Other spiritual advertisements promise channeling penguins who receive esoteric mathematics from another galaxy (yes, someone in Sedona, Arizona, claims to do this), effortless communication with the "other side," multiple-multiple orgasms, workshop soul retrievals, astral projection, distance viewing, alien abductions, and see-God-now psychedelic cocktails from Amazon vines.

Is it important whether these promises bear fruit or not? I met a master of kundalini yoga who carries a photograph that puportedly shows him levitating. I used to show people this photograph and found that it usually received two types of reaction. Some showed immediate, visceral disbelief, with shouts of "This is a fraud and a lie!" Others showed just as much enthusiasm and complete acceptance of the truth of his power to levitate. Furthermore, they wanted to know how he did it and whether they could learn to fly. But seldom would anyone ask, "What difference does it make to float above the ground?" Some of the sacred tricksters I know might shout back this answer: "About as much difference as bending a spoon or straightening your penis."

Displays of prowess simply don't touch the heart. Rather, they seduce our desire to have power over our bodies and our natures, internal and external. All of this miracle stuff is unimportant when compared with the experience of divine love. When the spiritual teachers of the world's great religions talk about getting distracted along the spiritual highway, these are the detour signs they are referring to. Healing is another matter entirely.

Over and over again the Bushmen encouraged me to teach others about their shamanic way of relating to the Big Love. They believe that if something is true and good, then it should be shared. I have no interest in anything that must be kept secret. If it is born out of the God of love, then it can be shared with everyone. I believe everything else too easily becomes a mind game that conjures illusions of magical power, and I personally have no use for that.

One of the most sincere healers I have ever met was Dr. Robert Fulford, whom Dr. Andrew Weil wrote about in the opening chapter of his best-selling book, *Spontaneous Healing*. On the basis of his clinical records, Dr. Fulford, who practiced osteopathy in Tucson, Arizona, may have been one of the most effective physicians who ever practiced: he was one of those physicians whom other doctors made referrals to when they were unable to help their own patients. Dr. Fulford usually helped his clients without resorting to medications. He was famous for treating chronic ear infections in infants and children, but he rarely used antibiotics. Instead, he found a way of working with the life force.

I met Dr. Fulford in a roundabout way. In 1995 I was holding an improvisational performance called "The Life Force Theater" at the Open Center in New York City. This was my way of trying to introduce people to spirited expression with minimal use of overly serious spiritual metaphors. I placed my work in the context of improvisational performance. A freelance writer who planned to do an article for *Esquire* magazine spoofing some of the "far-out things" happening in the spiritual arena called the Open Center and inquired of their more outrageous programs. Mine was mentioned. Gene Stone, the writer, showed up at the performance, as did an Italian television crew that was covering the event for a different sponsor. Gene stood in the back row of a sold-out theater, pen and pad in hand, ready to describe the over-the-top conduct he assumed was going to take place.

Like the beginning of a Bushman healing dance, my approach in such a performance is to start with absurd teasing and humor, doing what, on the surface, looks like a deconstruction of anything serious, religious, or spiritual. As the crowd becomes relaxed and allows a few vibrations of giggling to move through their bodies, the lighting, drums, and music begin shifting the mood into unknown territory. This is when the shamanic ecstatic sound making, body movement, and vibrant touch enter the stage and the place goes electric.

At some moment of heightened frenzy in this performance, I ran to the back of the room, grabbed Gene, and pulsed him with my hands. I watched as the writer moved into ecstasy. After the performance, Gene and I met and he said writing a parody about the work would be impossible for him. He told me that he was the writer behind Dr. Fulford's forthcoming book, *Doctor Fulford's Touch of Life: The Healing Power of the Life Force*. "You have to meet Dr. Fulford. You have so much in common and the two of you will really hit it off."

Gene Stone put me in touch with Dr. Fulford. When I first went to Fulford's family home in Ohio, where he had retired, we talked for a full day without interruption. I introduced him to the shamanic practices of the Bushmen. Placing my hands on his body, I showed him how the life force could be used in that traditional way. Dr. Fulford immediately discerned and acknowledged the uniqueness of the hands-on work of Bushman shamans. The Bushman way of energized touch, he said, answered the medical riddle he had spent a lifetime trying to solve. He spent the last years of his practice helping his patients in the same way that Bushman shamans work on each other. You might say that he was the first Bushman osteopath.

In my work with ecstatic touch I often go straight to a person's left shoulder, holding it with my right hand while placing my left hand over the person's heart. Then the n/om, chi, spirit, life force, or whatever you wish to call it is pumped through that person's body via strong vibrations that are typically syncopated and polyrhythmic. Doctor Fulford found that my vibrational work with my hands and body operated in the high frequencies he associated with spirituality and love. "When you can work at that frequency, you don't have to pay attention to treating body symptoms and psychological problems. Bodyworkers and most healers use vibrations at a lower frequency, which are effective for mending sickness. But when you can get those higher frequencies going, let them do their thing because they have the same benefits associated with body healing, but they also have the advantage of triggering spiritual development."

I believe Doctor Fulford was talking about the level of mind that Bushman shamans aim to connect with in their shamanic interaction with others. For him, the lowest frequencies are more about control, manipulation, and influence, whereas the higher frequencies concern beauty, freedom, and love. The good news is that all the benefits that come with the use of lower frequencies are included when one works with spiritual vibrations. One can choose to stay away from the seductive currents of power and head for the Big Love.

I knew Dr. Fulford during a time when I accepted all invitations and opportunities to demonstrate the activation of the life force. I did so without any conscious intent for a specific outcome. I would sometimes give a lecture while conducting a live demonstration, allowing my hands to do the energy work on their own, outside of my conscious awareness. People often reported a tingling sensation going from the top of the head to the bottom of the toes. It was not uncommon to hear someone say something like "You know about subtle energy work; consider this nonsubtle work!" Some people reported feeling heat throughout their bodies while others felt hot on one side and cold on the other. Many people felt drunk afterward, even after only a few seconds of receiving the energy. They felt high and euphoric (as did I), and almost every public demonstration resulted in someone teasing that this was the cure for drug addiction because it had the same desirable outcome with none of the problems.

Throughout the 1990s I felt like a spiritual gas-station attendant, mostly in the positive sense. People would come to me, one after another, as if to say "Fill 'er up please!" The quality and outcome of each person's experience was determined by the expectations, beliefs, and desires she brought along. For someone spiritually attuned, the experience would more likely be a spiritual one, perhaps seeing a religious icon or deity or feeling spirit in the person's heart. When I touched a young man in a ceremony in New York City, he and I both were propelled backward over a chair. The man went into mystical rapture, saying, "I see the Great Mother's light!" Afterward, we had a meal together and I mentioned a recurring dream I'd been having about a lama who lives in a cave, sitting on a tiger-skin rug. Ian's eyes opened wide as he replied, "That's my teacher. We've been living in Kathmandu and Nepal. Someday I've got to introduce you."

Others saw Jesus or felt saints upon them. Whatever their experience, I had nothing to do with it. It seemed that I was only holding the electrical cord that plugged them into a source of energy that charged the filament of their own desires and expectations. Some people just wanted to be "buzzed," so they vibrated, shook, and acted out in a wide variety of ways. There was almost always someone who took on the role of a wild beast in the jungle; they would jump on me as if attacking me in the middle of the Serengeti. I believed that if I consciously tried to handle them, I could get physically hurt. So when attacked and wrestled with, I would go into a trance and let my body be automatic, with no interference or resistance from my consciousness. It was a small miracle that I survived those wrestling episodes with my body still intact.

Some people passed out and had difficulty regaining consciousness. Paramedics were called on several occasions. And whether they consciously meant for it to happen or not, some women and men had their erotic sensitivities aroused. If you had walked into some of those shamanic performances, you might have heard singing, moaning, crying, laughing, or shouting, all at the same time. It was kinetic free-form play and I was a ball of fire, sometimes out of my mind but always fully in my body. It was a roofless circus of the body electric.

During that decade, but especially between 1994 and 1998, I would be called to travel through one dark night of the soul after another. It seemed that the more light that the shamanic work brought into my life the more darkness would subsequently enter, as if trying to chase the light away. I received every kind of imaginable praise and offer as well as every kind of threat. There were phone messages that sounded like excerpts from *The Exorcist* and death threats describing in intimate detail how I would be tortured and murdered. One woman, who I never spent any time with, claimed my spirit had entered her room and had sex with her and that she was giving birth to an invisible spirit baby.

Another woman claimed I had the spirits plant a radio transmitter in her brain, causing messages to be sent to her from God.

As they had with other liberal faculty, the conservative administrative elements of the Catholic university where I was working instigated an old-fashioned witch hunt, trying to get students to say things against me—like I was inappropriately "practicing Indian medicine" in the classrooms. The minister and deacons of the Black church I attended were ready to go to war with them on my behalf.

It was beyond my imagination how so many dark forces could fly out of Pandora's box at once. Mev used to say to me back then, "How can we tell anyone what is happening to us? It isn't believable! I wouldn't believe it if I heard it about someone else." But we garnered strength from the few who did see what was happening.

I didn't know which was more worrisome: the fear of being killed or the anxiety of being set up by false accusations. Yet I understood that I had opened some kind of box, the contents of which my culture had difficulty accepting, and I nearly lost my internal compass bearings due to the unrestrained backlash. In my heart of hearts, I knew I would have to come to terms with bearing partial responsibility for the nightmare that had been unleashed. After all, I did open the box. Yes, both heaven and hell were present, but there was too much of the latter.

I agonized over whether I was too open to any and all spirits and deities, allowing for everything—good *and* bad—to come in, whether I wanted it or not. If the outside world wasn't bad enough, the inside world also went to hell. I fought demons in the middle of the night. Once I woke up feeling something on my belly. I looked down and hallucinated a small dwarf sitting on my chest opening up my abdomen. A voice uttered, "You won't be able to experience what you feel." I quickly swiped that thing off me and cried out to Jesus for protection. I experienced my flesh starting to dematerialize; soon it began feeling like butter. I lifted my right hand and tried to feel my body but my hand went through my skin. I then realized, in that visionary other world, that I was unable to experience the materiality of my physical body. Several days later I again felt the beginning of this dematerialization experience but there was no dwarf to be seen. I tried to remain neutral about it and did not give it any importance. Whether lucid dream or alternative reality, there was no doubt that I was having a difficult time trying to manage it.

All of this was taking place at the same time that I was witnessing, or imagining that I was seeing, materializations. The Zulu sanusi Credo Mutwa gave me some advice during that period: "Write down the name of every object that has materialized and then take the first letter of each of those names and you will discover something." The word that came forth was *epopt;* I found out that this was a Greek word meaning "to be admitted to the highest grade of the Eleusinian mysteries, the great vision of light." I didn't know whether to take this message seriously or not.

This was a very crazy time in my life. I remembered Carl Jung's autobiographical book about his struggles during the confrontation with his unconscious. It seemed to be part of the price of exploring this experiential territory.

During the night I often fought other demons that threatened to take away my life force. One night I woke to hear a scratching sound outside my window. When I looked out I saw a mythical beast—a lion's face, green body hair, an orange mane. It terrified me. A week later, I found out that Walking Thunder, my Dine medicine woman friend, had a similar vision on the same night. She believed a curse had been put on both of us. She went to an elder who conducted a ceremony on our behalf; my inner voice directed me to suspend attaching myself to any belief about the meaning of the vision. I tried to give it no importance, thereby not feeding its power. Instead I focused my attention on being inside the radiance of the Big Love. The beast never returned.

Suffice it to say that I found myself in the midst of spiritual oppositions, contraries, conflicts, and wars, battling things I felt I could not defeat. It wasn't limited to the dark side, but it was the co-presence of both extremes: brilliant heavenly light and the scary darkness of hell. At times I didn't think I could make it through these haunting ordeals and, I must confess, there were moments when I felt like pressing the escape button.

If all that wasn't enough, amid armed campaigns to weed out "witch doctors," I dodged bullets several times in South Africa and I barely escaped a false kidnapping charge set up by government officials when I stayed with the Guarani Indians in lower basin Amazonia. Government intelligence agents warned that I should stay away from certain places and cultural groups.

Trouble was stirred up because I had bumped smack into what may be the last great taboo: the African body electric. Propose or mention a frenzied African ceremonial dance and you will often find yourself facing a desperate fear that seeks to attack and destroy. Whether the audience is agnostic, religious, or New Age, the idea of electrified bodies in Africa scares the hell out of many people. Like voodum in Haiti or hoodoo in historic New Orleans or Sanctified Church in Harlem, almost all African forms of spiritual practice are grossly misunderstood and discriminated against. African forms of spiritual practice are most often seen as "evil black magic" or orgiastic practice. This is what I found myself up against.

During this particular time I hit an existential bottom. At the lowest ebb of desperation and fear, I decided to spend even more time with the Bushmen as a means of learning more about how to live in the midst of these challenges.

In September of 1997, on the day before I left for Africa, I played some basketball with my young son in our backyard. After we put up the ball and came inside the house, I asked him if he had any questions that he wanted to ask me in case I had to be away for a long time. Children are naturally intuitive and he didn't miss a beat. He climbed on the kitchen counter, sat down, and started to talk.

"Dad, tell me about God and what life is all about."

For the first time we had the kind of father-son talk I had always hoped for, and a bond was created between us that nothing could sever, not even a distance of nine thousand miles. I asked him to remember what had happened to him several years before. Back then,

Scott had gone to bed one Saturday night and as we always did, Mev and I joined him in his bedtime prayers and songs. After turning out his bedroom light, I made a silent prayer asking that my son be given an experience that would let him know firsthand the reality and truth of spirit. I wanted him to appreciate that there is more to life than Nike shoes and video games.

No one but me knew that I had made that prayer. We all went to bed and fell asleep. At three o'clock in the morning, Mev and I were awakened by Scott's screams.

We jumped out of bed and ran into his room as fast as we could.

"Scott, what's going on?"

"I don't really know," he said, shaking. "I think I had some kind of dream, but it was really real. I saw myself being chased and shot in an alley and then I died. I went high into the sky and there I met God. God told me how everything works."

Mev and I began to weep. Our souls were penetrated by what we heard. Scott had received a sacred vision. We hugged him and explained that something very special had happened, specifying how other cultures around the world believed that what he experienced was the most important gift a person could ever receive. Out of my own curiosity, I asked, "What did God say to you?" Scott yawned and replied, almost nonchalant. "Dad, I'm too tired to talk anymore. I want to go back to sleep." I never again asked Scott what he had been told—elders from different cultures taught me the wisdom of leaving those matters private for a while. Doing so helped preserve the sacred power of the dream. The less told or even remembered, the more deeply a dream would settle and anchor into his unconscious mind, becoming an invisible, untouchable resource and inner power for his entire life.

Now, a year later, Scott and I recalled his vision, but remained silent about its content. We talked for an hour, which is an eternity for a child, and at the end I looked deeply into his sparkling blue eyes and angelic face, wondering how long it would be until I saw him again.

When I gave him a farewell hug, my sorrow was inconsolable. That was the condition the Bushmen found me in when I arrived again at the village of Ngwatle in Botswana. I had fled to Africa with no date for coming back.

That year the blind old Bushman shaman, Motaope, along with the other shamans, wrapped their arms around me and said it was necessary for me to go through all of what was happening. In the past, I thought I had mastered the life force and was being a beacon of light. Perhaps I was, from time to time, but now I was lost. There was nothing to do but remove myself from the world I knew and jump off a cliff. I was a free-falling being who, one more time, landed in the arms and hands of the Kalahari Bushmen.

11
Kalahari
Homecoming

IT IS SUMMER IN THE KALAHARI; the month is January and the year is 1998. Opening the front flap of my tent, I step out to see the predawn African bush coming alive. Moisture hangs in the air and the earth smells fresh and clean. I hear small animals scampering about. The sky above, painted by an invisible hand, is changing by the moment, until gold takes over and fills what was once the evening void. The desert sun is in its morning ascent, bathing the irregularly shaped thorn trees and bushes with light. The birds conduct a symphony of trills, shrieks, warbles, and whistles. In a rare lull, a beautiful solo songline is voiced.

Most of the large-animal sounds, particularly the cries of hyenas and jackals, belong to the night. They are quieted by the morning wake-up calls.

The early morning air skips across my arms, carrying the hope that other breezes will soften the day. At this moment, which will quickly lapse, it is not possible to imagine that it will become so hot and stagnant that no one will be able to do anything in the afternoon except hide under the partial shade of a camelthorn tree and nap until the evening moon arrives.

I think to myself: this is the same beginning to the day that people of the oldest culture on earth have experienced for thousands of years. I feel a tingling thrill dance upon my spine as I meet the same desert that the Bushmen of the past and present have experienced. I never sleep through the beginning of a Kalahari day. Dawn in the Kalahari offers a pure and thorough cleansing to my inner being. Dawn everywhere is the ancient incubator of hope, waking the longings of my soul to dare to consider what it would otherwise shy away from imagining.

I am not surprised that Africa is considered the cradle of human origin. As my sangoma friends are fond of saying, Africa is the Mother continent. But there is more that chronicles how Homo sapiens began than excavated skulls and bones. The Kalahari Desert of southern Africa is home to what is possibly the earliest form of human spiritual expression. The spiritual culture of the Kalahari Bushmen is older than those that created the monasteries of Tibet and Europe and the ceremonial lodges of North and South American Indians. The Kalahari Bushmen, one of the most endangered cultures on earth, have been relating to God since before words were written and civilizations established. Their spiritual expression is still alive, moving itself in the shaking bodies of today's Bushmen in arguably the same manner as it moved in those of their ancient ancestors. Indeed, rock art images that date back to the Stone Age leave little room for doubt about this.

My thoughts are interrupted by the distant sight of an old man making his way through the tall pale yellow grass. With him is a younger man who is dancing as he walks. Stopping to pull up a root from the sandy ground, the young man sings: "Ah-ee-ah, ah-ee-ah, ah-ee-ah, ta, ta, ta, ta, ta, ta, ta, ta."

They keep walking. These are Bushmen, tribesmen of the oldest inhabitants of southern Africa (and one of the most romanticized cultural groups in anthropological circles). As I watch these two move through the dry grass and patches of dense shrubs, I think of how their forebears once lived in the fertile land farther south near Cape Town, where there was plenty of water and game. That was thousands of years ago. At that time, the Bushmen painted fantastic images of themselves and the animals they hunted. I have studied these rock art images, some of the oldest "picture books" ever recorded, located on rocks and cliffs throughout the countryside of South Africa. Since then, the Bushmen had to move to the scorching deserts in what is now Botswana and Namibia, a desolate and difficult terrain that few others cared to visit.

The old man keeps walking across the sand. To the government of Botswana he is simply a "remote area dweller," someone the government hopes will not be seen or heard by the rest of the world. The government is doing all that it can to take away the Bushmen's way of life, trying to chase them off their traditional hunting grounds. The president of Botswana, Festus Mogae, once described the Bushmen as "Stone Age creatures for whom there is no place in the modern world."*

I know the old man who walks in the distance. I estimate him to be around seventy-five years old. It is hard to know the age of an elder Bushman. The old ones don't count years. The first time I asked a Bushman how old he was, he told me that he was over three hundred years old. That's when I stopped asking.

This old man, the senior member of his community, is one of my teachers. He is a well-known shaman in the southern Kalahari Desert, a region occupying the southwestern corner of Botswana, near the border of Namibia.

The Bushmen who live here are known as !Xo Bushmen. The physical appearance of the Bushmen in the north part of Botswana is more yellow and golden; here they have intermarried with other, more black-skinned, African groups and so are regarded as "black Bushmen." They call themselves the Balala.

The elder Bushman's name is Motaope. He is blind. He is regarded by all the surrounding villages as a "big shaman," someone who helps heal the sick as well as revitalize everyone's well-being. He also helps other Bushmen become shamans. Although he is blind, he is quite capable of navigating the desert unattended. Today, however, he is traveling

---

*Reported by John Simpson, BBC World Affairs, on BBC News, August 15, 2002.

with the younger shaman, Tete, a man he has taught to doctor the sick with plants and to use a special kind of healing touch. Tete dances and sings to the plants before he takes them to be used as a medicine for those in need.

Motaope and Tete are getting closer to my tent. I can see the old man in his worn-out brown clothes and torn jacket. He has slender hands and feet and tightly curled hair; he is about five feet tall. These men know how to survive in this harsh environment. The Kalahari is a vast sweep of aridity stretching over a thousand miles. Its heat burns the skin and its thorns pierce the flesh, but these are nothing compared to the treacherous sting of its scorpions, who hide behind stones and brush. In this remote country of thirst and the ever-present threat of fatal dehydration, the old man has an understanding of plants and animals that helps his people survive.

From the material point of view, Motaope, shirt bursting forth with dangling threads and shoes so worn that his toes stick out of the front, looks as poor as any third world citizen could look. Yet he is one of the spiritually wealthiest beings on earth. I see that his hair is still graying and that his walk is slow and deliberate. As the old blind man approaches, I see his long, dirty fingernails pointing to me.

I remember when I first met him. Motaope, whose name means "tell it again and again," said to me, "I know Bushman medicine like the palms of my hands. I am very happy to tell you what I know because this will make my knowledge travel further into the world. I am very old and wish that my knowledge be told and recognized for the power it holds."

Tete, which means "a feeling of wonder," is a mercurial, elflike trickster. Quick to laugh, sing, or dance, he can, without notice, change his mood and countenance. A mustache and a slight beard on his chin, he wears a well-worn knit hat with an orange rim on its bottom. I have never seen him without that hat. Sporting a dirty T-shirt and a soiled, much-stained tan jacket, his pockets overflow with the roots he has picked and stored for future medicinal use.

I have seen these two men many times before, walking across the desert sand looking for plants, but today there is something more deliberate about the old man's motion. Motaope is walking in a straight line that aims directly at me. I can feel his approach in my bones, as if there is a tightrope between his body and mine, pulling him toward me as it pulls me toward him.

Tete pauses, points to a small, leafless twig poking out of the ground, and begins poking the soil with his digging stick. Within a minute he unearths a tuber that looks like a sweet potato. Later in the day, when he cuts it open, it will drip water, providing a refreshing drink on a parched afternoon.

My wife and closest colleague, Mev, is also awake, mixing freshly boiled water with instant coffee to make her wake-up brew. Beverages are the equivalent of Kalahari gold, the most valuable thing a Bushman can have in the desert. In Botswana, the word for happiness and money, *pula,* is the same word as for rain. I remember asking Motaope about his favorite childhood memory. He replied that he liked recalling a time when it had rained after a long drought. His mother had collected some water with a leaf and then given the children a few drops each on their outstretched tongues. The main challenge of Kalahari life has always been finding water, especially after the pans dry up following the brief rainy season. Bushmen have a knack for finding water in the desert, though, not only in its melons and roots but also in natural pockets deep below the sand. Somehow they are able to locate it. They dig down and suck out the water with long straws. When their mouths can hold no more, they let the water drain into an empty ostrich egg shell, which is then stopped up with a tuft of grass. Then they bury the shells in a place secured for future use.

Mev and I often marvel over how the Bushmen's lives have traditionally revolved around their search for water. We are mindful of it every time we take a drink. Unlike these traditional Bushmen, who only bathe with the juice of desert cucumbers or animal fat, we haul in all of our water and limit ourselves to washing once every three or four days, using only a cup of water.

Now Mev leans forward slightly, holding her hand over her eyes to screen out the blinding sun, and watches Motaope and Tete as they near. She also knows that something important is about to happen. She is wondering what the Bushmen are up to as she prepares a drink for them. They have changed both of our lives in the past and every trip brings new lessons and learning. She, too, senses that there is something different about their approach this morning.

I step forward and embrace Motaope with open arms. His body is small and slender, quite pliable. His face is broad and flat with a wide nose covered with tiny craters, indentations that make him look deeply weathered and wizened by the seasons. His quiet eyes look as though they have joined the few scattered clouds overhead while his remaining teeth glisten as he smiles and makes a welcoming sound of homecoming.

We hug, my fingers brushing along his coat, feeling many holes and unraveled threads. With his thick lips close to my ear, he gently murmurs, "Umm, umm, umm." I respond in kind. It's the sound he makes when his heart is open. It is an old familiar sound.

"It's good that you are back. This is your home. I saw that you were coming in my dreams." He talks to me through our interpreter.

"Yes, Motaope, my heart is happy to see you."

"Ah-ee-ah, ah-ee-ah," Tete sings. He starts to dance. Tete has the deep brown eyes that are characteristic of all Bushmen. It is the same color brown found in an antelope's eyes, penetrating and mysteriously intimate. Almost all Africans believe that a Bushman can see further than other human beings. Their powers of vision are legendary. Tete looks us over, moisture gathering at the corners of both eyes. All the while he is singing: "Ah-ee-ah, ah-ee-ah, ah-ee-ah . . . ."

A physical jolt comes through the old man's weathered body and he jumps a few inches off the ground. I feel that jolt enter my own body. It feels as though I've been hit by lightning, what I call "Bushman lightning." This convulsive body jerk jolts me into spontaneous movement. Soon Motaope and I are shaking together. Our legs, hips, bellies, arms, hands, and heads shake and tremble. We are plugged into some kind of electricity. This current is not AC or DC. I call it SC—the "spiritual current" of the Bushmen.

We shake together in a coordinated pattern interspersed with jolts and movements that trigger various choreographies of kinesthetic expression. Our hands rub each other's backs, sides, bellies, and hearts. Sometimes our knees bend and lower us to the ground. The shaking doesn't stop there, but lifts us up again. "Ah-ee-ah, ah-ee-ah, ah-ee-ah, ta, ta, ta, ta, ta, ta, ta, ta." Our energetic embrace escalates until we each let out shrieks that sound like a giant bird screeching in the air. It feels and sounds to me like a release of mounting tension. Now we tremble more smoothly at a higher frequency. This vibration is invisible to an outside viewer but more intense from within. In this new phase, it is impossible to speak an intelligible sentence. Only improvised wild noises, a raw sound poetry, comes out of our mouths now. "Eeh, eeh, eeh, ah eeh!" We greet one another and the vast open space of the Kalahari with trills, shrieks, warbles, whistles, and songlines.

I feel as alive as it seems could be humanly possible. My heart is fully open. Love runs through my muscles and veins. On both Motaope's face and my own are the tears that so often attend overwhelming joy. From years of being together in this way, we know that if we don't stop we may pass out, plunging upon the millions of grains of sand that are beneath us and possibly entering another realm, the spiritual universe of the Bushmen, a place where ropes connect each Bushman's belly to every other Bushman's belly, making real a fervent connection that is absent and unseen in ordinary waking consciousness.

"Yes," I hear Motaope say, "it is good to be with you again, my son. Good, good," he repeats in his dialect marked by clicking sounds, as I continue to shake with my eyes closed. "We need to dance tonight. Yes, this is good."

Motaope has started cooling me down. He doesn't want me to travel into the spiritual universe right now. He pats my sides and head with his leatherlike hands, wiping his perspiration onto my skin. Our foreheads rub against each other while Tete, smaller in stature than the old man, stands on tiptoes to massage both of our heads in a gentle stroking way, trying to cool things down spiritually.

I gather myself to ask, "How are you?"

"Life is as it always is and I am happy that you are back. The Big God has sent you again."

This is how Bushman shamans greet each other—through touch, movement, vibration, trembling, shaking, sweat, smell, wild sounds, and simple songs. It is a sacred intimacy seldom performed or even heard about elsewhere in the world. It is the reason I am in the Kalahari this morning. It is what Bushmen shamans live for. It is the fabric of their spiritual life.

Bushman shamans all over the Kalahari previously taught me to be comfortable and exploratory with ecstatic body states and a heightened sense of awareness. They showed me how it is possible and even necessary to stay grounded in the earthiness of life and death while reaching for the highest altitudes of the spiritual sky and the furthest depths of the spiritual underworld. In a way, they taught me to fly—not flight of the aviary kind, but in the way of a wholehearted soul let out of its cage and permitted to soar, on full throttle, into the most intense experiences of intimate bonding. In these realms there can be a heightened relationship not only with immediate loved ones but with ancestors from the past, animals, plants, and Earth as a whole. This is the stuff of classic mysticism, whether Christian, Islamic, Jewish, Buddhist, Hindu, Native American, Siberian, Amazonian, or any of the other sacred traditions that treasure direct experience of the divine life force.

Really striking about the Bushman way of sacred communion is how unpretentious, earthy, and playful the Bushmen are in seeking, holding, and sharing it. There are no upper classes of people with specially colored robes, distinct haircuts, or membership totems. They are, as my grandparents used to say, "plain folk." It's probably not possible to choose a Bushman shaman out of a random line-up of Bushman citizens. There is no mark of importance that distinguishes a shaman from anyone else in the community. They are also no richer than anyone else.

Among the Bushmen, rigorous sharing, rather than competitive hoarding, is more valued and socially expected.

But wait until a shaman gets a hold of you in her dance. She may shake you up, inside and out. In the dance, shamans become transformed into master handlers of ecstatic expression with extraordinary methods of contact and communication. Healers and witch doctors all over Africa believe that the Bushmen are the strongest shamans and fantasize that they have miraculous powers. However, in the same way that it is nearly impossible for most people to "see" a Bushman shaman outside of the dance, it is not always possible to "feel" their transformational touch during a ceremonial encounter. You must be ready, prepared, perhaps "rewired" to receive what they have to offer. Otherwise you will experience nothing. This holds true for all Bushmen as well. Each Bushman must wait until she is ready to greet and embrace the shaman's touch.

Becoming a shaman is all about preparing for that touch, holding it, transforming it, and sharing it with others. The "it" I am talking about is a great mystery. Known as n/om, it is variously talked about as a kind of spirit, an energylike electricity, and a divine power. Its source is love, arising from the deepest kind of passionate relationship human beings are capable of experiencing—the same overpowering love that touches a couple when their child has just been born. This current of love has a humbling aspect. Its power is so great that it can knock you over and flatten you to the ground when you are open and prepared to be hit by its lightninglike impact.

I am not referring to something akin to a magical potion made by a mythological sorcerer that converts you into a superhero. N/om is something more potent and magical than anything ever described in a fairy tale. The Bushmen's spiritual gift pierces the sheltering armor of your psyche, deflates its ego-centered self-importance, and then paradoxically fills you with a spiritual essence that cannot be confined. This "filling" arises from an unspeakable mystery, compassionate love so strong that you feel gentle empathy for everyone, including your enemies. This has nothing to do with any quest for power that conquers foes and adversaries. It is the transforming Big Love that Jesus of Nazareth spoke about, the love that dares to love one's enemies. This is the great leveler and equalizer, the wisest, most radical and most paradoxical teaching, the all-encompassing compassion of the Buddha, the holy grail of all enduring pilgrimages.

On this particular Kalahari morning, as Motaope and I embraced, I was well on my way to entering more deeply into their most beautiful and extraordinary secrets.

That morning, immediately after our shaking embrace, Motaope took a few steps to his side, crouched, and turned his head toward me to give me his news: "Today we will make you a true Bushman shaman. You have felt our power and you are familiar with using it. We accept your touch as the healing touch of a Bushman shaman. The Big God now wants you to know everything about our ways. He has asked that we bring you inside our community like we have done to each shaman since the beginning days of our first ancestors. You are ready to experience these things. It is time to make another Bushman shaman."

Mev squeezed my hand. We had traveled the world numerous times, finding different shamans, medicine people, healers, and spiritual teachers, usually led to them by a visionary dream. She had supported every step of this journey even when it threatened our economic stability, my professional reputation as a scholar and teacher of psychotherapy, and our personal safety. We had traveled through heaven and hell together.

I said a simple prayer in my heart, words I remembered PaPa saying: "Lord, I surrender my life to you. I ask that you take me and use me as your servant. I will not stand in the way."

12
Initiation Night

I NEVER TOLD MOTAOPE THAT I HAD COME to the Kalahari on that trip with a desire to fully surrender myself to a greater power. Yet he saw that something was different in me. The day before we arrived he had set out straight toward us. He had been in another village and, awakening in the middle of the night, said to Tete, "Brad has come back. We must leave now and meet him." Motaope's dreams, like mine, sometimes told him what he must do.

Following his early morning announcement, he added, "You are ready to become a true shaman, a big doctor, and learn all that we know. Life has prepared you for this. We want to fully initiate you into our traditional ways."

Motoape said that he wished to start the process right then. He took his hands and gently placed them on my belly. His fingers were vibrating and I could feel them deliver a tingling sensation into my abdomen. His black hair, consisting of thick round clusters, what Europeans call "peppercorn hair," rubbed against my forehead. As he touched me, he softly sang a song. At first I didn't know that he was doing anything different from what he and dozens of other Bushman shamans had done to me over the years. I had felt this energy and had learned not only to be comfortable with it but to enjoy receiving it and giving it back.

This time it was different. As Motaope touched my abdomen, I began to feel sick. The nausea strengthened and I began throwing up.

"Come with me," said the old shaman as he reached for my hand and led me to a quiet place in the bush.

"This is how it is. Stay here until I call for you. I am making you a Bushman shaman."

I spent the day in that spot under a thorn tree fighting severe diarrhea, vomiting, and abdominal cramps. Drop by drop, I felt all of my life force drain away into the ground until I couldn't lift a hand or a foot. With no willpower left to fight the pain, I finally gave up and let it overtake me. Rather than oppose it, I surrendered.

I remained prone in some kind of deathlike state for the rest of the day, reflecting back over my journeys, marveling at some of the inspired miracles I had beheld but also humbled by the times I had been quite ignorant and foolish. Once Mev and I had driven eighteen hours to the Montana/Wyoming border to meet some medicine men at a gathering near the Great Medicine Wheel. When the meeting was over, a medicine man we didn't know asked for a ride to his home in Pine Ridge, South Dakota. We pulled into his place just after midnight. It was in the heart of the Badlands, an eerie place. The medicine man asked us if we wanted to do an *inipi*, a sweat lodge ceremony, with him. We looked at each other and thought, "Why not?" We prepared ourselves to join him in this traditional ceremony.

When we entered the tent the medicine man sang a song, made some chants, and asked us to pray. After a while he said, "Open 'er up." I immediately obeyed and began to offer a chant. "Open 'er up!" he shouted again. I reached more deeply inside myself and began to sing a song with as much power as I could gather. "Open 'er up! Open 'er up!" he bellowed. I thought to myself that I'd never been pushed this far this fast. I reached inward and tapped the deepest part of my unconscious mind—I began speaking some form of glossolalia; that is, I began speaking in tongues. Mev joined in, doing the same. The medicine man immediately threw a bucket of water on us. I remember thinking, "My God, this is unbelievable!" Out of me came the sound of thunder. I felt like I was entering another dimension.

At this our medicine man host opened the entry flap and demanded that we get out of the sweat lodge. He seemed afraid and began asking what language we had spoken. He said he heard us say his secret spirit name. He was clearly rattled. Our immediate survival instinct was to do nothing that would escalate his fear.

The whole fiasco had taken place because of a simple miscommunication. When he said, "Open 'er up," he meant open up the flap to the tent to let in some cool air. We thought he meant for us to go deeper into prayer. We sat quietly as he vented his fear, anger, and upset. We then respectfully thanked him, got dressed, and left. We were in our Toyota in the middle of the Badlands in pitch dark and didn't say a word for several minutes. Then, at the same time, we both let out a hysterical burst of laughter. "Open 'er up, Open 'er up," we shouted out as we drove ourselves home. "Yep, the Gods were crazy tonight inside that wigwam."

Ever since that bizarre inipi we decided that we would never accept an invitation to participate in a spiritual ceremony out of curiosity. We had to receive a spiritual calling or a dream before accepting such an invitation or taking off to a faraway place.

I thought about this as I sat in my deathlike state of awareness, recalling the spiritual events of our past. I was clear about the call to be with the Bushmen. I felt I was supposed to be here, and this clarity helped me accept what was happening.

As the Kalahari sun disappeared from the sky and evening came on, I looked out over the horizon, viewing the small traditional grass huts and the more contemporary mud ones that made up this village. Each Bushman could carry every one of his possessions on his back. Yet there is more to the Bushman life than what meets the eye's first glance. Look closer and you see that the Bushmen live in a complex ecology, one in which death can be hiding behind any bush or under any stone. So many things can kill you out here. Snakes such as the dreaded black mamba can kill you within hours if you ever have the misfortune of being bitten. One of the villagers had died from a mamba bite. There were tree snakes equally as toxic. I had already come too close for comfort with two mambas and two deadly tree snakes in previous trips, not to mention the morning when I discovered a puff adder outside my tent. Poisonous snakes, ravenous lions, and toxic plants and trees out here can kill you in an instant. The Kalahari is a place where you have to be careful where and how you walk.

I notice that some of the Bushmen are piling tree branches to make a fire. When they don't have a match available, they still know how to make a fire by rubbing two thin sticks together. They make a pile of dried leaves, then place one stick inside a hole that has been carefully cut into the tip of the other stick. When they spin the stick between the palms of their hands, it only takes a few seconds for smoke to appear. Then the dry grass bursts into flames. Tonight they were starting the fire in this old way.

I knew they were preparing for a dance. People were joking with each other like they always do before a dance, often with lewd and earthy remarks.

"You better have a big penis tonight," someone shouted, "so we can hear it drag the ground when you dance." Everyone was giggling, teasing, and joking. Everyone except me. I was lying prone on the ground wondering if I would ever feel well again. The thought of walking, let alone dancing, was totally unimaginable.

As the community gathered around the fire some of the older shamans came over, grabbed me by my arms and legs, and dragged me to the dance area. They were laughing and teasing and didn't seem to be concerned about my condition. One of them, Mabolelo, picked up a twig and threw it at a couple of rib-thin dogs that were yapping over a scrap of food, telling them to shut up. "Looks like you're ready to dance all night," Tete jests.

"You bet," I summon the energy to say, "and you're going to learn a few steps from me tonight." Tete loves to be teased as much as he enjoys teasing. He starts dancing, making fun of the new steps I might teach him.

We make it to a spot just outside the fire circle and they place me on the ground. I am facing the village huts. I see old Motaope moving toward me. He wears a leather dance apron and nothing else. He carries the carved blonde-wood dance stick with black markings and a smooth curved end that is always by his right side. He is already talking and singing. His short rhythmic dance steps pound the earth, stirring his internal n/om, his spiritual power. He is deeply calm and intensely focused. Bent forward, feet hammering the ground, he sings: "Ah-ee-ah, ah-ee-ah, ah-ee-ah, ta, ta, ta, ta ta, ta, ta, ta." He is getting close now. He starts talking but my interpreter is not with me. All I hear are the sounds of a language full of sharp pops and clicks made with the tongue brushing against various parts of the mouth.

The old shaman is in no hurry. He has all night to build up his internal energy, becoming less Motaope the man and more Motaope the shaman. Within half an arm's length from me I smell his sweat. I know his sweat smell—ancient, musty, dirtlike. More earthen than human is this shaman's sweat. Teardrops of the Kalahari herself drip off his body. Heavy sweat signifies that his power is activated. It is the Bushman shaman's medicine and power.

As Motaope reaches to touch me, I close my eyes and yield completely to him. There is no strength in my body. I can muster no emotional response. I am an empty, unresistant, naked soul whose body has been silenced by pain and exhaustion. The other shamans gather around us singing and making those shrieking sounds. I can't tell where the sound stops and the touching begins. I know Motaope's hands are on my belly, but it feels as if the communal sound is doing the touching, pulsing, and shaking. African rhythms are inside the sounds and they travel through my skin, directly into my heart. I am floating in this ocean of pulsing touch and sound.

"Hi-ee-ah!" I suddenly shout and become aware that I am no longer nauseous. I don't even feel my belly. Slowly and surely my body becomes lighter and lighter. I am a two-hundred pound man who now feels less than twenty pounds. The same hands that earlier had made me deathly ill now make me feel better than I have ever felt in my life.

Before I know what is happening, the men are lifting me up and draping me over Motaope's back. I am glued to his body with the help of the shaman's sweat. Motaope lifts one foot and then another, and I feel his feet as my feet. He bends over and my back also bends. As he sings my voice makes the same sound. Moving inside the circle where the women sit around the fire, I hear them clapping their hands and singing the songs of their sacred dance. As the transformed shaman, Motaope bends over and touches each person, shaking the person with his body and vibrating him with his fluttering hands. I feel that I am doing the same. I see, hear, smell, and feel what he does. We are indistinguishable in my field of awareness.

I keep my eyes closed, letting go of all introspection and internal commentary. My mind is swept along by rippling currents of energy coupled with flooding rivers of sweat. I am becoming like Motaope, effortlessly and spontaneously doing what a Bushman shaman does in a healing dance.

It has been said that Bushmen are beautiful because of the grace of their movements. While their swaybacked carriage makes their bellies stick out, their long and slender legs with lean muscle and fine bone make them appear to be gliding when they walk or run. To watch a Bushman walk or bend over to pick up a root is to witness part of a great dance. Everything in a Bushman's life seems like a dance.

I have no idea how long I have been draped over Motaope's back. It seems like hours. I open my eyes and feel a thunderbolt of shock go through my system: Motaope is not there! I am inside the circle doing the healing without him. Other shamans are helping me the way they typically help Motaope. They promptly notice that my eyes are open and that I am fully aware of the situation. I am drinking in the moment, deeply registering how I am participating in their ancient practice.

The men gather around and lead me outside the circle. Once again they sit me on the ground facing Motaope. I watch as they take off the long, dirty string of dance rattles that is wrapped around his ankles and calves. Made of dried cocoons, filled with pieces of ostrich shell and tied together with homemade strings, Bushmen wear these rattles to make a percussive sound when their legs move in the dance. The elders finish removing Motaope's rattles and, with excited hands, proceed to wrap them around my ankles.

When I stand up, all the men line up behind me. Motioned toward the fire, I begin dancing. My legs lift themselves without effort. The contact of my feet on the sand is revitalizing. A full moon is overhead. The fire sends its sparks into the sky looking like thin lines of light that reach toward the heavens.

I approach the inside of the circle and notice that the women are peeling off their blouses, exposing their breasts. This amplifies their singing and the energy I feel circulating in my body. We are all united in some kind of highly charged way, not describable with the language of sexuality. This is something else—a raw energy moving through hearts and souls that are wide open.

I see the black lines on the women's cheeks, worn for decoration, their necklaces and earrings made of broken bits of ostrich eggshell. They spend days making the beads and lacing them through tightened strips of sinew. In front of the fire's warm glow, the beads look like stars twinkling around their necks, bouncing upon their breasts. Most of the younger women have babies slung over their backs in a hide sling or piece of cotton cloth. The babies contentedly bounce along with the rhythms of their mothers' clapping hands. Everyone is in the dance—young and old, women and men.

The hypnotic music is sung by the tightly woven circle of women, their legs and knees loosely falling against one another. They clap rhythms that are synchopated and complex, singing various strands of undulating melodies. They form a circle of sound and bodies that is, in turn, circled on the outside by the men who dance around them. The shamans are inside the women's circle, near the fire. Circles within circles reach out into the cool evening air to lasso the spiritual energy of the cosmos, grab it, and tightly hold it inside the pulsing heart of the ceremonial community. Men bring their songs to the women's music, adding more layers of sonic tapestry, blending more pathways of connection, generating more spiritual energy.

The Bushmen are celebrating their newly initiated shaman. All the energies of life flow through us, undercurrents of earth and overcurrents of sky, bioelectric fields of plants and animals, magnetically charged attractions of intimacy and relationship, both sacred and profane. This is a genuine awakening of soul. Bushmen know that soul is not a concept for theological debate. It is an awakening of life. It is the birth of pulse and rhythm.

I dance all night, touching and shaking my body with other men, women, and children. Is this a kinetic holy grail, an answer of the body to the mind's search for the meaning of life? In this primordial dance we find grace and the holy love, sacred kindness, and eternal joy that we all desire.

As I dance and shake, my material body feels as though it is dissolving. That is my experience. I become a cloud floating in the air. Images shift. Some people look like cloudy X rays. I see dark spots on others that cry out to be touched. I act without thought or understanding. My hands are dowsing rods. They feel the tug of other bodies that want to be touched and shaken. All of this happens in a mind that is not mine but is all its own. This mind is outside the boundary of my skin. It is the mind of the dance. Everyone inside the circle is minded and mended by this greater pattern of connectivity.

Conscious thought recedes further and further until a silence fully occupies my inner space. I have become a human electrical transformer, a carrier of the life force. With one arm plugged into a cosmic socket, the other arm reaches out to anyone who wishes to make the hookup and feel the current.

As the life force surges through me, I am aware of my metamorphosis. I have this awareness even though I have lost the ability to speak, both to myself and to others. When I step outside of the dance circle to approach Mev, no words are able to come out of my mouth no matter how hard I try. Only wild sounds and untamed shrieks can be vocalized. "Ah, eeh ah, ta, ta, ta, ta, ta." It is difficult to stand up. I am sometimes dizzy. My sides ache and my belly is pumping like a hydraulic piston, causing me to stay bent over. My legs stomp the ground like a powerful machine driven by an unknown force.

Mev, accustomed to the wild, energetic movements of Bushman shamans, calmly comes to me with a drink of water to help cool me down. She knows the power of the Bushmen's touch. Held by Motaope and other shamans, she has felt vibrations get triggered inside her own body. Her way is to remain calm with this energy and let it naturally settle within her. My bent is toward allowing it to encourage other forms of expression. We are a husband and wife team, not unlike other Bushman shaman couples, joined together as Kalahari yin-yang.

As quickly as night enters and disappears upon the desert, the dance finds its own beginning and end. At the start, a single woman sings fragments of a song, adding her own simple clapping. Slowly other women join in, one by one, until a chorus has coalesced. When the music is strong, the shamans lead the way to the circle, the young shamans-in-training behind them. The men dance round and round the women, making a furrowed path in the sand, the same path that can be seen in ancient rock paintings of the dance. There is great power in that furrow. It holds the impact of a dancing shaman's interaction with the earth. The dance has its up-and-down cycles, hitting a peak of arousal and then dying down for a period of rest, only to start up again. Finally, when it is ready to end, the community spontaneously declares the final moment with a ritualized cadence of four special beats in which everyone participates to mark the finale.

As the dances have always ended over many thousands of years, the dance and the night come to a close together. Motaope and the others make their way back to their stick and mud huts while Mev and I return to our hut made of canvas, aluminum poles, and metal zippers. Lying on our cots, I look to Mev and tell her that I still feel like a cloud. I feel nothing but vibrations. She confidently replies, "Don't worry about it, Brad. It's a natural thing."

Many years before, when I first began receiving huge infusions of spiritual energy into my body, I panicked one evening. I couldn't stop shaking. It kept getting more and more amplified until I was flopping on the floor like a fish out of water. Mev simply turned toward me and, directly addressing the energy rather than me, shouted, "Stop it now!" The shaking stopped and I fell into a deep, relaxing sleep.

I contemplate aloud what a strange journey it has been. Starting as an academic systems theorist and circular thinker who practiced with psychotherapy, I stumbled into the heart and soul of the world's oldest mystical traditions. Mev jumps in: "Remember, Brad, you have a mission. And it's a big one at that. Be patient and wait for the dreams to direct you. You know how it works. Now let's get some sleep."

I remain awake. The sun will rise in a little while anyway and I want to watch the day begin, to enjoy the moments when the rising sun makes things fresh and new again.

A few hours later, Mev turns to her side and yawns, looking as though she has had a good night's rest. Soon everyone gathers around the morning campfire, sipping tea and coffee and nibbling on crackers we brought. The air is still cool. I sit with the group and listen with half an ear to the morning chatter.

I feel a light tapping and then a tug on my shoulder. Turning to my right, I am startled to see twelve African women dressed in long green gowns with collars up to their chins. They are standing in front of an isolated island of thornbushes. Lined up next to one another, hands pressed against their sides, they stare at me with eyes of fire. I take on their collective gaze, a string of twelve sets of eyes with blazing light as bright as the stars. They don't speak, but their eyes are sending me something. I feel a rippling current pass through me. I catch my breath and turn to ask my Bushmen friends about these people.

"Who are these women? Are they from here?"

"What are you seeing?" Tete calmly asks.

Everyone looks at me as though no one knows what I'm talking about. When I turn to get another look, I practically fall off my canvas-backed chair. They're not there! They have completely vanished into the morning desert air. Did I hallucinate them? What precipitated this waking vision? What is this about?

Motaope laughed hard when he listened to me asking about the women. His face broke into little folds crisscrossing his forehead. I noticed how extraordinarily small his hands were, though I knew there was enough power in his fingertips to light the Kalahari sky. He was wearing the necklace I had given him last time, a necklace made of old trade beads that probably had been carried from one end of Africa to another. The old man stood up straight and lifted the finger I had grown accustomed to seeing when he wanted to underscore an important point. His right hand stretched out over his head with that dirty, pointed fingernail aimed toward the sky. His mood quickly shifted to a serious tone and he prepared himself for a speech.

"The ancestors, especially the shamans from the past, sometimes come down and look at a living shaman. They want to see what God is doing with this person. Today they looked at you. If you were weak, you would have been scared and run away. Since you are strong, you were able to look at them. It's very good that you could handle twelve of them. They are going to teach you something. Since they're women, maybe they will teach you how to be a woman shaman."

Motaope and the other men can't hold back their desire to tease me. They immediately start laughing without restraint and prance about like women, curling their fingers for breasts.

"Every African woman has something important to teach between her legs," Tete quips.

I join in the absurd revelry and we all topple to the ground, overcome by laughter. "This is very good," Motaope says, and after a long pause, he gets serious again. "Sit down. There is more that I have to say."

"I know what is going on in your life. You don't need to tell me. My dreams have already shown me what you've been going through. As you gain spiritual power and a greater capacity to love, there will be people who are jealous of you and will try anything to hurt you. They may want you to give them something you are not able to give even if you wanted to do so.

"It is the Big God who chooses the shamans. A person can't decide on his or her own to be this way. No one in a right mind would want to go through the challenges and ordeals that come to us. Yet some people are looking for power and importance and they think that you can give it to them. When you don't deliver, they want to kill you. If they can't have it, then they don't want anyone else to have it. Of course, they seldom admit this to themselves," he said.

"There are also people who sincerely open themselves to our shamanic power and then find themselves experiencing their own hidden desires and wishes. If they are looking for the gods, hooking up with the power may help bring this about. If they bring fear, the power can feed their seeds of worry and concern. Remember that you do not determine other people's experiences. You only help bring forth the power that helps mobilize them to find what they seek. If they seek the wrong things, they will blame you for the experiences your power awakens in them.

"We, the Bushmen shamans of this part of the world, know that there are people out there who may try to hurt you. We have been busy making you some things that will provide protection."

Motaope turns to his son and asks him to hand me the medicines that have been gathered. He reaches into his own jacket pocket and pulls out some sticks, plants, and roots. Some are short and fat, others are long and thin. I notice that they still have pieces of dirty sand clinging to them. He places all of this mixture into some hot water and waits for the mixture to brew. Sipped slowly out of a tin cup, it tastes as though I am drinking the Kalahari desert. The old man, his son, and the other shamans are nodding their heads in approval. It is a bitter and strong concoction, causing me to sneeze and grimace.

When I finish drinking every drop, Motaope instructs the men to hand over to me some specially prepared items to carry with me, magical items whose specific details I promise never to reveal.

"These things will protect your family from harm. Stop worrying about others. We have taken care of them. Anyone who acts badly toward you will find their actions turned against them. Now listen very carefully, for this is extremely important. You must never get angry with anyone. Anger will be your greatest temptation, as it is to all shamans. You will sometimes want to use your power to destroy those who threaten to harm your family. Sometimes this must be done, though it is very rare. We have taken on this responsibility for you. You, your son, and your wife are protected by the Kalahari Bushmen.

"Now get on with your life. Don't stop being a Bushman. We want you to touch others like we touch and tell the world what you have learned from us. We regard you as a Bushman shaman who knows the healing way. You and I are lucky. The Big God was good to us and gave us a special gift. Go home and never forget that the Bushman ancestors are always with you. If you dance, you'll wake us up and we'll be there. You have come to spend the rest of your life in the Kalahari. We want you to go everywhere and take the Kalahari with you. In this way, you will never leave us."

13
Caribbean Spirit Traveling

IN JANUARY OF 1999, Mev and I traveled to the island of Saint Vincent in the Caribbean. There I found the African women I had seen in my Kalahari premonition. Dressed in green gowns, these women, part of a mystical group called the Shakers of Saint Vincent, taught me about other dimensions of the African spiritual universe.

The Saint Vincent Shakers, also called Spiritual Baptists, believe that the most important spiritual teachings take place in dreams. They accordingly seek spiritual knowledge though intense prayer fasts that are overseen by elders wise in the ways of spiritual journeying. To enter this classroom, you must first have a dream that shows you the person who will oversee your pilgrimage into spirit. That person is called a "pointer," because she has the expertise to direct you to the spirit world.

While in Saint Vincent I dreamed of a man named Archbishop Pompey. In the dream he told me, "I have God's number." Later that evening I awakened to find my right arm lifted toward the sky and my upper body partially lifted off the bed, as though someone had grabbed my hand, pulling me upward to the heavens. There was a power and influence from the spirit world that I had to acknowledge. When I found Pompey, a man most of the islanders knew about, and told him the dream, he replied, "Yes, I do have God's number. It was given to me. You have dreamed this and now you can enter my school and learn from the spirit."

I was prepared for a weeklong fast and given instructions for the ritual they call mourning. The pointer, following his dreams about me, selected particular colors of cloth bands and dripped symbols in candle wax on them before wrapping them tightly around my head. Then I was ritually put away in a little room at the back of the praise house. Elders came every morning and evening to pray over me and to sing sacred songs. My task was to pray around the clock as I thoroughly examined my life, carefully scrutinizing and facing all of my sins, wrongdoings, and shortcomings.

I lay there reviewing my life, recalling my past failings, fears, terrors, and sufferings and ready, I hoped, to allow them to take me down as far as my psyche could bear and then to go further, breaking through the veil of ego and self-concern. I was mourning my life and asking God to take me in his arms. After years of surviving the extreme polarities of light and dark, I sought to be fully available to the Creator with no resistance to his direction.

I doubt I'll ever forget the moment of my breaking. After praying through a day and a night, I hit bottom and, on some deep existential level, gave up the life I had previously known and been attached to. With convulsive tears, I cried out, "Take my life or let me die." Then I felt and saw the white garment of Jesus come over my body. His arms reached around me and he started to lift me up. I wailed, "My burden is too heavy for anyone to lift!" He then placed his hands on my heart and a song was born inside me. I began to sing:

> *I'm walking up, yes, I'm walking up,*
> *I'm going to see my Savior.*
> *I'm walking up, yes, I'm walking up,*
> *I'm going to meet my Lord.*

The moment my fist hit the floor to provide a rhythmic beat, an actual thunderstorm burst forth outside the room. On and on I sang, every drop of rain washing away my past, cleansing me, bringing forth new spirit. I eventually fell asleep and had a dream. In the dream I was at an airport that consisted of a tall middle building with lower buildings connected on each side. I walked into the middle one and beheld an elderly man perched high above me, dressed in a white pilot's uniform. I was told that he was the "chief pilot." I stared at him and noticed that he also was wearing a white pilot's cap. A voice said, "Remember everything he shows you."

Immediately I was surrounded by innumerable loops of misty light, some in almost circular form. The loops shot out in different colors into the distance like roads to faraway places. I remember seeing brown, dark red, and blue ones on my right. The patterns were breathtaking in their complexity and beauty.

The moment it struck me that these paths of light could transport me somewhere, I was immediately taken away along one of the paths. I dropped into a place I never had seen before. I stood before a mountain and saw a gigantic gift box wrapped with a red ribbon on its right side. The box started sliding down the mountain, slaying anyone in its path.

In further dreams I learned that this was the gift of the holy spirit, the n/om, kundalini, or chi that is a power so strong that people can be spiritually undone by its force. Throughout that week I had one dream journey after another. Sometimes I was shown medicinal potions or practices for activating the spirit; sometimes I was taken to faraway places where spirits taught me ancient wisdom. I went inside mountains, traveled within the sea, journeyed to Africa and the holy city of Zion. There I found the holy grail and drank the blood of Jesus that it held, feeling my insides catch on fire. In the mourning room of that tin-roofed praise house, with a volcano on one side and the Atlantic ocean on the other, I lay with six colored bands wrapped around my head, a wooden cross in my left hand and a lighted white candle on my right. I entered the visionary world of spirit and met my teacher, Ezekiel.

"Yes, your grandfather has told me all about you," Ezekiel introduces himself. "He said you are prepared to see the Wheel. He has done his job well and now I will be your teacher and guide. You have entered my school. Today and for the rest of your life, I will teach you many things. I know how much you loved your grandfather. It is because of him that you've been cared for and why you are with me today. I'm here to guide you every step of the way, one step at a time.

"I will show you the Wheel. See how it turns and churns." In my vision I look over a cliff and see a monstrously huge wheel-shaped fog beyond measurement. It is mist, wind, and white light. "Yes, grandson," Ezekiel goes on, "this is the power of the holy ghost. This sacred wind is sent down to open hearts, revealing hidden matters of the spirit. A moment has been prepared for you to see the source of spiritual sight and inspiration. Behold the force of life! Look closely, for you may only see it once in your lifetime. The next time you kneel before it you will no longer belong to earth. Behold the four sacred winds, the circles within circles, moving round and round in every direction. Be overcome by the Wheel, the circle of life, and know that it will never stop turning as long as light and dark are conjoined."

In another dream I am on a tall building and hear a warning siren. I realize that the place is on fire, so I go to the window and open it. It is too high to jump, but I notice some power lines that I can jump onto. I wonder whether they will electrocute me, but I have no choice: I must either jump for the line or be burned by fire. I jump, reach for a line, and *whoosh*, I find myself in the Kalahari dancing with the Bushmen and other African tribes. The line has taken me back to Africa. A poem is born in my mind.

> *Suffering waves from Africa way—*
> *A bloody coming, that Slavery day.*
> *Into the ground you went.*
> *Planting seed,*
> *Harvesting crop,*

Burying your own.

Gods wept, men sweat.
   And Jordan rose.
Deep and furious its fervor,
Churning, pulsing sounds of night,
   Bodies baptized in tribal light.

Ring the bell, let it tell
   The way of a faraway isle,
Where heaven and hell pierce the soul,
   Enabling sight within the dark.

Mourn with pilgrims of sorrow,
   Enter the tomb.
Pray with the password,
   Enter the womb.

Open your unseen eyes,
   Enter the baptismal pool.
Feel the anointing,
   Enter the mystery school.

Joyous waves from Africa way—
   As second coming, this spirited play.
Into the ground you go,
   Planting seed,
   Harvesting crop,
   Burying your own,
This passage into Africa way.

In Saint Vincent I experienced the ropes and lines that enable you to travel in the spirit world. Those lines are not only highways for travel; they are also power lines for plugging into spirit. And they are telephone lines that enable you to make a call to spirit, or even to God if you have the right number—literally a password or symbolic code received in dream.

I had many teachers in Saint Vincent, including Mother Superior Sandy, Mother Samuel, Mother Pompey, Mother Ralph, Mother Doyle, Mother Ollivierre, Mother Haynes, Bishop John, Pointer Warren, and my pointer, Archbishop Pompey.

I was particularly moved by the words and presence of the beloved spiritual elder, Pointer Warren. Before he died, he talked to me about the spiritual lines. "In the world of spirit, there are lines and ropes. The lines usually go across while the ropes hang from the sky. Those are powerful things to see. Only those on a high spiritual path see the ropes. When you see one, concentrate on it and go toward it. Reach for it and don't let go. It will take you somewhere. Jesus is the light of the world. He shows himself in the light."

I talked to many shamans in Saint Vincent who loved Jesus. They all had seen the light and traveled along the lines. They also knew that the source of their spiritual ways came from Africa. Mother Haynes, who was my guide to the spiritual elders of Saint Vincent, explained, "We came from Africa. If you ever get sent there on a spiritual journey, you will get a green robe when you return. There is a color associated with every line and place. You receive that colored cloth when you come back to yourself."

Mother Haynes and I both went to Africa along the spirit pipeline and discovered, like every other Shaker who travels there, that there are twelve tribes, the same tribes of Israel that are described in the Bible. In the Saint Vincent spirit world, those tribes can be traced back to Africa. I remembered my vision in the Kalahari of twelve women dressed in green robes. I knew there was a connection among all the spiritual traditions I had experienced. Could they be tied together, connected through the loops, circles, lines, and ropes that shamans see in vision? Did this network of highways constitute the sacred circle of spiritual life? Everything in my spiritual life seemed to come down to this question.

It was time to go back to the elders of the oldest living culture on earth. I prepared myself to return to my Kalahari home.

14
Stinging Truth

IN MARCH OF 1999, Mev and I set off again for the Kalahari. When we were finally within a two-day drive of Motaope's village I began thinking of how I would thank him one more time for all the knowledge and help he had given me. That night when I sat down near the campfire, the most poisonous scorpion in Africa, the bark scorpion, stung my right hand, on the tip of my middle finger. It felt as though I had received a thousand volts of the material world's electricity. I was miserable all night long, unable to relieve the pain.

I considered how odd it was that I felt a shock passing through the finger and hand that Bushman shamans use to revitalize and heal one another. I remembered what Motaope had taught me about the current that shamans use. He said it was the spirit that makes us shake and tremble. Once it starts inside you, it is there forever. Motaope had started shaking as a child after seeing a divine light during a dance.

"Anyone who has seen that light is one of us. When you see that light, you immediately know how to shake and heal. When you touch a person with this shaking, the power of spirit flows through them. That is the secret of healing."

Mev and I finally arrived at the village. We saw Tete and Matope, Motaope's son, running toward us. They weren't dancing or singing.

There was sadness in the air. Motaope's son spoke. "My father said you were on your way. He passed on two nights ago. His last words were, 'Tell Brad that he should know that although he may think he can't see me, I am here. I will always be in the Kalahari.'"

He continued, "He said you would understand what he means. He wanted you to discover that he will always be in the Kalahari, waiting for you."

I wept as I recognized that my finger had been stung at the same time that the old shaman had passed away. I told his son and the other shamans what had happened with the scorpion.

"Yes, that's the way these things happen. He is here, but in a different way."

I walked to the mound of sand where Motaope had been interred.

"He is buried with all the gifts you ever gave him. They are with him."

Over the years I had brought Motaope everything he had dreamed of having. The final thing he had requested was a piece of paper that said he was a doctor. He had heard about doctors in other parts of the world who had such a document. I had an artist design a beautifully laminated diploma that declared him to be a "Doctor of Bushman Medicine." He carried it with him wherever he went and was buried with that diploma.

Everything Motaope owned could still be carried on his back. He remained a Bushman to the very end.

There's only one thing Bushmen can do when their hearts are broken. We gathered the wood, started a fire, and began the dance. I was only beginning to appreciate how loss and grief, pain and suffering are the keys to unlocking the deepest mysteries of the Bushman spiritual universe.

We start to dance with Motaope's spirit all around us. It's in the scorpions, lions, birds, sand, fire, water, trees, in every living plant and animal, in the sky and stars. His voice and touch are present. "Ah-ee-ah, ah-ee-ah, ah-ee-ah, ta, ta, ta, ta, ta, ta, ta, ta."

Now I am blind, like the old man used to be, and can't see his spirit. I dance more and sing and shriek and touch and shake. I enter the Bushman spiritual universe and receive new eyes, the same eyes Motaope used to get in the dance. Now I can see the old shaman, but he's not wearing tattered clothes. He is a body of light, a figure that glows with a line above his head, stretching to the sky. His kind, gentle voice is still with him: "Umm, umm, umm." He is there with his grandfather and all the Bushman shamans who ever walked the African continent.

I love to say the word *Kalahari*. It carries its own rhythm. It seems to dance and sing itself across the landscape. "Kalahari, the goddess of sand, with dancing grass, singing wind, and vibrant sky, bring down the ancestors!"

I remember the last words Motaope spoke to me as though he were saying them this very moment. "God brought you and me together. This makes me very happy. I see you in my dreams. I know what you are doing and I protect you. You must tell everyone about our medicine. That's why we were brought together. Please teach them to shake and touch. Bring them to the fire where we dance. Every person needs to meet God through this experience. It teaches us to forgive and love everyone. Go and love as a Bushman. Let the dance show that we are truly one people, one family, one circle of love."

15
Tested in Bali

FROM THE BUSHMAN SHAMANS I LEARNED MANY astonishing things in the course of less than a decade. I had passed through stormy seas and come to a calm place, a peaceful place inside that let me know I would be able to move on with my life. Then, in September of 1999, I faced an unexpected test. I was confronted with a terrifying unexplainable presence and I did not know if I would survive the encounter. It was, in some ways, a final examination, checking out whether my training was sufficient to handle the powerful currents brought forth by the oscillating universal forces of good and evil.

I spent an entire night in Bali trying to survive an encounter with a giant being that I later found out was believed to be Jero Gede Macaling, the god of the *balians,* the traditional shamans of Bali. It opened the Balinese spirit world to me and taught me more about the perils of being a shaman.

At two o'clock in the morning on the day I had arrived in Bali, I lay awake on the bed of a Balinese guest room located in the family compound of my guide and friend, I Wayan Budi Asa Mekel, whom I call Budi. Without warning I hear what sounds like the whole right side of the room collapsing from either an explosion or an earthquake. Frozen with shock, I don't know where to go for cover. I switch on the light—we still have electricity. There is an unusual quiet that feels like it precedes an unknowable storm.

I decide to get out of bed. As soon as my feet hit the floor, I hear a huge stomping on the roof. I worry that vandals are trying to break in but soon realize that this sound is too loud to be made by a human being. I am stricken with horror: some sort of great creature is up there. Step after step it walks back and forth on the roof. With each step, I hear falling rocks and sand.

I run to the window and shout for help but no one responds. I wonder if everyone else has been killed. I try unsuccessfully to analyze the situation. I pray. But the stomping continues.

There is no way to express how frightening true horror can be. One's fright can become so extreme that logical thinking is quickly spent and you are left frozen, in the paralysis of knowing you are having an encounter for which you have no preparation.

All I can think of is whether I will get through the night and see the sunlight one more time. I understand now why ancient people worshiped the sun. It provides a passage out of the dark terrors of night. I cannot imagine spending another day in Bali. As my thoughts turn in that direction, the door starts rattling like someone, some thing, is trying to break in.

I surrender to the fear, allowing it to take me into the deep focus of trembling, desperate prayer. "What am I to do?"

A voice responds. "We want you to know about the left and right ways of Bali, both our dark and light sides. There are secret things you are to see, hear, and feel." I remembered how I had read about magical drawings used by Balinese shamans with both good and bad intentions. I think aloud, "I'll have Budi gather up some of those drawings and send them to me. That way I don't have to stay here any longer."

The instant I say that, I hear and see a flock of luminous birds fly into my room right through one wall and out the other. The stomping ceases and the door becomes still. "This can't be true," I mumble to myself. The stomping starts again. I realize that I am having a conversation with this mysterious presence.

"Okay, I'll study the drawings, but help me, don't frighten me."

A vibrating sound fills my head and I begin to feel altered. My body feels like it is changing its form. My fingers stretch and my face twitches as it tries to take on a different shape. I am in the midst of a Balinese spiritual reality I do not understand. My concentration focuses further, allowing the shamanic forces to give instruction and guidance.

When the sun came up, I ran out of the room to find Budi's helpers preparing breakfast. My emotions were unglued. I started to sob telling Budi what had happened. They immediately recognized what had taken place. "Yes," Budi answered, "you have been visited by the Big God of our shamans. We call this one Jero Gede Macaling. He wants you to do something. This is very rare. I must take you to our most powerful shamans and they will help you."

And so I was guided on a mysterious adventure that took me throughout Bali. In ceremonies with mediums, I heard over and over again that Jere Gede Macaling was pulling me into the interactional dance of the left and right sides of Balinese shamanism. I was finally taken to the island of Nusa Penida, where the Big God lives. There I was accepted as a balian and initiated into the Balinese mysteries by Jero Gede Macaling. I lived in the crack between day and night, the twilight zone where spirits enter and exit at will, the slot between two worlds.

I eventually returned to the room on the main island where I had been almost scared to death. Following the advice of several balian mediums, I prepared to spend the night there. Again I was awakened in the night, but this time I only heard the gentle sound of rain. I actually thought it was raining inside my room, but I didn't bother to turn on the light. I assumed it was my imagination. The next morning I found that every personal possession and piece of equipment I had in the room was wet. My papers on the desk were wet and even my clothes inside an armoire were soaked. But everything else in the room was dry. That morning Budi and his workers examined the roof of the room and found that it was filled with sand and rocks. Those materials are not used when they build a roof. I remembered the sound of the stomping and how the sand and rocks had slid down the roof.

Shamans are familiar with the death and resurrection show. Facing the dark, losing themselves in uncertainty and the unknown, time and again they are reborn into the light. This reentry into life gives them the capacity to reach out to others who have lost their way. Rather than fixing, they hold the hand of the one who is in pain and walk straight into the dark with him. Trembling with fear, they pass through the ordeals of night. Upon their return to the Big Love's shining light, they shake with ecstatic joy. That's the shamanic journey that can transform and heal.

16

This Little Light of Mine

MY SPIRITUAL HEART OF HEARTS has found one of its truest homes in the soul of the African-American church, or what their elders simply call Black Church, particularly when it is sanctified and anointed with that old fashioned holy ghost power. After my experience in Bali I couldn't wait to get back to Black Church. I am specifically referring to those communities of parishioners who love to worship together and bring down the Big Love so that they may experience forgiveness, redemption, graceful healing, and a lifting of the spirits of every man and woman, child and infant, to live each day with a continuously deepening affirmation of peace and thanksgiving.

When a Black Church, or any church for that matter, loses the centrality of love and becomes either a social club or an angry group making a list of who is really saved and who is not, the good spirit of the church departs quickly. To me, old-fashioned religion is a love bath, a baptism into the power of love that has no limits, no fancy entry requirements or specific conditions. It is simply about love for the sake of love.

I feel very fortunate to be part of the Black Church community. I believe that this has been an important factor in my learning to be a

Bushman shaman. The Bushman way is dedicated to the same Big Love that I find in the authentic Black Church. If you can't feel what takes place inside those church walls, then you probably don't stand a chance of understanding or becoming deeply intimate with Bushman spirituality.

There are (at least) two things that anyone setting out to become a shaman can learn from the Black Church. As a church mother told me, "First, church is all about bringing down the 'love current'—that spirited electricity that makes you feel all tingly inside. Second, you have to catch on fire—spiritual fire, that is—and to do so you gotta get dirty for the Lord." By this she means not be embarrassed to let yourself get caught by the spirit. I propose that this is also what you need to know about Bushman shamanism. It is all about getting down and being available for the spirit and bringing forth the love current.

When that love comes down on a congregation, miracles of the spirit take place. I have seen the holy light hover over a church service in the same manner that I have seen it hover over a Bushman healing dance. It is the same illumination that I experienced in my earliest mystical encounter. The strongest and purest church services feel essentially the same to me as the strongest and purest dances in the Kalahari. In both, I have seen this light, felt my body tremble and shake, danced in the shaman's way, and allowed the spirited sounds to come through me.

It is not always easy for a Black Church congregation to maintain and cultivate the deepest forms of expression that are brought about by this kind of coming together in an intimate, emotional way. There are challenges brought by seminary-trained clergy, who want to move the church from its "overemotionalism" and make it more intellectual in scope. This can be a tragedy. Emotion and intellect do not have to cancel each other out. They need to foster one another rather than be at odds. The other challenge for the church is the same that faces any person who suddenly starts feeling the holy ghost (or kundalini or n/om) power. You can too easily believe that you have seen, heard, or felt the Absolute Truth. You then concretize your visions and take yourself too seriously. That's when the church starts to turn away from the deepest practice of love, which is always improvisational and childlike, and instead becomes more dedicated to evangelizing and propagating particular beliefs and "right answers."

The best home for spirit is where there is freedom of enthusiastic and playful expression. This includes the freedom to laugh at what you say and even to make fun of it, exaggerate it, say the opposite—and in so doing, reduce any overimportance given to words. Absurd teasing and play set the stage for moving on to a spiritual experience. In the same spirit of free expression, go ahead and bring in the current, bring down the light, but when that experience has played itself out in the moment, get over it. Don't allow the experience to make you feel important or special. Get back to work. Life will get you ready for the next service.

In poor church communities, where people worry about getting food on their tables, transporting themselves to see a friend or to get medical care, and perhaps even about surviving gang warfare, the ordeals of everyday life bring them to their knees. They survive by making it from one church meeting to the next, one step at a time, praying for help to get through the week. As troubling as their conditions are, that context has a positive side: it prepares them to work with the spirit. When you are at wit's end, at the end of your existential rope, and your mind can't figure out what to do, you are in a good place to do some work with the Lord. When you get to church in a down-and-out state of mind, it is easier for you to give it up for the Lord. That's one way of becoming empty, a vessel ready to receive the gifts of spirit.

When church really happens, the whole gathering comes under the influence of the spirit of improvisation. I've seen services where the preacher can't even give the sermon. When he opens his mouth to talk, the holy ghost grabs the preacher and brings forth from him a loud noise, sending a bolt of electricity through the congregation. Music, more than preaching, keeps the service going. If you want to understand Black Church, look past the choir and the preacher. The keys to the Kingdom are in the hands of the church organist or pianist. They invisibly conduct the spirit's entry, even though they look as if they are accompanying the preacher's inflections and the congregation's mood.

It is more accurate to say that there is a circular connection where no one is really in charge—not preacher, congregation, choir, or organist. They are all moved, at the same time, to be under the influence of spirit.

This is what is meant by the interdiction "Let us bring ourselves together into one mind," whether those words are prayed in a sweat lodge or a Wednesday night prayer meeting in a holy ghost church. When that happens, the music, the dancing, the shakes come on everyone. This is sanctified church. For me, there is no better place or feeling than being taken by the spirit in a rockin' and rollin' Black Church.

Some of my most powerful dreams and visions have been mystical encounters with Jesus. I have walked with him in my dreams, flown with him, touched him, talked with him, and have hung with him on the Cross. Once he handed me a glass of white light, looking like glowing milk. When I drank it, I felt a warmth trickle down the insides of my body. As it flowed, it turned my insides hot and triggered the sensation of electrical energy. It brought forth the inner heat, the shaking, the feeling that the Divine is both inside and out.

Ever since Jesus handed me that drink of light, I find that I experience it every month, sometimes every week. When I lie down at night, I pray to Jesus. His name is the first word, the second word, and the last word in my mind before I fall asleep. When I call upon his name, I immediately feel a high vibration come over my head. I sit with that current as it sends the revitalizing life force throughout my body. At its peak, it pours some kind of warm liquid down my insides. I don't feel it on the outside of my body, only on the inside of my skin. As it did the first time I drank the holy milk, it makes me warm and electric.

What a glorious life I have with Jesus! It is not the same Jesus that I hear associated with cold-hearted fundamentalists who show hatred rather than love or church services that feel like funerals rather than love baths. Jesus is my most sacred word for the Big Love. I respect—in fact, I think it's wonderful—that other people have other names for this sacred love. It is not the word that matters but the relationship you have with the word in making the hookup with love. I would never tell others that they need to change the name of their God, prayers, dance steps, or any aspect of their spiritual practice. Growing up with parents and grandparents who used the name of Jesus as an evocation of divine love helped make me who I am, but there are many names, evocations, roads, and realizations of the Divine. It doesn't matter how you find the Big Love. Just get there!

I do believe that every spiritual pilgrim, if raised in a religious setting, must find a way home to the spiritual roots of childhood. Whether you grew up in a Catholic home or a Buddhist household, it is important to stay on whatever path you are on and don't stop walking until it circles all the way back to your home. Other traditions along the way can teach you what you forgot about your own and prepare you to embrace your roots, but they will never be your family of origin. If you are Jewish and find the Buddha, hang out for a while and then move on, or even do as Sheldon Kopp suggested in his book, *If You Meet the Buddha on the Road, Kill Him!* If your teacher isn't helping you find a way to love your own spiritual roots, then she is sadly disconnected from divine love, no matter how much lip service is given to it. But if your teacher helps you return home, you will find your house to be a different place, your family spiritually richer for all the new "cousins" of your childhood's tradition you bring back with you. Now you can rejoice in the realization that you came from one love that has given birth to so many divine offspring in the form of the world's religions and spiritual practices.

All missionaries, whether Christian or Buddhist, too easily get confused. They shouldn't be adopting the lost; they should be returning them to their cultural homes. True spiritual leaders want people to love their parents, families, and cultural roots.

My earlier life as a cybernetic thinker, psychotherapist, and university teacher was accompanied by a timidity to publicly utter any "Jesus talk." To converse about God with others, I resorted to intellectual abstractions and elaborate discourse. It was easy to talk about Zen Buddhism, Dzogen Tibetan practice, or yuwipi ceremonies; it was obvious that others were impressed with such discourse. But say the "J" word and the room cleared. The Bushmen changed all of that for me, as did my time studying with the other spiritual healing traditions I have been involved with. The Bushmen opened up my inner spiritual life and made my heart feel more connected to my mind.

If you could get inside my head, you'd see that in the course of each day I am almost always in a spirited ceremony. The music and dancing never stop inside of me. The songs I have received in my dreams, some original and others well known, are always playing. Every day I dance with the Bushmen and shake with them, and I dance down the aisles of a backwoods Black Church in Louisiana. I do this through the powers of my mind. I am drunk on the spirit twenty-four hours a day. I don't care if this makes me seem crazy. I want to be a divine fool, filled with spirit and inspired with each breath of every moment.

When I feel down, scared, hurt, or worried, I just call out the name of Jesus. I say it over and over again until a song bursts forth. When I feel high, happy, comfortable, and filled with joy, I say, "Thank you!" I am born again in the moment. The name of Jesus takes me around the world. He is my spiritual skeleton key for opening the doors to other spiritual traditions and practices. I say, "Yes, Jesus," and then find that I'm singing with the Bushmen or dancing with the Lakota or meditating with the Buddhists.

This is what it means to be a Bushman shaman. The Bushmen I have met also walk around, filled with song and music, always waiting to be touched by the spirit so they can shake, dance, and touch one another. A shaman is a live wire with a direct connection to God's power station. The current is always flowing. Whether a danger or a pleasure comes my way, it has the same effect—it increases the inner voltage. When someone threatens me or puts me down, I feel the inner current warm up. Jesus is there waiting. The spirit and the life force are there. When I meet a pleasant person the current also warms up. All things, good and bad, bring me closer to God. Even when I am momentarily tripped and get angry, irritable, or worried, eventually I get back to the current.

The shamans I have met all vibrate and feel the inner warmth trickling down their insides. That's what we talk about when we hang out together. Once you have felt this experience, you know without a doubt that life in the current is the only way to live. When I am spiritually tuned, which requires constant attention, I fear nothing because I know that anything I face, whether good or bad, is just another log to throw onto my inner fire. For me, the best way to stay tuned is to bring forth some spirited gospel music and start shaking for the Lord.

The old hymn, "This little light of mine, I'm gonna let it shine" sums up the shaman's life. A fire lights up the inner world, bringing forth imagination and love. When the challenges of life come your way, when you encounter pain and suffering yourself or witness it in others, throw the suffering into the spiritual fire. The flames will become larger so that the light can shine onto the world, showing others that there is another way of seeing and being in the world. Step into the fire, be the light, and sing the praises of illumined joy.

Following my ordeal in Bali, I met a taxi driver in New Orleans named James. He's known by some of the other drivers as a healer because his faith is so strong that his prayers and touch can help people in their time of need. I asked him how he came to have his faith.

"In 1958 I was robbed in my cab. They said, 'This is a holdup, get both hands up; don't try nothin', don't say nothin'. Give us your money.' They made me climb over the seat and get on the floor with my face to the back of the seat. They held a knife against my head and a gun on my back and shouted, 'Don't look at us or we'll kill you.'

"But they weren't in charge. God was in charge. That's when I had a personal experience of Jesus, when I was lying there on the floor of the cab. I saw him and felt his touch. He threw his arms of protection around me and saved my life. That's when I turned over my life to him. I made him a promise that very moment that I would serve him for the rest of my life. What he did for me he will do for others. But you have to believe.

"Ever since that moment I have received a blessed life. I experienced a new birth back then and I want to tell everyone about it. 'Let your light shine before men that they may feel good works and glorify the Father who art in heaven.' I praise God and love him. I will not let anything separate me from the love of God.

"When my life was threatened that night, I personally felt the power of Jesus. He held me and I felt a heat go through my body. I immediately had no fear. He gave me a power and I knew right then that I would be able to help others by touching them. I knew it without any doubt. That's how strong the experience was. The warmth of Jesus's touch filled me with certainty and knowing.

"The heat in my body made me feel like I was being lifted up above the situation. As I realized that Jesus was touching me, a song was whispered into my ear. I hummed along with it. The song only has three words and I have never stopped singing it. The song simply says, 'Just be nice.' That's it, but it gives me great satisfaction. It was a gift from God. It is my song. 'Just be nice.' The thieves let me go and I didn't stop singing that song for three months. I just sang it over and over again.

"Jesus took care of me and he has given me a long life. I'm past seventy-four years of age now, even though I don't look it. I thank him. He saved me and I am not afraid of dying. My purpose is to do good for others. Even to this day, I still say and sing those words all the time: 'Just be nice.' Those are the words God wants me to say and sing. Those words still bring tears to my eyes. The holy spirit brought all of this to me."

That story touches the very essence of shamanism. On the edge of death, wondering whether you will live another moment, spirit touches you, filling you with warmth, peace, and certainty about the purpose of your life. In that joyous, transforming moment, a song comes on you— the only tool a shaman needs. When the song is sung it brings back the inner warmth, healing your soul and the souls of others. This is true of shamans in the Kalahari, the Amazon, and South Dakota, and in the taxis in New Orleans.

It is impossible for me to imagine a shaman without a song, without the inner heat and body shaking, and without the love of God. These things constitute the core of shamanic presence. A shaman's technology of the spirit is nothing more than passionate connection to life. Getting on your knees to pray makes you closer to the Big Love, which in turn makes you closer to others. When you are a part of the bigger circle of divine love, you are not irritated because someone says God is a "he" or a "she" or that divine relationship is instead expressed through the name of Buddha or Rumi or Muhammed or Kuan Yin. You look past the literal words, whether skillfully articulated or not, and look through your spiritual eyes, through the lens of your heart. Being spiritual comes down to being about whether a person is *in* the spirit, not whether they say or do the "right" thing.

You can dance down the aisles, speak in tongues, or preach the gospel and not have the spirit. It's easy to put on a show for others in the name of religion. Getting into the spirit, however, has more risk. You might not look hip or put on a polished performance in that state. That's what that church mother meant when she talked about "getting dirty for the Lord." You might jump and holler and roll on the ground while singing praise. Or you might fall asleep. There is no telling what you might do when the spirit gets on you.

The spirit can come on you when you're hitting a drum and shaking a rattle, or when you hear someone else pray with sincerity. The strong shamans are moved by anything that carries the life force, n/om. They are in love with all of life and all the ways the life force can be turned on and shared with others. In this regard, yogis, shamans, mystics, saints, and bodhisattvas have no significant differences other than costume and style. They all seek to be buoyant—that is, to remain afloat as life preservers to anyone swimming in the divine ocean of love.

During my fieldwork in Saint Vincent, I had a dream about visiting the first rare bookshop I ever went to as a child. My mother had taken me to this place in downtown Kansas City, located near a restaurant called the Italian Gardens. In the dream an old man is sitting in a chair outside the front door. As I walk near him, he says, "Welcome. We've been expecting you. Go right in." We walk in and immediately I see the tall antique bookcases, going all the way to the ceiling, filled with leather-bound books from long ago. When an elder woman comes out of the back room, she asks what I am looking for. I reply, "I want the books by Swedenborg." As she goes back to search through their collection, I notice a book catalogue on the counter. I open it to a section marked "Esoteric Christianity"; it has three pages of listings but all the titles are in Latin. Before I can get my books my mother says, "We have to go now. The shop is getting ready to close."

I woke up wondering who Swedenborg was and what books he had written. I prayed for another dream that would provide further guidance. I fell back asleep and dreamt that I was sitting at a round table in a kitchen in the back of an old house. I look over my right shoulder at the back door and see a round loaf of bread float through the middle of the door. It continues floating until it rests on the plate in front of me.

I woke up, fell asleep again, and had another dream. Now I'm looking at the kitchen wall and seeing a face that goes back and forth between being a skull and having flesh. It has eyes of fire. I see a man's face covered with white paint, a wide glistening silver arrow on his forehead. Other symbols and ancient writing are scattered over the man's face. I ask him who he is and he replies, "I am Zacharias, prophet of the Lord. There is a line of prophets."

That was the end of my night of dreaming.

The next week I did some research online. I found that Swedenborg, a renowned scholar and scientist who invented the field of metallurgy, while in his fifties had a powerful vision of the mystical Christ that changed the course of his life. He stopped writing scientific works and began writing books about his spiritual visions. He decided to publish all of those books in Latin; many years later his followers referred to his orientation as "esoteric Christianity." I ordered his book *Journal of Dreams* from a used bookstore. When the book arrived the following week, I read the following account of a dream Swedenborg had on October 13, 1743:

I saw also in vision that fine bread on a plate was presented to me; which was a sign that the Lord himself will instruct me since I have now come first into the condition that I know nothing, and all preconceived judgments are taken away from me; which is where learning commences . . . .

Zacharias, whose name means "Yahweh remembers," was a Biblical prophet who once received tidings from an angel that his elderly wife would give birth to a son. He couldn't believe that such a thing was physically possible, so God punished him for not having enough faith and took away his ability to speak. Zacharias and Elizabeth did have a son, whom they named John. Upon John's birth, Zacharias found that his speech returned, but this time he was filled with the Holy Spirit and began to prophesy that his son was the forerunner of the Lord. His son was John the Baptist, the saint who baptized Jesus of Nazareth.

In my own life, I sometimes have been so thickheaded that no matter how many miracles I witnessed, I still carried doubt. My intellectual mind would construct a theory of how the experience was due to some form of hypnotic suggestion or hallucination. But as it finally sunk in that there was a Greater Mind at work that I was unable to doubt any longer, I lost both my doubt and my faith. There was no need to exercise believing in something if you held it to be a solid fact. I knew firsthand the validity of the Great Mystery and had no need for faith. At that point, the sacred dreams spewed forth. I believe the dream of Zacharias was a lesson for that time in my life.

I am in London visiting a rare book shop, Jarndyce Books, at 46 Great Russell Street, directly across from the British Museum. I ask the owner, "Do you have any books by Swedenborg?" With a puzzled look, he replies, "We don't have any, but I assume you know that the Swedenborg House is right around the corner." I phone the place but they are closed.

The next day I return to find that the Swedenborg House is where public meetings are held and books about and by Swedenborg are published. I walk in and see the walls filled with rare books. One of the staff members, a young man named Stephen McNeilly, walks into the room and I introduce myself.

I immediately tell him my past dream about going into a rare bookshop and asking for Swedenborg's books. "That's the reason I came here today."

Stephen's face lights up, "I believe it. You see, I had a dream of going into a rare bookshop, too, and seeing one of his books. That was the first time I ever came across his name and it's the reason I work here today."

Swedenborg believed that his dreams taught him to have a "feelingful understanding" of life. Cheyenne elder William Tall Bull once said to me, "You don't need any more teachers. Just listen to what the spirits tell you. Pay no attention to anyone else." Like Swedenborg, I entered an inner academy, where dreams were the texts and spirit was the teacher. Swedenborg's "feelingful understanding" means that, when spirit infuses our knowing, we see with the mystical organ of the heart. We learn to see-feel and hear-feel, with deep relations to divine love and compassionate expression.

I am remembering a day back in 1994. Deacon Amos Griffin, head deacon for New Salem Missionary Baptist Church, is on the phone. "Brad, please come down to the church tonight. We want to talk with you."

"Okay, Deacon Griffin, do you want me to bring something?"

"Just bring yourself," he says with a slight chuckle.

I am the only white man in this inner city Black Church and Amos was one of the holiest persons Mev and I had met. He was the inspiration for our "A.Q." standard, reminding us of the importance of non-judging love and service.

I drive to the church and meet Amos and his friend Roy, another deacon. "Brad, we want you to be a deacon with us." I don't know what to say. I am honored, but I'm also nervous because they don't know that I regularly participate in Ojibway and Lakota ceremonies, something the church might not understand. I thank them for the honor and say, "I need to pray about it and then let you know."

Later that night, I realize that I can't be a deacon because the church would perhaps feel deceived if they found out about my openness and love for other religions. I respectfully decline, saying, "I'm not ready for being a deacon. I prefer doing volunteer work like cleaning up the church. Please let me know what you want me to do." Amos and I pray together. My heart is broken as I recognize that I will never have both of my feet inside his church.

A shaman is always an outsider, someone who can't fully belong to any bounded form of worship or belief system. A shaman is free to love God in all of his or her forms and cultural settings. The missionaries who came to convert the Algonquin Indians in northeastern America were sometimes told the Indians had already seen Jesus, "the one walking around with the wolves." When I talked about the missionaries with the Bushmen, they couldn't understand why the white man's Jesus lived in a pile of papers (a book) rather than in one's heart, or why others would rather talk about him than sing and dance with him. Behind Jesus, Buddha, Mohammed, and any other spiritual leader is the fire of love. Its beams of light link every possible manifestation of the Big God's transformative love.

I always want to go back to the Bushman's dance, moving around its fire, seeing the lines that take one to the truths behind all the world's religions, doing so with tear-based love rather than fear-based knowing. Jesus, a holy name that evokes God's Big Love, is at home in the Kalahari circle dance, as he was in the story told by the *The Acts of John* in the Gnostic gospels. There, Jesus, too, held a circle dance with his disciples and revealed its mystical secrets, things long known and practiced by Bushmen underneath a canopy of moon and stars.

17
Ropes to God

IT IS THE BEGINNING OF THE YEAR 2000, the start of a new millennium. Following a New Year's Eve party with my family in Times Square, I depart for the Kalahari, this time to the village of Djokhoe, in the Otjozondjupa region of northeastern Namibia. It is a flat landscape of scrubby vegetation dotted by baobabs, red umbrella thorn, strands of camelthorn trees, and blackthorn acacia. There I have a dream that makes no sense to me. In the dream I behold an ostrich egg suspended in midair. It is about three feet in front of me. As I stare at the egg, I watch it crack open right down the middle. After it splits apart, I notice that the left half of the egg has two thin lines around it, one red and the other green. The right side is totally white. In the dream, I simply stand, mesmerized by the cracked-open egg. When I wake up, the image seems still to hang in the air.

Filled with vibrant energy, I begin singing and shaking, anxious to tell the Bushmen. When the sun rises I walk quickly to the Ju/hoansi Bushman shamans. Immediately upon hearing my report, they become unusually excited and start dancing. The oldest shaman, Cgunta, finally speaks. "You have experienced our most important dream. When you see the egg open up like that, it means that the rope of light that goes to the Big God is now open to you. Only Bushman shamans have this dream.

We don't talk about it if you haven't seen it. You have to dream it before we can talk. I had that dream, as did my father and grandfather. It is our oldest dream. The ropes to God have been opened for you."

That night I go up the rope. In the Bushman visionary world, I see a white shaft of light and begin walking toward it. As I come close, my body begins floating upward, smoothly and effortlessly. I feel as if I am riding an elevator straight up into the sky. Somewhere at the top my grandfather is waiting. He walks me to the Big God and I am surprised to see that God has so many arms and hands. As I get nearer, the Big God reaches out and, with a slow, whirling movement, touches me with every one of his hands. We quietly stare at one another and I feel the Big Love quivering my heart. My grandfather quickly comes up and pulls me away, speaking gently. "Now you must go back." I float down to the ground and begin weeping as my Bushmen friends comfort me. They know I have seen the Big God. We dance throughout the night.

In another dance dream, I travel to my grandfather's church. I show him how I dance with the Bushmen and explain how they opened my heart to return to the Black Church, which in turn brought me home to the words he taught me as a child. "Yes, grandson, your journey is bringing you full circle. You are coming home."

From country church to intellectual career to the Bushman's dance, I feel that I am returning home, embracing the truth of what I had lost along the trail. A wheel is turning.

One month into the new millennium, I learned that the red and green roads are horizontal lines that take you to other villages and places, both in this world and in the imagination. They are like the colored lines used for spiritual traveling in Saint Vincent. The vertical ropes, on the other hand, take you to the Big God. With those ropes you can climb up to the sky or down into the underworld. In the Kalahari Dreamtime, God is in both places at once.

Many shamans find the horizontal ropes and experience traveling in the spirit. But only those with strong inner heat and spiritual love see the ropes to God. Those ropes take you to the primal realm of the ancestral spirits, to the mythic place where the oldest ones, including the Big God, resides. There you learn songs, dances, and ways to heal. For the Bushmen, that is the most important theological seminary, medical school, and academy of performing arts.

I have spent over a decade learning all I can about these ropes to God from historical accounts, rock art drawings, conversations with other Bushman shamans, and my own personal experiences. Once I went halfway up the sky and found a room waiting for me in a cloud. When I walked inside I saw my wife and young son. Scott called me over and said, "Look Daddy, I've drawn a picture of Jesus for you. And I want to give you a song." He began singing "Jesus Loves You" in a soft, sweet voice. That was one of my strongest trips up the rope. When I came down I wept and wondered what it meant to see my own son, not at his present age but as a young child, rather than seeing an ancestral spirit from the past.

I went to the other Bushman shamans and told them about my experience. "That's very good," Toma Dham replied. "You are learning that this rope is about the Big Love. The ones who teach you the most important knowledge are those we love the most and feel closest to, whether they are living family members or relatives from the past. I have also gone up the rope and met my son. That's a very strong experience. The Big God really loves us."

He went on. "The rope is like a string of ostrich egg beads. Each bead is someone you love, with your family members being the most important. But when you get filled with the Big God's love, you love everyone as though they were your close relatives. That's why a shaman has a string of beads that sleeps in his or her heart. When the Big Love gets inside you, the string shoots up to the sky. It is a string of love, made of the sacred light. It goes all the way to the Big God."

My Bushmen friends believe that the Big God is filled with love. His love is so vast and infinite that he wants to share it with all living beings. That's why he sends down the songs. They are the only means by which he can deliver the love he feels for us. The Gods speak with music; they seldom if ever use words. The Bushman's God has sent a song to everything that lives—butterflies, bees, trees, plants, birds, elephants, giraffes, elands, and all the living creatures of the world. All of God's creation has a song. It is the shaman's job to hunt for the songs. We wait, trying to catch and share them with others.

A Bushman shaman is a receptacle for holding the Big Love. Opening your heart to catch a song, you bring all the love it contains into your body. When the love current enters it constitutes pure n/om. As it moves through your insides, your belly gets tight and begins to pump. It feels like it is contracting and squeezing the song into a tiny arrow so that it may then reside within you. When it comes time to shoot a song arrow into another person, your belly begins shaking again, heating the arrow and melting it down until it is a steam that can be released from your body. That's when the shaman becomes like Cupid, shooting hot arrows of love into others.

Malevolent shamans, however, do know how to reverse the love into hatred and shoot a dirty arrow, one that aims to do harm, bringing sickness or even death. That is sorcery, and the cost is extreme. The arrows do not fly in a straight path. They fly through the person at whom you are aiming and, like a boomerang, come right back to pierce you. If you shoot an arrow of harm at someone, it will hurt you both. My Bushmen friends say that you only have a limited amount of times that you can shoot the dirty arrows and then you will die. They should only be shot to protect the ones you love. Unfortunately, sometimes shamans get greedy and mixed up, thinking they can manipulate others to do whatever suits their whim. Those shamans end up taking a big fall.

On the other hand, if you send a clean, white-hot arrow of love, that arrow also comes back to you, but this time it replenishes your spirit. The same is true for healing. When you take out the dirty arrows from others that cause sickness, your own dirty arrows come out with them. In this way, you also get some healing. That's one of the benefits of being a shaman. What you do to another is also done to you. That's why the shamans feel the best after a dance. Whenever a healer says that a healing ceremony took away a significant amount of his life force, it means that there wasn't enough love involved. Heat those arrows to a white-hot temperature, burning away all the dirt and self-centered desires and fears, and you'll be invigorated by every healing encounter. That's one of the secrets of the Bushman shamans.

When a Bushman shaman goes up the rope and visits the village in the sky, she then can bring the whole village down to earth, superimposing it on the dance ground. The other Bushmen know when this is happening. This is the ultimate moment in a Bushman's life, to dance with all the ancestral spirits and to feel the heightened n/om that is available during their immediate presence. The Bushmen dance to bring down the sky and be with all their relatives. From this perspective, they never lose the ones they love. The ancestors just go somewhere else and return when there is a strong dance.

Many amazing things happen to the Bushman shaman during a dance. As the arrows heat up inside the body, they cause it to bend over, and you experience a pumping movement in your abdomen. This is the pumping up of the n/om, comparable to what yogis call the rising of kundalini. As it is pumping, a guttural sound often comes through you, sounding like the rhythmic percussion of a drum. I believe this is the origin of African rhythms. All Bushman shamans and ecstatic technicians of the African diaspora are intimately familiar with this. In Saint Vincent the shamans call this *'doption,* referring to how the spirit adopts you and turns you into a human drum. Pointer Warren describes it this way:

> 'Doption is another special gift from God. When the spirit adopts you, you must move and let it come out. It will bring a special sound that sometimes sounds like a drum. If you are deep in 'doption, it can give you a vision and even take you on a spiritual journey. 'Doption is

communication from the holy spirit. When it pulls on you, it can give a spiritual sight. When it's on you, you can prophesy, see into others, and even heal them.

Mother Samuel, also from Saint Vincent, says that "'Doption is when the spirit gets into your belly. When you feel it making your body tight, you must stand up and stomp the ground. This is a very strong experience."

Bushmen know when a person is transforming into a shaman. The spirit or n/om becomes so strong that the shaman starts slowly, stomping in a deliberate way, and begins making grunting or percussive sounds that involve such vigorous breathing out of the nose that it can bring on a nosebleed. This is not a pretty dance. In fact, it can be argued that the shaman's dance is not a dance at all. Dance, typically regarded as an aesthetic form with identifiable choreography, is, at most, a warm-up for the shaman. It prepares the shaman for being grabbed by automatic movements and shaking. As the n/om gets hotter, you see the shaman's head and body going up and down in a bent posture, looking like a rope is pulling the body. Bushmen believe that a rope to God is, in fact, pulling the shaman's insides up and down. When they see a shaman stomping it looks like he is climbing; as Bushmen see it, the shaman is climbing a rope to God. In healing dances the shaman progresses from dancing to shaking and then to pumping and climbing the ropes to God.

"Do the lines have to be shaken in order to turn them into circles?"

My question amuses the old shamans, who love to talk about these matters.

"The only line you need to worry about," Cgunta Boo replies, "is the one hanging between your legs." As his uncontrollable burst of laughter starts to hurt his ribs, he grabs his side.

"It seems to me," as I join in the jousting, "that a little shaking down below can make a pretty straight line." Now we've all lost it and there's little chance of getting the conversation back on track. We tremble so much with amusement that no one can utter a complete sentence.

When the giggling subsides, Toma tries to come back to my question. "We shake because things must change. It doesn't matter whether they change from lines to circles or whether they change from circles to lines. Things must simply change."

Cgunta Boo doesn't want to stop teasing. "Just like your curled up circle wants to become a line. That's the line you want to climb!"

There is no way to stop the Kalahari circus of ceaseless teasing and word play. Today's serious talk has become fodder for one joke after another. In this conversational turn lies a key to knowing what it means to be a Bushman shaman.

18

The Gods Are Crazy

LATER THAT SAME NIGHT, after being mercilessly teased, I think about how scholars such as Mathias Guenther have proposed that the Bushman's beliefs are "multifarious, inchoate, and amorphous." There are so many variations and constant changes in the Bushman's concepts and explanations that anthropologists conclude Bushman spirituality is "a confusing tangle of ideas and beliefs, marked by contradictions, inconsistencies, vagueness, and lack of culture-wide standardization."

When I asked the Bushmen about their concept of change, I learned something that never has been recorded by any anthropologist. It was the old shaman, Cgunta, who replied, "Our most important idea is *thuru*; that is, the process in which one form changes into another form. The word refers to how we shapeshift into a lion, but it also refers to how we see God and all of life. The endless recycling and changing of forms that we see in nature constitutes the core practice of our spiritual way of being in the world." With those words, I immediately understood the inconsistencies and constant morphing lamented by anthropologists. They actually represent a circular and inherently cybernetic epistemology, unseen and unheard by less circularly attuned outside observers.

I remembered when Sam Gurnoe, an Ojibway elder, said to me, "These circular ideas are something my people live by. Our ways are open to you. Maybe they will help you become more intimate with your own." Now, after years of being away from academic work, I find that the Bushmen are natural cyberneticians. They think circularly—that is the secret to knowing how they know. They have pulled me around another circle.

Over the years I presented my findings about the way the Bushmen experience their spiritual universe to scholar and rock art scientist Professor David Lewis-Williams, founder of the Rock Art Research Institute in the Department of Archaeology at the University of Witwatersrand, Johannesburg, South Africa. He is an originator of the shamanistic hypothesis of rock art; that is, the idea that prehistoric rock art images depict the experiences of indigenous shamans. After several trips to the Bushmen, I would come out of the Kalahari and meet with Professor Lewis-Williams to discuss what I had found. He encouraged me to continue my research. He later wrote:

> The real breakthrough came when Brad began to participate in Bushman healing dances. Eventually, after many astounding experiences, the people accepted him as a "doctor," a *n/om k"xau*, one who is believed to possess and control a supernatural essence or power that can be harnessed to heal people with physical and social ills. At once, hitherto closed doors began to open . . . . The mutual high regard and esteem between Keeney and his teachers is patent. The Bushmen want the world to know, as fully and as accurately as possible, what they truly believe. (Keeney, *Ropes to God*, 161).

And I would like to invite you now to take a step inside the Bushman's circular way of knowing. Imagine sitting with me in the Kalahari sand, talking slowly about an alternative way of knowing that bends the common lines we use to distinguish and make sense of the world. Let's start with their understanding of the Big God.

According to the Bushman's circular way of understanding, the Big God has two sides—a stable side called the Sky God (which is mirrored by the God underneath the ground) and a constantly changing trickster side. Cgunta once drew this distinction in the sand:

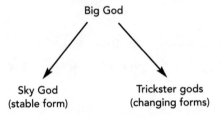

The trickster side may be good, bad, or somewhere in between. Trickster is always morphing, moving around the circle of all possible forms of God. As it was sketched for me in the sand:

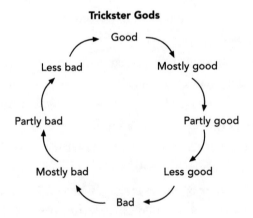

At times you can use the trickster god to help you, but you must be careful because it is always shifting its form (and therefore its trustworthiness) through the process of thuru. The circle connecting the good through bad forms shown above is only one example of the many faces of the trickster. It also can be met in the circles that connect wisdom and ignorance, beauty and ugliness, sacred and profane, or light and dark, with each circle holding the many variations and gradations of the trickster's expression.

Here we find how the gods are crazy: they never remain fixed in one form. This is the key insight to the Bushman spiritual universe. The constantly changing forms, the ceaseless thuru, are the source of n/om, spiritual life itself. Stated more formally: when the circle of all possible forms is taken as a whole without the fixed distinctions of chronological time, it constitutes the eternal sphere of the stable sky god. This circle of eternity embraces—that is, consistently loves—all of creation. And that Big Love is the source of n/om.

Along these lines, the Big God may be expressed as a circular relationship, where God's stable, loving presence is born out of trickster's changing forms:

(stable love / changing trickster forms)

Stated in the language of cybernetics, the whole of God is a set of simultaneous interactions of God's changing forms (or parts). (Consider contemplating this circular riddle: the particular trickster forms are the carriers of time-specific interactions that we chop out of the whole to imagine their participation in various processes that constitute the whole.)

For the Bushmen, the movement behind each change and transformation is expressed as thuru. This movement is seen in everything from the changing seasons to the shifting moods of every individual as well as in the trembling and shaking of the shaman's body. It even applies to how the Bushmen comprehend the passing of their beloved family relations. Not surprisingly, they see the ancestral spirits as having two sides:

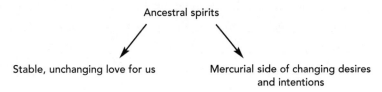

Ancestral spirits

Stable, unchanging love for us   Mercurial side of changing desires and intentions

Here the ancestral spirits embody the now familiar circular pattern:

(stable love / changing trickster forms)

where their never-changing love for us is born out of their changing desires and intentions. In other words, the trickster side of the ancestral spirits shifts through the process of thuru in the same way that it does for the trickster gods. Overall, the ancestral spirits always love us and want the best for us, but the trickster mercurial side is always changing. Sometimes the ancestors miss us too much and want to shoot an arrow that makes us ill, perhaps killing us, so that we can be reunited with them. At other times they are only looking after our well-being. When they notice that we aren't taking adequate care of ourselves, they may shoot a few arrows to make us feel a little tired or sick, so we'll be reminded to take some action for our health. For the Bushmen, this is a reminder to dance.

Anthropologists learned first about the ways Bushman shamans depicted the malevolent side of the ancestral spirits, causing harm, illness, and death. This perspective saw healing as a battle with the spirits and protecting the living from their harmful influence. Then scholars started to become aware that for Bushmen, "healing makes our hearts happy" (see *Healing Makes Our Hearts Happy: Spirituality and Cultural Transformation among the Kalahari Ju/'hoansi* by Richard Katz, Megan Biesele, and Verna St. Denis). Healing, then, could be paradoxically viewed as a love feast taking place within an antagonistic battlefield. This broadened, though easily confounded, our understanding of Bushman shamanism.

In 2003, Dr. Megan Biesele, a scholar of Bushman culture, came to my home to discuss my experiences with the Bushman shamans. Once associated with the Harvard Kalahari Research Project, she is an internationally respected anthropologist who has worked with the people of the Kalahari for over thirty years. The author of *Women Like Meat, Healing Makes Our Hearts Happy*, and *Shaken Roots*, among other works, she has taught at both the University of Texas and Rice University. Now the coordinator of the Kalahari People's Fund, which she cofounded as a nonprofit advocacy and education group benefiting Bushmen communities in Namibia and Botswana, she was delighted with how my work contributed to understanding Bushman spiritual practices. Dr. Biesele returned to the Bushmen after meeting with me and studying my books *Kalahari Bushman Healers* and *Ropes to God: Experiencing the Bushman Spiritual Universe*. Upon her return, she wrote:

> One of the mightiest lessons to be learned from working with healers in the Kalahari is that transcendent strength emerges, can emerge, only from humility. Bradford Keeney's work is an informed meditation on this ancient religious paradox as expressed in current practices of the Ju/'hoan San (Bushmen) of northeastern Namibia. It is informed not only because Brad has "been there" to visit and dance with Ju/'hoan healers, but because he knows whereof he writes, having traveled "ropes to God" himself for much of his life, in many places in addition to the Kalahari.
>
> Brad spoke to healers like /Kunta Boo and =Oma Dahm after dancing with them for many hours. There was no question in their minds but that his strength and purposes were coterminous with theirs. I know this not only from the books, but from talking myself, a year or two later, with /Kunta, =Oma, and others who had danced with Brad. They affirmed his power as a healer and their enjoyment of dancing with him. His work honors them by taking the details of their healing tradition in an effective way to a wider public, as they requested him to do.
>
> Brad's work gives a Western reader a close experience of the empowering details of Ju/'hoan healing. It makes abundantly clear how necessary such details—culturally specific but universal in their ability to effect human transformation—are to a community's taking

concerted action to heal itself. The convictions of the healers who have time and again "traveled the ropes" and seen beyond the ordinary world would be meaningless without the enveloping matrix of belief they create by communicating details of the journey to others.

Understanding and belief are enhanced, among the Ju/'hoansi, by a comprehensive ideology regarding relationships with known, beloved ancestors. Ju/'hoan people are in active, routine contact with relatives who have gone from the mundane sand-surface but pursue a parallel "human" life on another plane, usually in the sky. Anthropologists have emphasized the whimsical and often punitive nature of the interest Ju/'hoan ancestors continue to take in the affairs of the living. Because of what he has seen on his own rope trips to the sky, Brad Keeney has brought up incisive questions about this relationship. "Aren't the Ju/'hoan ancestral spirits more often seen with love and trust, rather than as adversaries?" he asks. This is a good question, one which has made me think—despite my own years of work on this tradition—very hard. I hope more light will be shed on this question by the Ju/'hoansi, now that we are finally asking it.

There is another insight of Keeney that resonates well with my understanding—and I believe it will be backed up eventually by what the Ju/'hoansi tell us when we ask the right questions in their language. That is that any process that endlessly changes form is God. In other words, the fact of growth, maturation, transformation itself is the concrete expression of God's existence, for Ju/'hoansi. Already we have verbal corroboration for this idea in their myths, their rituals, and the phenomenology of their spiritual technology. I feel sure further talk with them will enrich the corroboration. Brad's work is to be commended for insisting on this large vision.

It is a vision which opens into the light, just as the Ju/'hoan healers fervently seek to "open their chests" to heal. Much can be done now to refine and further enlarge the opening into understanding: his work is an important beginning for that process. It takes its place as the newest (and in many ways the direction-pointer) among others about the healing traditions of the Ju/'hoansi.

I found that Bushmen shamans simply aim to activate the process of thuru, helping move one mercurial form of the ancestral spirit to another. Bushman shamans know that the ancestral spirits are principally here to help us. When all their possible forms, desires, and intentions are taken together, there is only love and a desire to help us live.

Furthermore, a shaman can't heal without the help of the ancestral spirits. Shamans require feeling a wholehearted connection with their ancestors. The longed-for loved ones of the past provide the main resource for opening the shaman's heart. Bushman shamans feel the love and help of their ancestral spirits as they try to heal others in the community. At the same time, they try to block or remove any harm the ancestral spirits may have caused. Yes, this is contradictory to a dualistic way of seeing the distinction between help and harm. However, it fits an epistemology of circular relations.

On the level of everyday life, the Bushmen also see every human being as manifesting two circularly related sides:

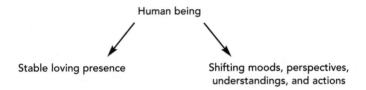

Human being

Stable loving presence

Shifting moods, perspectives, understandings, and actions

Being alive may be defined, in Bushman terms, as how our changing trickster forms maintain a stable loving life. Here the shifting forms cover the wide range of human feelings, including happiness, sadness, jealousy, altruism, attraction, and repulsion. Bushman shamans understand the ever-changing side of our emotional lives and shape-shifting relational patterns. All married couples, for example, go through one affective form after another. We constantly shift our emotions and patterns of interaction. Passion and intimacy move to anger and withdrawal, interspersed with caring, parenting, friendship, and so forth. For Bushmen, health and well-being are understood as the uninterrupted transformative action of thuru. As long as the forms keep shifting or moving along the circular path, there is life (that is, love) in the relationship. All the forms, when taken as a whole, constitute a stable, healthy relationship. Family therapists with a systemic view have tried to articulate a similar understanding. For the Bushman shaman, any effort to maximize any particular form (or minimize another) is to block thuru's life-giving movement. That is what the shamans try to prevent from taking place.

Bushmen see all participants in life, from the gods to the ancestral spirits and the community of the living, as requiring constant change. Their view echoes the practical wisdom articulated by cybernetician Heinz von Foerster: "If you want to find yourself, change!" Stand this saying on its head and you have the message: stay the same and find yourself lost (or symptomatic). Whenever the circle of forms stops moving, the circular string is broken. This is when healing is necessary.

Bushman shamans are capable of many orders of change and transformation. In addition to experiencing the recycling climates of human emotional life like everyone else, they have learned to merge themselves with the ancestral spirits and the gods. As their bodies express movement into these shifts, a dancing of life's differences and oppositions is let loose. This is when thuru takes hold of inside and outside, transforming and juggling one opposite with another, doing so as the body shakes, jerks, and trembles. The movements are an enactment and realization of thuru, a Kalahari version of the dance of Shiva. Sharing the shaking touch helps activate thuru in others. In this whirling mix, dirty arrows are exchanged for new arrows of healing, inspiration, and vitality.

The shaman cannot do this work alone. He or she must interact with the ancestral spirits and gods. This, in turn, takes the shamans to the heart of the Big God's love. There they are absorbed into the divine Big Love, with trembling hands for delivering birth, death, and resurrection.

From the Bushman's "well-rounded" perspective, life is an unbroken circle of transformed states, identities, and particularities. The lines that connect all conceivable forms make a circle of circles, a sphere like Mother Earth. This "mind of nature," to use Gregory Bateson's metaphor, can be depicted as a large-scale conversational pattern, where the participants take part in the conversations of the biosphere. The circular perspective brings us within the dominion of earth rather than outside it, encouraging us to be responsible stewards rather than exploiters.

Circular understanding can also help set us free from the bondage of rigid mind-body dualisms. Consider this reframing of the old mind-body conundrum:

mind (conversational pattern) / bodies (expression of the participants)

Here the *patterns* of interacting bodies constitute mind. This shift orients us toward appreciating diverse embodiments of mind rather than placing mind outside of the body. And this shift encourages us to be more mindful of the centrality of our relationships rather than remaining blinded by self-centered illusions.

In the Kalahari, the conversational mind of the dance (where no words are spoken), may be understood as:

(healing dance / shaking interacting bodies)

where the expression of thuru through shaking bodies brings forth the world of the dance, an eternal moment when all ancestors and creation are present through the evoked arrows of love.

Bushmen implicitly know that life's interconnectivity and wholeness are generated by a circularity of ever-changing forms. Like Ezekiel's wheel, n/om, kundalini, chi, and holy ghost power are all brought about by circles that never stop turning. Each circle swallows itself, then gives birth to the circular process that created it. In this circulation, the mind of nature is not separate from the body of nature. They are joined by the formless form, no-mind, and absent-body of thuru. Keep in mind that I am referring to nothing less than a mystery that can never be named or known outside of being within its embrace.

If a trickster is unable to keep changing his wardrobe to bring thuru to a halt, a circular string will break. Consider the words in Bleek and Lloyd's *Specimens of Bushmen Folklore* of the /Xam Bushman who was dying from wounds inflicted by a white farmer: "I would altogether talk to thee, while my thinking strings still stand."

Broken strings refer not only to death but also to situations in which opposite sides of a relationship have pulled themselves apart. My Bushmen friends tell me that other cultures have broken the strings with them, suggesting that the interaction has been a unilateral push or pull rather than circularly reciprocal. These same cultures, black and white alike, have broken their strings with the animals and plants, where there is no co-respect, co-learning, cooperation, and co-love. Bushmen seek to live another way: they reside within the circles of life. They surrender to thuru as a way of being inside the Big God.

The Ju/'hoansi Bushmen of Namibia use the same word, G//aoan, to refer to God, devil, and ancestral spirits. On the surface it may appear confusing and contradictory to have one word attached to all these different meanings. But when we recognize that "devil" is simply a way of pointing to the "trickster" aspect of their spiritual universe (rather than marking an opposition between good and evil), we find that their understanding is neither dualistic nor illogical. Again, it is circular, with different aspects or forms brought forth by ongoing processes of transformation.

G//aoan is the supreme shaman who never stops practicing thuru, first changing into its broadest form of expression—a stable sky god coupled with a morphing trickster. Out of this yin-yang, complementary relationship are born the ancestral spirits that likewise have a stable, trustworthy side and a trickster side that can be either benevolent or adversarial. Finally, we have the thuru of the human shaman where, on one side, we find a trustworthy servant always devoted to helping others, while the other side is a trickster shifting between light and dark, vision and absurdity, movement and stillness.

A shaman is a master of thuru, capable of dancing across many realms. She has an awareness that good can give birth to evil and vice versa. Knowing this, the shaman sees the suffering of others as something brought about by the laws of rigid dualisms, where evil and good, devil and God, are considered separate and in a holy war, one side determined to destroy the other. This is the folly of the human world. It is the grand illusion and mass spell that must be broken. The way out is to see the world circularly, realizing that all things are related and created through their interaction. Destroy one side and the string is broken. Then all sides perish.

In Bali I learned that the tension between good and evil is called *sakti*. The Balinese shamans believe that no one really has sakti in the sense of having a force or power inside of them. It is more accurate to say that a spiritual person is "fighting for sakti" than to say that they "have sakti." As my Balinese colleagues put it, if we say that you have sakti it really means that you are in a battle for it. If there is no evil attacking you, there is no sakti in the situation; but if someone is trying to kill you and you are still alive, you are *in* sakti. This is an important concept to the Balinese, and outsiders who study their culture usually don't understand it. You never win a battle because the important fights keep going on. If you are winning, then there is sakti.

Similarly, no one really has n/om. But when you are shaking as a shaman, fighting to bend the lines into circles, there is n/om. You are in the midpoint of all imaginable contraries. There wind moves, spirit breathes, n/om flows.

The shaman's body holds on to all opposites and differences, embracing all sides and voices. Inside these polarities a whirling wind originates, whipping the shaman from side to side. Waves of energy express the inner contradictions of human existence. Love and hate are held next to each other, neither side allowed to run away. The wheel turns. Altruism and selfishness face off but neither crosses the line. The wheel turns again. Good and evil stand their ground, facing one another. Again the wheel turns.

In contraries lies progression. In the body of the shaman, the wheel of life (and death) turns and spirited current is generated.

15
Trickster
Shaman

IN THE EARLY PART OF MY ACADEMIC CAREER, back in the
1980s, I was introduced to the Zohar, a book of Jewish mysticism.
Many years later I had a dream about the Zohar. I subsequently found
out that the first printed copy, made in 1588, resided in an archive in
Venice. I traveled to Italy and met the volunteer worker at the Renato
Maestro Library and Archives of the Jewish community in Venice, who
found the manuscript in the storage area of the library. The night before
I was taken to see it, while resting in my hotel bed, I felt the spiritual
current pouring inside me. I went into the Dreamtime.

*I'm driving a car along a road stretching across miles of wheat
fields. I pick up a hitchhiker, a young man who is quiet and has every
appearance of being friendly. We drive along without saying a word
until the road comes up to a black gate, the entrance to a park filled with
children at play. The young man says, "Please stop the car and I'll open
the gate. We need to pass through here to get to the other side." Finding
no reason to disagree, I follow his suggestion and enter the park.*

Halfway through the park the hitchiker says, "Please stop. I have something I must do." I stop the car and the man hops out, grabs his suitcase from the back seat, and opens it. To my horror I see that he has an axe. His facial expression changes, becoming the crazed look of a madman. I see that he is possessed by evil and is preparing to harm the children. I run to him, struck with the realization that I must gather the courage to exorcise this young man. I take a deep breath and place both of my hands on his chest, my right hand over his heart. I am paying no attention to his axe. I speak loudly as I stare directly into his eyes, flaming beads that radiate hot anger. I say something that I must respectfully not disclose in print. My words are delivered with unambiguous authority.

A powerful current rushes inside my body, traveling from feet to belly. When it arrives at my belly button, the internal energy swells and pulses several waves, sending energy straight up my spine and out of my head. The current is so strong that it takes my entire insides with it.

I remember how the Bushman shamans taught me that healing another person requires taking out the "dirty arrows" from his insides. When you do that to another, your own "dirty arrows" are drawn out, too. As you cleanse the other, you cleanse yourself. In this dream, the exorcism of the young man not only cleansed me; it removed my insides. I was only left with skin and no internal matter. To my surprise, my skin wasn't human. It was the skin of a fish. I looked like the remains of a fish on a dinner plate following a meal.

I woke up, still feeling the pulsing energy, startled by the experience and not sure what to make of it. Then a voice spoke: "The light will always be with the dark. But you can choose the dark wisely. As others have done before, you can be with those who suffer naturally, whether from injustice, poverty, or severe illness. Be with those and the dark will provide a good marriage with your light. If you do not choose your dark, it will seek its own form, which may be the evil fire of hell itself."

The next morning, after my late night dream, I was taken to see the ancient copy of the Zohar. I discovered that it is filled with marginal notes and extra handwritten pages dated 1558. I was aware that this might be an important discovery for the study of Jewish mysticism. I found out that the Zohar speaks of good and evil and offers the advice that "a person should take care not to make himself visible to the dark forces of destruction." The rabbis told me what I heard the night before in the Dreamtime and discussed a passage from the Zohar:

> Before there was the wheel, there was the idea of the wheel. Thoughts
> have influence . . . they run the world . . . spin a world.

Over and over again, the shaman finds God and then sees dark forces hiding behind the next corner. While fasting and praying in the desert, Jesus finds Satan offering one temptation after another. Swedenborg dreams of God but can't stop desiring flesh. Sanctified parishioners dance to the Lord on Sunday morning but in the middle of the week feel hatred toward the fat cat, bigoted politicians who hold their people down. Social activists living by the "small is beautiful" mantra generously give offerings to help others but then lust to buy something new for their secret stockpile. We are all on the same ground, saint and sinner alike. In the eyes of God, the lamas, yogis, priests, rabbis, and shamans are no different from hard-time convicts. They learn this firsthand, with difficult struggle.

The shaman must die over and over again to become detached from any side of a treacherous either/or. It doesn't matter whether you are too good or too bad. Either way, you have to enter the mourning room and go through the resurrection experience. In this way shamans live to die, though they do everything to avoid it. With each painful crucifixion comes new life and hard-earned wisdom. The shaman is both a trustworthy disciple of the good and an untrustworthy trickster, playing with all forms and ceaselessly shifting them into others. Shamans are walking tornadoes, embodiments of the four winds. They drive everyone, including themselves, to the precipice, the outer edges of our limits of knowing, trust, faith, creativity, absurdity, and forgiveness. They urge us to jump off the cliff and die with them and they leave us alone to suffer, but they show up later to help bring us back through the spiritual birth canal.

Shamans rip apart the commonsense axioms of self-help and professional helping conduct. They show how the general good is usually bad whereas the particular bad always offers a spiritual lesson. Shamans urge us to drop out to graduate, to laugh at a funeral, and to weep at a great meal. They teach us that true marital love is born out of the courage to accept those necessary times when both sides hate the other. They teach us that there should never be punishment, only forgiveness. We are too small to judge others, and our smallness and ignorance are our greatest assets. They bring us to our knees, and in doing so, we find ourselves closer to the gifts of spirit.

The shaman as trickster knows that the most important matters of life, those related to the heart and soul, those involving trust, love, peace, and goodwill, are embedded within slippery paradoxical patterns of complex interaction. They are not governed by the mores of business and the rationales of law. From the crazy shaman view, the essential ingredients of being human are always upside down and mirror-imaged. They are reversals of common sense. For example, do not trust anyone who says, "Trust me." On the other hand, sincerely saying that you are not trustworthy may provide the ground for developing some trust. Crazy wisdom and crazy trust make us suspicious of those who lazily invoke metaphors of patriotism, law, and duty, while we pay serious attention and listen to the offbeat sounds of the underdogs who dare us to love our enemies, take care of the planet, and dance wildly in the streets.

As a trickster therapist, I invited my clients to dive headfirst into absurd experience, turning therapy into a microtheatre of experimental interaction. I sent clients home to place words and images inside their pillows, attach strings to their television sets, and upheave their daily habits with prescribed nonsense, confusion, and sweet madness.

In a case conducted in the swamp country of Louisiana, my colleague Dr. Wendel Ray and I worked with a retired professional football player who had been diagnosed as "psychotic" by psychiatrists in a mental institution. He believed a voodoo intervention by his former wife caused his life to "freeze." Now in his second marriage, he was still frozen. One example of this: He still used the same bedroom furniture from his former relationship. He seemed unable to let it go. To release him from his curse, we began by having him cut out and dispose of a small piece of his bedroom lampshade.

He eventually removed all the furniture, burned it, and began feeling free. We immediately hired him as a consultant to help another family that revered football and had a twelve-year-old "psychotic" daughter that psychiatrists wanted to hospitalize. Our consultant took them to a playing field where he coached them to play a family football game as we made a video of their entire ritualistic performance. All participants found themselves resourcefully transformed and moved on to have productive lives.

As a trickster teacher I sometimes turned the classroom upside down. I banned students from reading their books while encouraging them to open a book at random, reading only one sentence. They were advised to play with the sentence in an irrational way, perhaps writing it down and placing it in their home freezer. In this way, their frozen imagination would begin thawing, along with their curiosity about the rest of the book.

Years ago I suggested to my doctoral students that it might be possible to make a bigger difference in the profession by advertising a strategically designed announcement of a book that wasn't written (nor would ever be written) than creating an actual publication. As an experiment, my students and I spread the rumor that I had written an article attacking the use of traditional research methods in psychotherapy. For nearly four years, articles were written in the field defending research from this attack, including a special issue of a journal. I had never written the article! That's the "mirage of power" brought about by trickster play.

On the cultural front, I wrote a book about wacky ways to watch the David Letterman show. While Letterman was hosting the Academy Awards, I was in the CNN studio discussing lunatic ways to play with canned hams while watching the show. Whether in therapy sessions, classrooms, or on the streets and the airwaves of popular culture, my trickster role was to shock, surprise, and trip up the observer into becoming the observed. The dissolution of this dichotomy, the difference between seen and seer, served to loosen the daily play of others, helping us be more readily moved by the winds of inspiration. These cultural stunts helped land me several opportunities to contribute to *Utne* magazine, writing about how crazy-wisdom tasks, prescriptions, and strategies can permeate our lives and spawn revolutions of spirit, turning the inner wheels of imagination and play.

Throughout history, sacred fools, clowns, and jesters have been called upon to act out the paradoxical nature of life's most mysterious truths. They shocked onlookers with their unpredictability and contrary participation. Whether they flirted during a solemn ceremony, laughed in a courtroom (thank you, Abbie Hoffman), or wept at a joke, tricksters have understood that they have accepted the responsibility of revealing the truth that can only be expressed through absurdity. Lao Tse, a poetic Chinese shaman, was on to this when he advised:

> *To remain whole, be twisted,*
> *To become straight, let yourself be bent.*
> *To become full, be hollow.*

Shamans not only retrieve souls; they also give birth to soulful expression. Shamans not only go on hedonistic thrill rides on the sci-fi channel; they also fall down on their faces and are then picked up by spiritual grace. Shamans do not limit themselves to hunting for power; they also sacrifice themselves freely to love. Shamans do not necessarily have special knowledge; they cultivate gardens of ignorance.

Shamans do not have to limit themselves to understanding or influencing the past, present, or future; they may behold the Great Mystery that throws them into speechless amazement. Shamans are not only warriors with harsh war cries; they are also lost pilgrims who weep when found. Shamans not only channel the spirits to give practical advice to others; they are also spirited channels in which silence or nonsense effortlessly flows. Shamans do not always shake a rattle; but they often shake. Shamans seldom have the answer; they are more likely to change the questions.

2⊍

Mending the Strings

THE BUSHMAN SHAMAN'S WORLD is filled with strings. There are vertical strings and ropes going straight to the Big God in the sky. Horizontal to the ground are strings for traveling to other places. They can take you to another village, another place on the earth. They can take you through bodies of water, amidst the stars, or to spiritual worlds not drawn on any physical map. As well, strings connect one person to another and to all the animals and plants. As the shaman deepens her wisdom, the perception of isolated people and "things," including plants, animals, and places, starts to fade. In their stead, the strings of connection become more illuminated. Life becomes understood in terms of the strings that connect.

In this world that emphasizes relationship rather than isolated parts, shamans learn to travel along the strings. They not only move their awareness from one place to another; they also shift the locus of identity to that of the other. In the dances before a hunt, the shamans experientially become the animal in this relational way. Doing so helps them know where to go for a successful outcome. When a string is traveled to meet an ancestral spirit, the shaman walks up to the spirit and merges with it.

The beloved grandparent from the past is now present, vibrantly alive within the shaman. There is a fusing into the one remembered and longed for. Similarly, the shaman may be absorbed inside the Big God, feeling one with its presence.

Climbing and traveling the ropes is less a walked journey than a transformation of moving from a consciousness of separate identities to one of nondualistic comprehension. The shaman becomes absorbed inside the gods, the ancestral spirits, the hunted animals, and the persons being doctored. The process of moving from linear separation to circular union constitutes Bushman shapeshifting. It would be more accurate to call it relational shifting, where the "I separate from the other" transforms into an "I inseparable from the other."

The job of the Bushman shaman is to help fix broken strings and to make them stronger. A string is made stronger when a shaman ecstatically opens his heart while reaching out to another. As this is done, the string expands its diameter. With the heart that open, the body shakes and feels highly charged. The African body electric expresses internal heat and vibratory movement and feels pulled in many directions by innumerable strings. As the intensity of this experience increases, the shaman's body feels smaller and seems to have less materiality, eventually feeling as though it has become an electrically charged cloud of vapor. This occurs while the string gets wider. Eventually a threshold, a climax point, is hit. At that moment, the shaman is able to travel along the string and go to the other side of the relationship. Once there, he becomes the other side. This process of transformation, thuru, is what the shaman does to strengthen the strings and make relations more vibrant. Thin strings must be empowered in this way so that important relationships are protected and given recharged life.

On the other hand, a shaman can constrict his heart and make the string thinner, doing so until the shaman can travel down the string. When the heart and string get smaller, the shaman is working with raw power rather than love, and this is seen as a bad practice. This playing with power to achieve purposeful outcomes can break strings and harm relationships. Bad shamans try to exercise control over others, restricting that person's capacity for openness and diminishing their love, while feeling an expansion of raw power within themselves that is aimed at achieving a particular end. This conniving brings trouble, sickness, and evil.

Bushman doctors believe that the Big God made them the First People for a reason. Their role in the scheme of things is to mend and strengthen the strings. In this way, they help keep our natural ecology alive. Bushmen shamans see the noncircular thinking and practices of many other cultures (and bad shamans) as breaking strings and endangering the survival of the natural world. Our hope for the future, according to them, is to keep dancing and working with the strings. As the Western world keeps breaking strings and disconnecting necessary relationships, Bushman shamans keep on dancing, trying to string things back together again.

Strings are metaphors for relationship while the process of moving from one side of a relationship to another is thuru, the process of transformation. The best string is the one that pulls you up to the Big God. This pulling is a longing for the Big Love. Another kind of string is attached to the ancestral spirits, who miss us as much as we miss them. When they tug on us, we have to be careful. The mutual desire for one another may bring about sickness and death as a means of realizing reunion. In the context of daily survival, Bushman hunters follow the strings that go to the animals. Those strings tug on them and bring them to their source of desired meat. In the interpersonal realm, longing for sexual union with another involves being pulled by a string, as does the desire to call another person to be more involved with you in an intimate way. Everything involving relationship and interaction involves a string that on an unenlightened level of awareness suggests separation of the assumed objects on each of its ends. On the heightened level of shamanic awareness, we find connection and the possibility of becoming the other. There we listen, observe, and touch the other to know who we are and (completing the circular perspective) find who we are not.

Bushman morality is simple and nonjudgmental. Like all human communities, with the Bushmen there are times when some people have heated arguments, steal, fight, exercise harm, or have extramarital affairs. These conducts are not seen as requiring punishment but are instead compassionately understood as the unfortunate consequences of having dirty nails and arrows that subject you to being pulled by bad strings.

The response to your misdeeds is for the community to call forth a dance and have the shamans pull out the dirty nails and arrows and replenish you with clean ones. This humane understanding of human nature makes Bushman society more compassionate than modern civilizations that declare war and punishment upon those who are judged as different, problematic, challenging, inappropriate, wrong, bad, or evil. For the Bushman, all difficulties require going to a dance, bringing down the Big Love, and getting over it. No one is invited (or encouraged) to be a card-carrying victim or criminal. Whatever the ailment, whether physical, psychological, or social, a Bushman goes to the dance and gets those dirty nails and arrows removed, helping bring everyone back to traveling along the good strings.

Bushman elder Toma explained to me that the Bushman shamans feel sadness when they see another shaman get onto a bad string. They do not seek public shaming and scolding, but rather they go to the shaman and suggest a cleansing. They call for a dance so they can pull out the dirty arrows. Sometimes a doctor who has fallen off a good rope has a dream of finding a cave. Inside the cave is a room for healing where the spirit shamans take out the dirty arrows and replace them with clean ones. When fallen shamans have been cleansed and revitalized, whether in spirit dreams or actual ceremony, the other shamans announce to the community that they are okay and now capable of being good shamans again.

Shamans who fall and are brought back to clean spiritual health become the strongest shamans. They develop a wisdom from their mistakes and recoveries that isn't available to those who haven't fallen. Furthermore, the shamans who help doctor the fallen one also get stronger and wiser when they provide compassion and cleansing rather than punishment for their colleague.

The Bushman shamans go on to say that the Big God is very wise and that humans are *made* to make mistakes as a paradoxical means of finding help. By this they mean that getting tired or physically ill, or making a mistake—whether at the level of anger, theft, or adultery—are ways the Big God reminds us that we need to cleanse ourselves, that we need to take out the dirty arrows and nails and put in the new ones.

Thus even the trickster side of God provides a way of helping us stay good and strong. As Tcqoe !ui once said to me, "Human beings are so stupid and lazy, they wouldn't bother to take care of their arrows and nails unless bad things happened to them." God's trickster side fools people into getting on bad roads and doing all sorts of wrong things as a means of getting them to the dance for healing and spiritual rejuvenation. With this in mind, Bushman shamans acknowledge problems, symptoms, sickness, and wrongdoing as resources. They bring us to the shamanic dance, at which fresh arrows and nails revitalize and retune us, putting us back on the good strings.

When Bushman shamans receive nails from the Big God for the first time, they usually see a sacred light and believe they are rewired in some kind of spiritual way, making them vessels for shamanic work. Bushman shamans refer to this as the time when you get your rope attached. They believe that this is what happened to me when I had my rapture experience at nineteen years of age. After that, the Big God and the ancestral spirits help guide your life. When you get your big string, the one that goes directly to the Big God, other strings on your body are also connected to it. Strings are attached to your legs, hips, arms, and hands, as well as a string that goes down the top of your head all the way to your belly and then up and out of your throat and mouth. All these strings are tied to the big string above your head. In this way the Big God can pull your strings, dance you, and use your body to express healing with others. That's the way the Bushman shaman explains the African body electric.

On one of my visits to the Bushman village of Djokhoe, I spent a late afternoon talking with the shamans there. After a while, we embraced and began giving each other nails. I looked over my shoulder and saw G/aq'o Dahm, a young man, intently watching what was going on. It seemed like his body was calling out to be touched. I walked over to G/aq'o and touched, vibrated, and shook him. In a moment of intense energetic interaction, I put some shamanic arrows and nails into his belly. He screamed, started jerking wildly, and jumped up and down. He had received his nails. The community was thrilled because until that moment none of the young people had accepted any nails or expressed any serious desire to become a shaman. They were too scared of being shamans and were too often distracted by the interruptions and seductions of what they heard about the material benefits in other cultures.

The next morning the elders gathered to hear what G/aq'o had to say about his experience. He told them that an unusual thing had happened when he had gone to sleep that night. He noticed pain in his shoulders and hips as he felt strings being attached to those places on his body. The strings began pulling him up and he became frightened and tried to stop it. Something had changed inside him, said G/aq'o, and he wanted the shamans to do the things to his body that would make him a shaman.

The elders offered their congratulations and said they were ready to guide him through the process. I encouraged him to continue and said, "The community has been waiting for a young man to get on a good string and lead the others. You will be a good shaman because you want to help others, can be serious and hard working, can be funny in an instant, and have a body that wants to receive the nails." Toma, one of the elder shamans, joined me: "We are waiting for a big shaman who can show us things. We are happy that you may become this person."

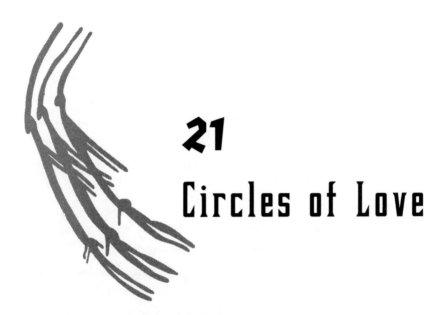

21

Circles of Love

IT'S NIGHT AND WE'RE DANCING AGAIN in the Kalahari. My insides are on fire. My solar plexus is tight and cramping; I feel I can't bear the strain anymore. Now the pumping action starts. Up and down my insides go, each bottoming accompanied by gigantic inner waves of convulsing, followed by an upward thrust. The dance is strong tonight. I can feel it and I can feel the women's clapping pushing my insides up and down. Sweat is pouring through every opening in my skin. I am made of pure fire and energy!

It's only the beginning of the shaman's dance and I want to move into the fire. I walk barefoot on the glowing red embers, flames spewing forth, and I feel nothing. It's not hot enough, I think to myself. I want to go back to it, bend over, and place my face in it like old man Cgunta. I start to throw my face into the fire, but the old women haul me back.

They pull out their tortoise shells and the medicine powder—a perfumed fragrance that helps cool me down. I'm on track again, and the energy that has been waiting to continue its journey grabs my body. I let out a wild scream, and that starts the pumping all over again. I am feeling the Big Love. I want to love everyone here. I look at Tcqoe !ui, an elder woman shaman. She and I have shared the shaman's way of making intimate connection many times before. I want to exchange the hot arrows with her. Looking at her, I escalate my feelings to a climatic release that is felt as a body jerk, sending an arrow into her belly, saying, without speech, "Come dance with me." She immediately stands up and dances toward me. We speak to each other without talking, sending what outsiders would think were telepathic communications. But there are no parapsychic phenomena here. We're only sending messages by way of the arrow. All strong shamans know this—it's the oldest mail delivery system on the planet.

Tcqoe comes and I wrap my hands around her waist; my body is draped over her back. We dance the shaman's dance together. We turn to face one another, holding hands, as we each shoot arrows into one another, doing it at the same time. We shoot them through our fingertips, through our eyes, and through our pulsing bodies. We are making a circle of arrows between us. The current is never stronger than this. It is so strong that I wonder if I will lose consciousness. It is spiritual lovemaking. All the love in the world seems to be passing through us, but not just for us. It is sent to everyone else in the dance. It is sent to her husband, Bo, the chief of the village, who is smiling with delight. I am named after him. It is sent to Mev, standing near my side, who was given Tcqoe !ui's name. This love, like our names, is not owned by anyone in particular. It is brought down like rain from the sky, available to all who stand under it.

Together, all the shamans walk up that rope. We dance around the fire, drawing near, backing away, going toward it again, and then quickly spinning around to face the many people sitting in a circle around the shamans' circle. Babies on mothers' backs, elders, and young adults all sit waiting for the shamans to touch them with their vibrant trembling hands and convulsing bodies. I, with all the other shamans, touch everyone, one at a time, removing dirty arrows with a screaming release, putting new arrows and thorns into them, all the while praying and loving.

The shaman Cgunta is in need. I join the other shamans and we fall to the ground around and on top of him, rolling around, all of us convulsing, making wild sounds from the other world, resuscitating his soul. We wipe our sweat, strong medicine, on each other. We blow, suck, sing, and screech like birds. There is no need for any rattles, feathers, or bones under this star-studded sky. One's inner heat, trembling skin, and opened voice are the only tools needed to express the calling of these shamans.

I feel my body disappear. It no longer carries the burden of weight. I have become a cloud, a fog of pulsing energy. In this nonmaterial form, I can "fly" anywhere, become anything, from lion to ancestor, and spread myself into a thin cord that goes to the sky. It is beyond intoxication. Sometimes I must be cooled down by Mev's gentle touch and stroking hands while the other Bushmen doctors help me regain focus. I am like a boxer running to his corner. Water is thrown on my face from time to time. Sounds of encouragement and attention stream past my consciousness before I step into the next round.

In the beginning, the vibrations jump-start all my muscles. My calves, knees, thighs, belly, arms, hands, and head start shaking. Then it turns to whole-body pumping that is so strong that it often hurts. Perhaps it is a kind of birthing. The shaman's body is trying to give birth to spirit. The transition feels like death to the inexperienced ones. We older ones have learned to accept the ordeal as the price we pay to enter the delights of being pure spirit. After the release, the highest-frequency vibrations descend on one's head. There is nothing left of you now but steam, white light vibrating through the night.

In the fog, the pulsing cloud sees with spiritual eyes not separate from smell, taste, hearing, and touch. As the old shamans say, "You can smell everyone's illness." You can also smell their desires and their soul. It is as primal as the primary brain can deliver. Sometimes pouncing about on all fours, growling, and wrestling with malevolent spirits, then immediately shapeshifting to tender nursemaid and high priest and priestess, there is no separation of gender, race, culture, species, or life form. This cloud can become everything or nothing without notice. Embodiment of surprise and unpredictability, the shaman tricks everyone, including the shaman, into falling outside the realm of the known.

Mystery is brought down from the sky and rises from the same—but different—realm lying below. Time evaporates and physical boundaries erase themselves.

Here, the gods enter and dance between the poles of the sacred and profane. The gods are crazy. If they didn't embrace all sides of every possible position, straddling light and darkness, pleasure and pain, delight and terror, they wouldn't be gods. The gods must be crazy or there would be no differences to make a difference. These gods invite us to jump off the cliff, go beyond all limitations of thought and experience, and throw ourselves blindly into their illogical mind. Shamans, mad as hatters, accept the invitation.

In the Kalahari, we become a wilderness party celebrating earth and sky, vaporizing all understandings and bringing forth movements of birth and death. We feel it is the madness of divine love. All the love dogs, love coyotes, love lions, and love gods show up, howling at the moon of infinite desire. In this free-for-all exchange of love, an elder can smile and laugh and say, as I remember one saying to me years ago, "I feel so much love in the dance that I even love the man who stole my wife."

Here we find the strongest medicine in the shaman's medicine bag— the prescription to love one's enemies. In this faraway desert place, devoid of modern technological conveniences, the spiritual circuits are all plugged in. With no more material possessions than what each person can carry on his or her back, we meet a people who have found what others elsewhere can't seem to hold onto, no matter how much education, wealth, and spiritual knowledge they accumulate. Here, among elders who have never read a book, I learned life's most important lessons.

Has the oldest surviving culture on our planet kept the first spiritual fire going for thousands of years? In some unexplainable way, perhaps they carried and delivered this fire to the rest of the world. Maybe it was hauled across oceans in slave-laden ships. Iron shackles cutting flesh and breaking backs could not suppress this inner fire.

An elder folk healer in Brazil, ninety-nine-year-old Otavia Alves Pimentel Barbosa, had known some slaves who had come from Africa.

They had taught her about the steps you can climb to the sky, going all the way to what they called "the field of birds." There the ancestral spirits reside.

In rural churches of the South, from Georgia to Louisiana and any place else where there's a swamp where old African American preachers used to fast for a vision, elders remember stories about ropes and strings. Some of their grandparents talked about being suspended over a spiderweb that you can only see when you are converted.

The Bushman shaman's truth has spread to every corner of the earth, from the dances of the Caribbean to the Jesus of the Black Church, who shouts and moves the spirit through all whose hearts are open to receive. It is in the temple of the cave-dwelling Buddhist abbot I met in Thailand. He connects long strings from his temple to trees in the forest, providing highways for spirit. The rope to the sky is also seen by some of the First People of Australia. Their shamans climb it into the Dreamtime.

The silver cord in the Bible, like the horizontal and vertical lines of the Bushman spiritual universe, is not a thing of the material world. The materialistic fantasies of supernaturalism fail to see what spiritual sight reveals. In spirit, all the senses combine to bring ecstatic experience. Bushman rock art drawings are renderings from a hand touched by spirited knowing. The lines are seen when God's music pierces the heart and is felt by the whole body. The heart-centered mystical organ of sight sees that the silver cords, the lines of connection, and the ropes to God are not lines of measure. They are sacramental evocations of relationship, lines that connect. And these lines go everywhere, taking spiritual pilgrims to their lessons. Over and over again, shamans learn that the lines can be bent into circles and that the circles erase our differences, providing an opening for the Big Love's entry.

In the spirit, all places and living beings are woven together by the lines of light, spinning a web of infinite interconnectivity. Here the soul is free to feel-see-hear-smell-taste any aspect of life, here or there. The lines of relationship are the arcs of the greater circles of life. They comprise the Mind of Nature. Its complexity of recursive interaction is so vast that we must speak of it as a great Mystery, a multiplicity of deities and gods, so far beyond our ability to discern and comprehend that to even get a glimpse of it leaves us speechless, or musing, at best, that "the gods are truly crazy."

In my daydream I see my grandfather. We are sitting in his old parsonage and I am twelve years old again. "PaPa, I don't want to be a preacher when I grow up. I'd rather play and have fun."

"Yes, grandson, I can see that it is too much to understand. But some day you will see that it takes a lot of suffering and pain and confusion to get free of all your worries. We just can't say, 'I am going to stop doing this because it is not good for me.' We have to keep doing what we shouldn't be doing until we drive it into the ground, until we get sick of it to such an extent that it is totally bankrupt and empty of any illusions of meaning. After that, we are free to do the right thing."

I wasn't sure what he meant, but I took a guess. "You mean like when I go to the circus, you let me order all the junk food I want until I go home sick, and that maybe one of these days I'll realize that I shouldn't order so much?"

PaPa laughed, nodding. "One of these days, after I am long gone and your bones and joints start to ache like mine, you'll feel the same about the whole of your life. You won't have to digest every experience that comes before you anymore. You can simply be content to be where you are and at peace with yourself. You'll come home and find that everything you have been looking for has been waiting patiently."

I am trying to understand his point. "But don't we have to go on a long journey in order to see that we are blind?"

"Yes, we are doubly blind. We don't see that we don't see. I will tell you this and I will say it one more time before I die. Grandson, you will become many things and accumulate many experiences in your life, and then you will lose everything. Only then will you wake up and find out who you are and why you were born."

I was confused, but then I remembered a story that my grand-mother had once told. "Your grandfather never wanted to be a preacher. He used to drive a motorcycle all over the flint hills of Kansas. Then he came back home and the spirit started working on him. He fought it day and night. He'd rather have done anything else. Then one night he woke up screaming and turned to me and said, 'There is nothing I can do to stop it. I have to be a preacher.'"

PaPa went on with his talk. "Yes, everyone fights being who he is. God made us that way so that when we find out the real truth, it will really stick. We won't doubt it if we have to work hard and travel many dangerous roads to find it. Someday, you'll wake up and say, 'I know why I was born and what I must do.' I'm saying this to you, Grandson, because I love you so deeply. I see myself in you and I feel a responsibility to warn you of the years and journeys to come. But know that my voice will always be with you. My hand will be there for you to hold and my heart will beat next to yours. Someday you will understand."

I am dancing again under the Kalahari stars, this time with the women shamans, in their !Gwa dance. After I dreamed their sacred dream of giving birth to a pulsing drum, they brought me into the woman's shamanic way. Rather than dancing around the fire in a circle, my feet are rooted to the ground as my whole body shakes wildly. The women's dance is from the song of the !gwa plant; it's roots are holding them to the earth. There's no traversing furrowed circles as is done with the men in the giraffe dance. As Texae put it, "We get our magic from the plant roots. That is why we stand in our dances like the roots in the ground."

Many anthropologists have assumed that the men's shamanic dance is stronger, but I have learned that this is not always true. The women have kept quiet about the extent to which they are involved in spiritual medicine and the fact that they are the power behind the men. The women doctors sometimes tell me that they are stronger than the men. At other times, they say that men and women have the same power. The strong women shamans never say that their power is less than that of the men. Sometimes I enjoy dancing with the women more than with the men. There are times when I feel that they have more heart and soul.

As I stand among them, currents of n/om are rippling from my feet toward my head. I see the rope. The women elders come to me and we hold onto each other, climbing the rope together. Entering the village in the sky, we see our beloved relatives. All our grandmothers and mothers, fathers and grandfathers, brothers, sisters, sons, and daughters are waiting to dance with us.

I see PaPa and Doe, along with my great-grandfather Keeney, whom I knew as a young boy. There is Ruth, my beloved mother-in-law, laughing and waving me toward the fire. I remember how she could hold out her hand in the woods and a bird would rest on it. She had a deep connection with nature. Her head looks toward the sky and then she looks at me, with eyes clearly focused, asking me to take a gift back to her daughter Mev. She says, "Tell her that I still love the birds and make sure that she looks in the backyard each morning."

There was no way I could then know that several months later our backyard would become home to a family of peach-faced love birds, a rare sighting in Tucson, Arizona. Though they are now part of a feral population in Arizona, they are indigenous to Namibia, where the Bushmen I am dancing with have their home.

I embrace Ruth and then I hug my grandmother and tell her how much I loved it when she used to scratch my head. The other Bushmen shamans are doing the same, asking their mothers and grandmothers to scratch their heads, the thing they loved most as children. This touching encounter with our dear loved ones breaks our hearts. I learn again that we can't be open to receive the Big Love unless our hearts are first broken. We convulse with tears of sadness and joy, grief and homecoming, lost moments and eternal returns. This is the entry to the heart of God.

There is no need to go in circles to find your home. Stand where you are and feel the roots and soil below. You can walk straight up to God from where you are planted. The women shamans know this. Most have given birth to daughters and sons. The mothers have held the truths of home even in their wombs.

We all collapse to the ground, weeping and shaking together. The old ones place my hands on their breasts. I feel the warm milk flow one more time inside my head, flowing from the top to the bottom, and right into the earth. Roots made of sacred milk, flowing in and out of earth's skin, are going everywhere, now looking like strings in the sky, spiderweb of Iktomi, circular webs holding God, horizontal lines intersecting vertical lines, holy crosses with outstretched arms embracing all people of the world, no matter their color or which sound they voice.

I dissolve into the greater pulse and feel the whole world having one heartbeat. In an instant I think of my grandfather, and with tears streaming down my face I say, "This is why I was born." In that heap of shaking mothers I feel a hymn being born that would make my grandparents rejoice. The song loses its words and soon becomes part of the improvised sounds of the night, bringing me back to the moment, with rivers of tears flowing from the mothers who baptize me into God's ocean of love.

22

Seen by the Original Ones

I HAVE DANCED ALL NIGHT with the Bushmen and have slept for only an hour. As I wake up and start to rise, I hear a voice. It says, "Tilt your head slightly to the right." I do so without any thought as to what purpose might be behind the instruction. Although I feel my head tilt, I realize that my physical body hasn't moved at all. Beginning to feel anxious, I wondered what was going on. Then the voice returned, "Don't worry. Enjoy yourself. Make sure to ask that you go all the way." The voice was reassuring and I immediately felt relaxed. That's when I started to float upward. I was hovering about six feet over my body, which was still lying curled up on a sleeping bag.

I no longer felt anxious but instead was exhilarated about the possibility of flight. I spoke out loud, saying "I want to go all the way." That's when I flew straight up into the sky, going past all the clouds and breaking out of the atmosphere. Within moments I was in the vast, dark void of outer space, flying so fast that I felt as if I had become a comet. A long trail of light was left behind as I sped through space.

Stars and planets could be seen everywhere, but what caught my attention was a planetary-sized bonfire in the distance. Its flames pulsed, making it look like a breathing fire, a cosmic dragon filled with unimaginable power. I felt free of its influence. I had escaped its tug on me. I asked again to go all the way.

Faster and faster I went. Then I remembered that I had been here before. The Guarani shamans had sent me to this place. And I had seen it in numerous spiritual ceremonies, including the spirit-calling ceremony of the Lakota Indians and in highly spirited country church prayer meetings. I was familiar with this black infinite space filled with bright stars and streaks of light. But I had never seen the big fire and never had I gone this far for this long.

The flight was thrilling and I wouldn't have minded if it never stopped. But then, without notice, I landed upon barren sand. There was neither bush nor grass within sight. There was only sand on the ground beneath me. In front of me stood several camelthorn trees with a small amount of green coloring in their branches. I stood still at first because it seemed as though I was being watched. Although it was silent, a spirited current was in the air.

The current entered me and my head began to tremble. Moving down my spine, it went all the way to the bottom of my feet. I felt a warmth and soon my belly started to shake and jerk. Then the current came up through my voice and I started to sing with a powerfully shaking sound.

My eyes closed and I saw nothing. I was only aware of hearing the vibratory sounds. Then I heard nothing. I could only feel. There was only an awareness of n/om. I was absorbed in n/om.

I don't know how long I was in that state of mind, but the next thing I remembered was seeing the Bushmen women shamans all around me. They were holding on to me, singing and rubbing their hands all over my belly. I wondered where I had been and where I was.

My journey had taken me all the way. I had gone to the Kalahari. Yet I was already in the Kalahari. Had I traveled to the end or the beginning, to the past or the present?

I looked up and saw Cgunta Bo and Toma Dham smiling. "Where did you go?" Toma asked. I started to tell him about flying among the stars. "Yes, this is very good," Toma responded.

"Did you see the fire?" Cgunta Bo asked before I could even tell him about it. "Yes, I saw it, but I didn't want to go near it. I flew right by that fire."

"That's important," Cgunta Bo replied. "That fire is the original ancestral fire. It can kill you. Never be tempted to move toward it. Did you go all the way?"

"Yes, I went all the way. When I started flying, a voice told me to ask that I be taken all the way. I went to a place where the ground is made of sand."

"Did you see the trees?"

"Yes, there were a few trees with a few green leaves on them."

Cgunta Bo was now very serious, as he carefully asked "Was anything else green?"

"No, Cgunta, only a few leaves on the trees were green. That's all the green I saw."

"That is wonderful! You are very fortunate. You were taken to the beginning of everything. That is where the Original Ones live. They were our first ancestors, the first Bushmen. Part animal and part human, they could communicate with all the plants and animals. Did you feel them watching you?"

"I felt it," I said.

"And they sent you back. We could see that they taught you more about the n/om."

I looked up and saw Tcque !ui, the chief's wife. She was coming closer to embrace me. Years ago, she had given me my Bushman name, Bo. She started speaking in her gentle voice. "The ancestors have given you their approval. Now we have nothing more to teach you. You are in their hands now. Whatever you need to know or receive will come from them. You have become a big shaman, what we call a *n/om kxao*, an 'owner of n/om.' The Big God sent you to help us save our ways. Now we will learn from each other, with the help of the ancestors."

The other women also came toward me and we all began hugging one another in a huddle of pulsing vibrations. After a few moments, we sighed together and opened our eyes once again. Tcque !ui resumed talking, saying, "We want you to tell others about the Big Love. Teach them to shake and open their hearts. Show them what it is to be a Bushman shaman."

As the women shamans helped me stand up again, I saw Tcque's husband, Bo, the chief of the village, walking toward us. Helped along by his walking stick, he was getting older with each visit. I wondered whether he would be there for the next visit.

Bo and I hugged one another as the rest of the community gathered in a large circle. Then he spoke. "We want you to tell everyone that you are a Bushman shaman from the Kalahari. This is your home. You speak for us."

23
Say Amen, Somebody

IT IS SATURDAY NIGHT, March 6, 2004, at the Grand Ballroom of the Omni Shoreham Hotel in Washington, D.C. I'm standing next to the stage with my band that features Kim Prevost, a New Orleans' first lady of jazz, gospel, and blues. Other band members include guitarist Bill Solley and keyboardist Ed Prevost, Jr., both from New Orleans, and our New York-based drummer, Jacob Rostboll. Our arms are wrapped around one another as we huddle for a prayer. I speak so that only we can hear, as the inner Kalahari vibrations shake my voice.

"Dear Lord, we ask that you make us vessels for your work. Open us and use us to help share the Big Love. Release any obstructions that we may carry inside and make us empty—clean instruments for praising your name. Take our hearts, our hands, and our voices and turn them to your service. We ask that you bring in the spirit. May this be an evening of great rejoicing and celebrative declaration of your gentle grace and soulful embrace. Let your light shine upon us and bring healing, awakening, a call to bear witness for the power of forgiveness and uncompromising love. For these things we ask, Amen."

We open our eyes and see the overhead chandelier lights dimming in the ballroom as a spotlight is thrown upon the stage. It is the Saturday night dinner and keynote address for the annual Psychotherapy Networker Conference, one of the leading national gatherings for psychotherapists. I have a surprise for the audience. They don't know that we have called for the spirit. There will be no formal speech tonight, no pontificating over expertise. Tonight we will try to bring them into a ceremonial space so they may feel what it's like to be lifted into spirited praise.

I look out over the audience and see some familiar faces. There are students of mine who I haven't seen for nearly fifteen years. They have come from all over the country. My students have done well for themselves and I feel a kind of down-home parental pride. Several of them direct graduate programs, another was the president of the national association for family therapists, another a dean, along with numerous tenured professors, institute directors, and the editor of an academic journal. Other faces in the audience are unfamiliar. I have been away from the field of psychotherapy for a long time and have lost touch with its trends and developments.

The director of the conference, Rich Simon, who also edits a successful popular magazine on psychotherapy, steps up to the stage. We haven't seen one another since I was a cybernetic theorist. That was over twenty years ago. He begins his introduction: "Brad began his career as an intellectual in our field and directed several graduate training programs. Then he disappeared and started hanging out with shamans. Now he's come back, bringing his knowledge, music, and stories about the global wisdom traditions. I call him the Elvis of Africa. I can assure you that he will take us past any boundary we have ever known in the history of this conference. It is my pleasure to introduce . . . ."

I run toward the stage, my band keeping pace behind me. With a microphone in my right hand, I exclaim my delight in being able to share some of the things I have learned from shamans around the world. "Some of my most important teachers are unable to read and write. And they are among the poorest people on earth when you consider the material things they own. But they have enormous spiritual wealth and know some things that may change your lives and help you become more resourceful to those who come asking you to help them in their time of need and suffering. You, the psychotherapy community, comprise the youngest folk healing tradition in the world. It is time for you to hear what the oldest traditions have been doing and what they have to say.

"The shamans I have known aren't interested in raising people's self-esteem. There's no psychology out in the bush. The shamans want life to hit you hard and knock you to the ground." The second I say that, Ed hits the keyboard, making a staccato musical punctuation that causes some people to jump out of their seats. "Say it, Ed!" I shout back to him. Now we are off and running.

As I continue talking, the musicians, one by one, join in and provide an emotional underscoring to the points that are being made. Kim intersperses some humming, then there's a guitar rift, a drum roll, and all along is the hang-on-every-word accompaniment of Ed's keyboard.

"Oh yes, I'm going to tell you something. I have to tell you something. The shamans want life to take you to your knees. You have to get down, way down, so far down that you aren't sure you'll ever get up again." I'm on my knees as I say these things and the band is rocking right behind me.

"Here's how it works: I'm talking about a psychotherapy of brokenness, a shamanism of brokenness, a theology of brokenness. You have to be broken in order to be remade. Being truly down is the only time you are able to sincerely ask to be lifted up. Kim, I'm almost ready for you to take them there."

Kim, who grew up in her father's Black Church, sings back that she's ready. "I'm ready, ready, yes, Lord, I'm ready. Want to tell it. Tell it tonight . . . ."

"First let me tell you who the shamans are. They may not be who you expect. I'm not talking about magic or superpowers or hidden secrets. I'm talking about something far more mysterious and wonderful. The shamans are the people who get broken and at their lowest moment they desperately and sincerely reach up, asking for help. They appeal to a mind that is greater than any single human personality or group know-how. They ask a Greater Power, a Greater Mind to come upon them, to touch them and make them whole again. It's the mind that Gregory Bateson spoke of when he talked about surrendering to the wisdom of the greater ecology of mind. Oh, yes, I've got to say it!"

"Yes, yes, yes, gotta say it," Kim sings back.

"Here's where I'm going. If you get real down and sincerely cry out for help, something very special may happen to you. I'm talking about the way the Big God reaches down and gifts you with a song. Yes, I'm saying that a song can be put in your heart in your greatest time of need. Yes, I'm saying a song is delivered when nothing else will help. Yes, I'm saying that the shamans bring down the songs. The shamans bring down the music."

Kim belts out an interlude: "I say A-a-a-a-a-men. Say it again and again!"

"Ladies and gentlemen, the shamans are the song catchers. They snare the songs that hold the power to heal our broken hearts and anguished souls. My grandfather and father were country preachers. Both of them knew that the great gospel songs were born in moments of personal suffering. I, too, learned firsthand about the gift of song. In the midst of my own personal challenges and difficulties, a song came to me and it tells you what I'm trying to say. Kim, help me out and bring us some of that 'Precious Love.'"

Kim and the band then sing a song that I wrote during one of the most troubled times of my life.

> *I've come to the end where all is forsaken,*
> *I turn to my Lord and pray,*
> *Please help me.*
> *I am broken, please take me and make me,*
> *One who touches your love.*
> *Precious is his love,*
> *Oh, how precious is his love.*
> *Jesus breaks and makes me so that I know*

His love will be one with me,
Precious is his love.

As Kim sings, I rhythmically move down the long ramp that goes into the audience. Audience members start swaying and dancing to the ballad. The room looks foggy as the twilight of spirit settles in.

Kim finishes the song and, without missing a beat, I shout out, "Bring on some of those Bushman rhythms!" A taped loop of the Bushman dance then comes through the sound system as the band improvises with it. Speaking more rhythmically, I begin telling them about the Bushman shamans.

"In the Kalahari, you dance in order to get ready for some shaking. There the shake is what matters. Let me show you what I mean." I jump into the crowd and let the spirited occasion shake my body. From side to side I see audience members standing up and letting their bodies wiggle and shake. "Everybody up. Don't worry about getting it right. There is no right other than letting it happen. Don't be cool or hip. Be free and let that shake come on you."

The place is starting to rock. I continue: "First you dance, then you shake, but that's only half of it. Let that shake grab your belly and lift you up and down. Come on and walk with me. Let's walk like the shamans." I look out and hundreds of people are stomping the ground, learning about the Bushman shaman's way of moving.

"Now, when you get to the Caribbean, this walking and stomping can take you somewhere. You can move this way and do some traveling inside the mythopoetic landscape. Here's how we go to Africa." The band immediately kicks in and we all move in the African way. "Now let's go to Jamaica!" We all bounce forward and backward, caught by the rhythms of the Jamaican revivalists. "And now Saint Vincent!" I show them how to move in the Shaker way.

"When you move like this, you can sometimes feel a sound wanting to come out of your mouth. Band, let them know what this sounds like." Now we are doing an improvised 'doption, making the gutteral rhythms that entrain the body into deeper movements. "All aboard," I announce.

"Everybody on the train. We're bound for some glory land. Let's go: 'umm, huppa umm, huppa, so happy, umm huppa, so happy . . . .'" The room is full of movement and sound. I run around shouting, "Thank you, thank you, thank you . . . ."

Sometimes the room looks like the Kalahari. At other times we are in the Caribbean. Then we are elsewhere. We are traveling in the spiritual Dreamtime.

"Kim, let's take them to church." The band kicks into a soulful version of "Leaning On the Everlasting Arms," beginning with a medium tempo and then building into a kicking pulse. The audience is in the spirit. We've taken them to Black Church.

"Kick it up one notch. Let's show them how things cook in New Orleans." Ed takes off, like he does when he plays for his father's Black Church in New Orleans, breaking into the old gospel tune "Jesus Is on the Mainline." We're bringing in the Big Love. You can feel it. Kim is shaking, Bill is bobbing, Ed and Jacob are tranced out. And I'm imagining my grandfather, praising him for his teaching. "Thank you, Grandfather," I shout out over the microphone. "Thank you for teaching me about the Big Love."

We continue, pausing to tell stories about Osumi, Sensei's healing work in Japan. The music shape-shifts into another cultural form and then we are in Amazonia, rejoicing over how the Guarani Indians bring down their song prayers. Wherever we go, it's like going to the perimeter of an outer circle, visiting a far-away tradition. But each spoke of the musical wheel brings us back to the center. There we enter the spirit of the African diaspora time and time again. Around the world we go, stopping periodically to refuel in spirited celebration.

I watch the audience move with me as we shift from the sounds and rhythms of the Amazon to those of Saint Vincent, southern Africa, Bali, and others. I realize that thuru will always have the last word: forms never stop changing into other forms. My Kalahari home has taught me to find peace with the changing forms. Bushman shamans, fully embracing thuru, welcome all voices, sounds, rhythms, and movements. We belong to the greater circle of changing forms. We belong to the Greater Circle.

Kim soon breaks into a ballad as people embrace and dance. I move around the floor and think of the time I met the daughter of one of the great psychotherapists of our time, Milton H. Erickson. I recall how Betty Alice Erickson, herself a therapist, and I talked about how most people missed what was most essential about her father's work: he was a healer who opened his heart to help others grow. We decided to write a book about his life from that perspective. Within months an influential Ericksonian leader admonished me, saying that Erickson should never be described as a healer. A week after that confrontation, I dreamed of meeting Dr. Erickson. I called Betty Alice and told her how he appeared in my dream. "Yes, that's how I see him in my dreams," she replied. I went on to say that he whispered something in my ear that sent a strong current through my whole body. Those words, spoken in the dream, unconsciously assured me that he was also part of the great circle of healers.

As the music continues on stage I am still in the crowd, embracing one therapist after another. I remember a dream I had the night after hearing that Gianfranco Cecchin, a renowned family therapist from Milan, Italy, had died in a tragic automobile accident. In the dream I received a telegram from him, saying: "Do not go back. Keep moving on with this work. Do not turn back." I also remembered my many conversations with my colleague Dr. Frank Thomas, a family therapist and conference organizer. He, too, had left full-time academic work and had become a student of the life force. We had reunited and become good friends.

I turned and looked at the musicians. They knew I was inviting them to hold nothing back.

Intensified pulse, movement, and musical improvisation make it now feel as though we are raising the roof off the ballroom as we move toward a highly charged, all-throttles-pulled-back crescendo. The crowd spontaneously forms a conga line, shaking around the room to rhythms and sounds of the African diaspora.

Yes, the Big Love was being readily transmitted, shared, and celebrated. Even psychotherapists can catch the spirit. Kim, Bill, Ed, Jacob, and I shouted out, "Thank you! Thank you! Thank you for bringing the Spirit!"

I remembered the words my grandfather had spoken when I was a fourteen-year-old boy: "Someday you will understand." Now, thirty-nine years later, I once again beheld the great mystery of the Big Love. With colleagues, friends, and loved ones, I recognized a current of truth that could be absorbed but never articulated. In that moment, shaken speechless, I understood.

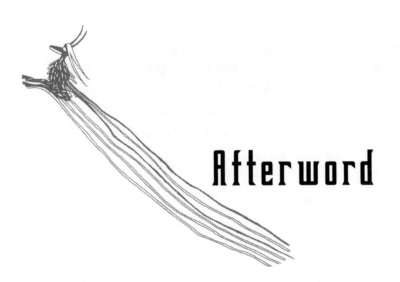

Afterword

THE HEARTS OF BUSHMAN SHAMANS hold an ancient spiritual fire. They were among the first shamans to work the spirit. In this uncertain time in our history, with unstable economies, highly infectious diseases, terrorist plots, and corporate-centered politics, we can benefit from the Bushman's time-proven wisdom. It can help us get through the forthcoming challenges and their promised dark nights of the soul.

Bushman culture has survived one form of attack after another, from warring tribes to insensitive (and often cruel) government policies. Efforts to help the Bushmen, whether carried out by missionaries or social workers, don't always evince respect or even awareness of the Bushmen's healing wisdom and deep spiritual roots. An exception is the Kalahari People's Fund, with its history of serving the people and their healing ways. Similarly, the Ringing Rocks Foundation has been an able servant to the Kalahari people. Both of these organizations deserve our support. As an ever more materialistic world threatens to destroy the sanctity of nature, all of us should consider listening to how the Bushmen have survived for thousands of years with great spiritual wealth, in spite of owning next to nothing.

All the Bushman elders I have met express their sadness over how "ignorant" other cultures are. They are fully aware that most people, whom they call "the line people," do not know how to be in the circle of life. We have broken the strings that outline the patterns that connect. The Bushmen, "the circle people," wait patiently for us to wake up, join their healing dance, and mend our ways.

I write this passage while sitting in the Kalahari with a group of women and men shamans. They are telling me that the most important thing for their future is to keep their ways alive. "There must be future generations of shamans to maintain our light of truth," Cgunta speaks out.

"Without the dance, we are nothing," one of the elder women adds.

They ask me to help them create a Bushman medical school, beginning with a depository of spiritual knowledge. We agree, with the financial support of the Ringing Rocks Foundation and the assistance of my good friend and outfitter, Paddy Hill, to build a hut in the village for this purpose and prepare to digitally videotape the oral testimonies, stories, and teachings of all surviving Bushman shamans. The hut will hold DVD players, a solar panel, and a DVD library of Bushman shamanic teaching, helping keep the wisdom of their elders, the ancient knowledge of the inner fire and the great fire, alive for those who hunt for it in the future. The Bushmen call this place *Thara tjua,* which means "shaking house."

Proceeds from the sale of this book will serve to foster the ongoing tradition of Bushman healing wisdom. I invite you, dear reader, to join all of us in helping keep the spiritual fire burning in the Kalahari.

I am sleeping inside my tent near the Bushman village. A noise outside wakes me up. It sounds like a branch being broken. I look out the front flap. With the help of the light from a full moon, I see a large elephant with fully developed tusks looking straight at me. I can almost touch its trunk, but I don't move and it doesn't move. Our eyes connect and stay locked onto one another. I ask the elephant, "Are you bringing me a dream?" Lifting its right front leg, it stomps the ground in affirmation, causing a small cloud of dust. We look again at one another and

I feel the living, pulsing vibrancy of our immediate relationship. Without announcement, the elephant spins itself around and quietly walks out toward the distant horizon, disappearing into the farther reaches of the dark.

Falling asleep again, I dream of the elephant. It tells me that I have found my home in the Kalahari. "These are the people to trust. Linked to the first ones, they will provide your earliest memories. You are here because it is your destiny. Know and accept that this is your destiny—to be here with the Bushmen and to be inside their spiritual ways. Tell everyone what you have learned. Be a Bushman and share your wealth of spirit with others."

The clapping starts, bringing on the songs and the lines that reach backward and forward in time. I walk toward the rope, ready for another pilgrimage into the matters of dark and light. The ancestors are dancing, teaching, healing, and mending the poetics of heartbreak and the soul's fall. Into the dark I go, waiting for the recurrent baptism in light.

I wake up, remembering the words of various Bushmen elders I have learned from over the years. "Your skin is the same as ours." "We love you and we dream of dancing with you." "We are on the same rope together." "Tell people we have sent you to teach our way of loving the Big God." "Let them know that we are the Circle People." With tears flowing like gentle rain, I fall back asleep, vowing never to leave the Kalahari Dreamtime.

I invite you to contact www.ringingrocks.org for further information on how you can contribute to conserving the healing wisdom of the Kalahari people.

Bibliography

Akstein, David. *Un Voyage a Travers la Transe: La Terpsichore Transe-Therapie*. Paris: Editions Sand, 1992.

Arguelles, José. *Charles Henry and the Formation of a Psychophysical Aesthetic*. Chicago: University of Chicago Press, 1972.

Bateson, Gregory. *Mind and Nature: A Necessary Unity*. New York: E.P. Dutton, 1979.

———. "Some Components of Socialization for Trance," *Ethos* 3 (1975): 144–55.

———. *Steps to an Ecology of Mind*. New York: Ballantine Books, 1972.

Biesele, Megan. *Women Like Meat: The Folklore and Foraging Ideology of the Kalahari Jul'hoansi*. Johannesburg: Witwatersrand University Press, 1993.

Bleek, W.H.I. and L.C. Lloyd. *Specimens of Bushmen Folklore*. London: George Allan & Co. Ltd., 1911.

Bleek, D.F., ed. "Beliefs and Customs of the /Xam Bushmen," from material collected by W.H.I. Bleek and L.C. Lloyd, *Bantu Studies* 9 (1935).

Bonhoeffer, Dietrich. *The Cost of Discipleship*. New York: Macmillan, 1966.

Brand, Stewart. *Two Cybernetic Frontiers*. New York: Random House, 1974.

Corbin, Henry. *Creative Imagination in the Sufism of Ibn Arabi*. Princeton: Princeton University Press, 1996.

Cox, Harvey. *Feast of Fools*. Cambridge: Harvard University Press, 1969.

Englar-Carlson, Matt. "Enough About Models and Abstractions, Let Your Therapeutic Soul Be Free: An Interview with Bradford Keeney," *The Family Journal* 11, 3 (2003): 309–14.

Erickson, Milton. *The Collected Papers of Milton H. Erickson.* Edited by Ernest L. Rossi. New York: Irvington, 1980.

Erickson, Milton H. and Jay Haley, eds. *Advanced Techniques of Hypnosis and Therapy.* Boston: Allyn and Bacon, 1967.

Fulford, Robert C. with Gene Stone. *Dr. Fulford's Touch of Life: The Healing Power of the Natural Life Force.* New York: Pocket Books, 1996.

Guenther, Mathias. *The Nharo Bushmen of Botswana: Tradition and Change.* Hamburg: Helmut Buske Verlag, 1986.

———. *Tricksters and Trancers.* Bloomington: Indiana University Press, 1999.

Ishii, Jozo. *The Essentials of Self-Healing Therapy.* Japanese booklet (in Japanese), 1928.

Jung, Carl. *Memories, Dreams, Reflections.* New York: Vintage Books, 1961.

Katz, Richard. *Boiling Energy: Community Healing Among the Kalahari !Kung.* Cambridge: Harvard University Press, 1982.

Katz, Richard, Megan Biesele, and Verna St. Denis. *Healing Makes Our Hearts Happy.* Rochester, Vermont: Inner Traditions International, 1997.

Keeney, Bradford. *Aesthetics of Change.* New York: Guilford Press, 1983.

———. *Balians: Traditional Healers of Bali.* Philadelphia: Ringing Rocks Press, 2004.

———. *Brazilian Hands of Faith.* Philadelphia: Ringing Rocks Press, 2003.

———. *Constructing Therapeutic Realities.* Dortmund, Germany: Verlag fur Modernes Lernen, 1987.

———. *Crazy Wisdom Tales.* New York: Barrytown Press, 1995.

———. "Dancing with the Bushmen." *Spirituality and Health* (June 2003).

———. "Ecosystemic Epistemology," *Family Process* 21, (1979): 117–29.

———. "Ecosystemic Epistemology: Critical Implications for the Aesthetics and Pragmatics of Family Therapy" (with Douglas Sprenkle), *Family Process* 21 (1982): 1–19 (also published as a chapter in Ronald Miller, ed., *The Restoration of Dialogue: Readings in the Philosophy of Clinical Psychology*. Washington, D.C.: American Psychological Association, 1992).

———. *The Energy Break*. New York: Golden Books, 1998.

———. *Everyday Soul*. New York: Riverhead, 1996.

———. *Gary Holy Bull: Lakota Yuwipi Man*. Philadelphia: Ringing Rocks Press, 1999.

———. *Guarani Shamans of the Rainforest*. Philadelphia: Ringing Rocks Press, 2000.

———. *Ikuko Osumi, Sensei: Japanese Master of Seiki Jutsu*. Philadelphia: Ringing Rocks Press, 1999.

———. *Improvisational Therapy*. New York: Guilford Press, 1992.

———. *Kalahari Bushman Healers*. Philadelphia: Ringing Rocks Press, 1999.

———. *The Lunatic Guide to the David Letterman Show*. Barrytown, N.Y.: Station Hill Press, 1995.

———. "The Medicine Man Who Never Had a Vision." Chapter in *The Mummy at the Dining Room Table,* edited by Jeffrey Kottler and Jon Carlson. San Francisco: Jossey-Bass, 2003.

———. "Not Pragmatics, Not Aesthetics," *Family Process* 21 (1982): 429–34.

———. *Ropes to God: Experiencing the Bushman Spiritual Universe*. Philadelphia: Ringing Rocks Press, 2003.

———. "Say 'Awe': Seven Tips for Soulful Parenting You Won't Find Anywhere Else," *Utne Magazine* (December 2003): 71.

———. *Shakers of St. Vincent*. Philadelphia: Ringing Rocks Press, 2002.

———. *Shaking Out the Spirits*. Barrytown, N.Y.: Station Hill Press, 1995.

———. *The Therapeutic Work of Olga Silverstein*. New York: Guilford, 1986.

————. "Tricksters of the World, Unite!" *Utne Magazine* (May–June 2004): 56–57.

————. *Vusamazulu Credo Mutwa: Zulu High Sanusi.* Philadelphia: Ringing Rocks Press, 2001.

————. *Walking Thunder: Dine Medicine Woman.* Philadelphia: Ringing Rocks Press, 2001.

Keeney, Bradford, and Jeffrey Ross. *Mind in Therapy: Constructing Systemic Family Therapies.* New York: Basic Books, 1985.

Keeney, Bradford and Scott Keeney. "Funny Medicines: Improvisational Therapy with Children." *Japanese Journal of Family Psychology* 7 (1993): 125–32.

Kopp, Sheldon. *If You Meet the Buddha on the Road, Kill Him!* New York: Bantam, 1982.

Kottler, Jeffrey and Jon Carlson with Bradford Keeney. *American Shaman: An Odyssey of Global Healing Traditions.* New York: Brunner-Routledge, 2004.

Krishna, Gopi. *Living with Kundalini: The Autobiography of Gopi Krishna.* Boston: Shambhala Publications, 1993.

Lewis-Williams, David. *Images of Power: Understanding Bushman Rock Art.* Johannesburg: Southern Book Publishers, 1989.

Mutwa, V. C. *Indaba My Children: African Tribal History, Legends, Customs, and Religious Beliefs.* Johannesburg: Blue Crane Books, 1964.

Osumi, Ikuko and Malcolm Ritchie. *The Shamanic Healer: The Healing World of Ikuko Osumi and the Traditional Art of Seiki-Jutsu.* Rochester, Vermont: Healing Arts Press, 1988.

Ray, Wendel and Bradford Keeney. *Resource Focused Therapy.* London: Karnac Books, 1993.

Swedenborg, Emmanuel (ed. by G.E. Klemmon). *Swedenborg's Journal of Dreams, 1743–1744.* New York: Swedenborg Foundation, 1977.

Varela, Francisco. "Not One, Not Two." *CoEvolution Quarterly* 11 (1971): 62–67.

Von Foerster, Heinz. *Cybernetics of Cybernetics.* Urbana: University of Illinois, 1974.

————. *Observing Systems.* Seaside, Calif.: Intersystems Publications, 1981.

Watts, Alan. *Psychotherapy East and West.* New York: Ballantine, 1961.

Walljasper, Jay. "The Luckiest Man Alive? Bradford Keeney Travels the Globe Searching for the Secrets of Soul." *Utne Magazine* (July–August, 2003): 46–54.

Weil, Andrew. *Spontaneous Healing.* New York: Knopf, 1995.

Whitaker, Carl. "Psychotherapy of the Absurd." *Family Process* 14 (1975): 1–16.

BOOKS OF RELATED INTEREST

Healing Makes Our Hearts Happy
Spirituality and Cultural Transformation
among the Kalahari Jul'hoansi
by Richard Katz, Megan Biesele, and Verna St. Denis

African Spirits Speak
A White Woman's Journey into the Healing Tradition of the Sangoma
by Nicky Arden

Zulu Shaman
Dreams, Prophecies, and Mysteries
by Vusamazulu Credo Mutwa
Edited by Stephen Larsen

Vodou Shaman
The Haitian Way of Healing and Power
by Ross Heaven

The Shamanic Way of the Bee
Ancient Wisdom and Healing Practices of the Bee Masters
by Simon Buxton

The Straight Path of the Spirit
Ancestral Wisdom and Healing Traditions in Fiji
by Richard Katz, Ph.D.

Aboriginal Men of High Degree
Initiation and Sorcery in the World's Oldest Tradition
by A. P. Elkin

Spirit of the Shuar
Wisdom from the Last Unconquered People of the Amazon
by John Perkins and Mariano Shakaim Shakai Ijisam Chumpi

Inner Traditions • Bear & Company
P.O. Box 388
Rochester, VT 05767
1-800-246-8648
www.InnerTraditions.com

Or contact your local bookseller